HEADLONG INTO FURY

A WWII Pilot's Riveting Story of Rescue and Redemption

An aged WWII pilot, his aging son,
and the war story that healed their wounded hearts.

HEADLONG INTO FURY

A WWII Pilot's Riveting Story of Rescue and Redemption

RON WHITE

Plain Sight Publishing
An Imprint of Cedar Fort, Inc.
Springville, UT

ISBN 13: 978-1-4621-1766-6

Published by Plain Sight Publishing, an imprint of Cedar Fort, Inc.
2373 W. 700 S., Springville, UT 84663
Distributed by Cedar Fort, Inc., www.cedarfort.com

LIBRARY OF CONGRESS CATALOGING-IN-PUBLICATION DATA

Names: White, Ron, 1956 January 14- author.
Title: Headlong into fury : a WWII pilot's riveting story of rescue and
    redemption / Ron White.
Description: Springville, Utah : Plain Sight Publishing, an imprint of Cedar
    Fort, Inc., [2016] | "2016
Identifiers: LCCN 2015038455 | ISBN 9781462117666 (perfect bound : alk. paper)
Subjects: LCSH: Kirkland, Frank James, Jr., 1921- | Bomber pilots--Biography.
    | World War, 1939-1945--Veterans--Biography. | Veterans--Biography. |
    LCGFT: Biographies.
Classification: LCC D790 .W4195 2016 | DDC 940.54/4973092--dc23
LC record available at http://lccn.loc.gov/2015038455

Cover design by Lauren Error
Cover design © 2016 by Cedar Fort, Inc.
Edited and typeset by Rebecca Bird

Printed in the United States of America

10 9 8 7 6 5 4 3 2 1

Printed on acid-free paper

To the men and women of the US Armed Forces of every generation, who more than self their country loved.

CONTENTS

CONTENTS

ACKNOWLEDGMENTS

The inspiration for this book is plain to see, sort of. My dad's war stories got me started but the motivation to complete the book emanated from Julie, my wife of thirty-five years. She was immensely supportive and always encouraging. Before the possibility of there being a book there was my desire to provide my children a legacy of hope and perseverance, essential characteristics for a happy life. The book was written with an eye toward their futures.

When I started this project I needed to understand aviation terms and training methods so I could carry on conversations with my dad about his World War II experiences. I was fortunate to find a copy of *Randolph Field: A History and a Guide*, a book compiled by the Workers of the Writers' Program of the Work Projects Administration in the State of Texas. Published in 1942, the book was written by otherwise unemployed writers in the last years of the Great Depression. The book's "Glossary of Airplane and Flying Terms" and Flying School "Slanguage" helped me learn the language Dad spoke as an aviation cadet at Randolph Field and other airfields in the Gulf Coast Training Center. The book provided the context for the pride Dad felt about qualifying for and being trained at Randolph Field: "The West Point of the Air!"

I also want to express my appreciation to Joseph Walker, author and syndicated columnist. Joe was so kind to read an early manuscript of the book and provide needed counsel and direction. For better or worse, Joe led me to believe my "labor of love" could become a viable book worthy of publication. That encouragement motivated me to work on the book whenever possible, which led me to a chance meeting on

ACKNOWLEDGMENTS

an airplane in October 2014. I was working on the manuscript, my laptop open on the little fold-down table in front of me. A woman sitting next to me asked what I was working on. I summarized Dad's war story for her. She told me she worked for a publisher and suggested I send a copy of the manuscript to her. Two weeks later I had a contract to publish the book from Cedar Fort. Thank you, Cindy Bunce, for looking over my shoulder on that JetBlue flight.

Finally I express my appreciation for the members of my Cedar Fort team. To my editors, Chelsea Jackson and Rebecca Bird—thank you for your careful eye for details, your patience, and your endurance. I am not sure how many requests a first-time author is allowed to make but I am quite certain I exceeded my quota. To my designers, Lauren Error and Kinsey Beckett, I wish you could know how proud my dad was of your book cover. He said with his picture on the cover and your design, the book was a sure-fire winner. Last, but not least, my thanks to my marketing manager, Brantz Woolsey, and his incredibly hard working sales staff. It is my great honor to be associated with each of you. Onward and upward!

INTRODUCTION

My dad flew B-17s in World War II, a class of bomber planes known as Flying Fortresses. His last mission was a raid on a German railroad yard in northern Italy. There was collateral damage: errant bombs destroyed a famous church and its priceless artwork. On the return flight, an angry nest of German fighter planes attacked Dad's squadron. His plane took heavy cannon fire and eventually succumbed to a rocket blast, crashing in Yugoslavia.

One consequence of the crash was the shattering of a dream, Dad's childhood dream. That is what this story is about. It has been seven decades since he bailed out of that plane, but his dream is still vivid to him, as is the pain he feels over its loss. This story also considers the people in that northern Italian village whose church was shattered by the bombs. Their response to the loss of a Renaissance treasure is a message of hope and determination.

Before getting to those stories, let me tell you something about my dad. He is of pioneer stock and spirit, his grandparents having been prominent figures in the history of the Arizona Territory. His family's legacy of service, industry, and sacrifice was his only inheritance. It endowed him with a sense of dignity as a poor child during the Great Depression and provided inspiration to him in combat. Long after the war was over, the traditions of his fathers continued to sustain him like marrow to the bones.

In November 1972, my high school football team rolled into the school parking lot after losing a first-round playoff game. We had lost in the first round the year before too, so I was pretty upset about it. I stepped off the bus, head down, not wanting to look into the faces of

1

friends and family who were waiting there to cheer us up. My plan was to walk to the locker room without speaking to anyone. My friend stepped out of the crowd and stood in my way. I looked up at him, but I couldn't risk talking because my emotions were so raw. To tweak a line from the motion picture, *A League of Their Own*, "there's no crying in football!"[1]

"Don't worry, Ron. You may have lost the game but your dad won the fight," he told me.

"What are you talking about?" I asked.

My friend explained that at halftime my dad had complained to the other team's officials about the loud speakers in the PA system on the visitors' side of the field. The volume was so high it was hurting the ears of our fans, particularly those of my then five-year-old brother, Jeff, who has Down's syndrome. At first they ignored Dad, and then they began to argue with him. He persisted in asking them to do the right thing by lowering the volume. They mocked him and suggested they would "kick his butt" if he didn't shut up and get back up in the stands.

Dad had no sooner said, "I'd like to see you try," when two guys grabbed his arms from behind and the third guy in front popped him a good one in the mouth. Dad threw off the two behind him and hit the guy in front with a combination that sent the man to the ground. He turned around and clobbered one of the guys behind him, who fell to the ground—out cold. By then the third guy jumped the infield fence to get away from the fists and fury of Frank James Kirkland Jr.

Upon hearing of the only victory our side experienced that night, I smiled and shook my head. *He did it again*, I thought. He is frail now but even back then Dad was not an imposing figure—kind of short, bald, with a bit of a paunch. But he was the toughest guy I knew, and I didn't ever want to be on the receiving end of any of that, although in my sixteen-year-old mind I wondered if I could take him.

The careful reader will note the difference in my last name and his. He is my stepfather, but I have been calling him Dad as long as I can remember. One of his fights was with my biological father when Dad started dating my mom after her divorce. My biological father said something nasty to Mom and *pow*! He got the FJK special: a knuckle sandwich.

Dad didn't fight to be mean; he fought in the name of fairness and justice, at least as he interpreted such things. One time a man thought

Mom was too slow coming off of a stoplight. He passed her car, honked his horn, and flipped the proverbial bird. Dad was in the passenger seat and made Mom follow the guy into the parking lot at Mayflower Grocers. After pulling the offender through the driver's side window, Dad taught him a lesson in good manners.

I'll admit there was a part of me that was afraid of him in those days. Discipline and good order were important to him. When I was younger there was always a stick inside the garage leaning behind the door. When I got in trouble, it was "Ronald, go get the stick . . ." As I got older I tried to keep my distance from him to avoid conflicts. It didn't always work out as I would have liked.

At the same time, I knew he cared about me like I was his own son. I still get emotional when I think of a Christmas day at his brother Al's house. I was eight or nine and very excited about all the Christmas presents under the tree. I tripped on a package and left a gaping wound across one of the beautifully wrapped gifts. Uncle Al laid into me pretty good, calling me clumsy and careless. Even worse, he said, "You're not even a Kirkland. What gives you the right to mess with our things?" Dad stood up immediately, put his arm around my shoulder and said, "This is my son. If he is not welcome here, I don't want to be here." He gathered up the rest of the family and we walked out the door and went home. I can't express how much love I felt for the man that day.

As I grew into adulthood and moved away from home, it was the fight stories and his many sacrifices that I remembered. He worked two jobs to put food on the table and oftentimes even a third so I could have that new Schwinn bicycle with a banana seat, an acoustic guitar from the pawn shop, or tickets to the Pro Bowl game at the Coliseum. Multiply those acts of generosity for me times six children and you've got a lot of overtime and side jobs. And they were not easy, "no sweat" side jobs, either. He poured cement, painted apartment buildings, fiber-glassed boats, welded Rose Parade floats. Whatever the job required, he did it.

I didn't think much of his war stories back then. I knew he was a pilot in WWII. The wheres and hows of it had been a mystery to me. And since I didn't know much about his life before or during the war, I really didn't really know *him* or, therefore, understand him.

All that changed five years ago when my mom died. I called him weekly from my California home after that. Our conversations fell into a steady pattern: "How you feeling today, Dad?" "You went to the doctor again?" "You don't like being doped up on that medicine, do you?" And a few more questions like that. After a few months, I decided to talk to him about the war. He came alive. I began to take notes. We spoke four or five times a week. We would hang up and many times he would call right back: "Ronald, I remembered something else about the Foggia Airfield Complex . . ." When I visited him in Arizona, I could tell that our discussions about his younger years were having a positive effect on him. I could see his fighter instinct kick in for a time and the glint return to his eyes.

A couple of years ago I got mad at him for driving to his mountain home in Arizona from the Phoenix area with Jeff in the car. They live in the East Valley with my sainted sister and her patient husband. Jeff wanted to see his home or rather, as he calls it, "his apartment," in Show Low. The drive would take them about four to five hours. Imagine a ninety-one-year-old man cruising up steep mountain roads with a forty-five-year-old son who could not drive or navigate. I envisioned Dad falling asleep at the wheel and missing a hairpin turn, the sound of Jeff's *Neil Diamond* music fading with the descent of their old blue Buick.

"I don't care if you go, Dad, just don't take Jeff with you," I implored.

"Heck, Ron! I can still fly an airplane," said the old man who had not flown since 1945.

He would not be deterred.

When I began to organize my notes about our discussions, it was simply to honor his life and secure his memory. I wanted my brothers and sister to have a record of what I had learned about him. Eventually, I realized he was teaching me things that I could apply to my own life, and to the lives of my children. His experiences growing up in the Great Depression; the racial attitudes of his hometown that so sharply shaped him, and his softening on that score; his determination to succeed as an Army Air Corps pilot despite the obstacles: they all left their mark on me. I also sensed a longing from him for the time when he was among the best and brightest, filled with purpose, having the time of his life.

The story that follows is based on his life and times, as he expressed them to me. There are a few characters and situations that are fictional. They were added to help tell his story in the larger context of the times.

Dad told me some stories from which I have imagined the dialogue, trying to be true to his memory of the events. In that sense this work is not a biography. I have not attempted to document and footnote each fact represented in the book.

I decided Dad's voice should be heard, so he is the narrator of the story. Of course the words are mine but they reflect the things he shared with me and portray feelings of which he only hinted, but which I believe to be true. The style is also a nod to his skill as a storyteller. If you were to ever meet him at a party, you could be sure you would be engaged in a lively one-way conversation for a significant amount of time. He is a good talker, one of the best. Listening was never his strong suit, though.

The story begins and ends with a discussion between Dad and one of his sons, although I don't specify which one. I have two older brothers and two younger ones. There are elements of the story pertaining to each of our lives, except for Jeff's. Dad didn't need to teach Jeff anything about how to get along in life. He came to us with a fully developed sense of his purpose: to love and be loved. He is the favorite son and brother.

Dad is not a perfect man. He has flaws like the rest of us. Even so, his life is an inspiration to me. By telling his story of triumph and tragedy in times of economic upheaval and war, I hope to help mend the broken wings of those who read it. If you haven't experienced any hardship in your life, you just haven't lived long enough. Read on, my young friend. Read on. Maybe Dad's story will prepare you for the day when the heat of the sun melts away the wax on your wings, and you feel you can no longer fly.

Notes

1.   *A League of Their Own*, directed by Penny Marshall (Los Angeles: Columbia Pictures, 1982), film; line adapted.

CHAPTER 1

Historians have a knack for finding the right words to encapsulate time. Terms like the Stone Age or the Renaissance are like crib notes to the past. Novelists, on the other hand, are skilled in the conjuring arts. With the wave of an ink-tipped pen, they can materialize the essence of man. Ernest Hemingway managed to do both things in describing the men and women who came of age prior to World War I. He called them the Lost Generation.[1]

In my opinion, though, the whimsical notion of being lost devalues a generation of Americans whose idealism and lives were shattered in "The War to End all Wars" and whose dreams of prosperity went dark on Black Tuesday. To me, the losses of the Great War were much more organic than Hemingway let on: men lost limbs, people lost lives, families lost fathers and sons. After the war, the Lost Generation was hit by the stock market crash, and their losses mounted for more than ten years during the Great Depression. They lost real fortunes in the stock market; life savings in failed banks; homes, farms, and businesses to creditors; and for tens of thousands, the will to live, some of them famously so from windows in tall buildings.

On second thought, Mr. Hemingway may have said it best after all. He captured a generation's soul with just two words. My attempt to improve upon those words takes up a full paragraph and corrals nothing other than, perhaps, my own visceral reaction to the unfortunate lives of people, long since gone, who meant so much to me. Undaunted, I press forward, writing on a related topic. It is the story of a boy from that era—a son of the Lost Generation. It is my story.

Life in the late twenties and thirties was harsh in my hometown of Phoenix, Arizona. Jobs were few, wages were low, and conflict was everywhere. From sputtering factories and fallow farms to tension-filled homes and empty-cupboard kitchens, people knew the only thing great about the Depression was its burden, and their suffering. Given these hardships and deprivations, my parents' generation learned to "use it up, wear it out, make it do, or do without," and pounded these values into the brains, muscles, and sinews of their little ones.

President Franklin D. Roosevelt took office a few years after the crash of '29, and became the nation's Motivator-in-Chief. On Sunday evening, March 12, 1933, he broadcasted a radio message to the nation about the banking crisis at the center of the Great Depression.

> My friends, I want to talk for a few minutes with the people of the United States about banking—to talk with the comparatively few who understand the mechanics of banking, but more particularly with the overwhelming majority of you who use banks for the making of deposits and the drawing of checks. I want to tell you what has been done in the last few days, and why it was done, and what the next steps are going to be . . .
>
> We had a bad banking situation. Some of our bankers had shown themselves either incompetent or dishonest in their handling of the people's funds. They had used the money entrusted to them in speculations and unwise loans. This was, of course, not true in the vast majority of our banks, but it was true in enough of them to shock the people of the United States for a time into a sense of insecurity and to put them into a frame of mind where they did not differentiate, but seemed to assume that the acts of a comparative few had tainted them all. And so it became the government's job to straighten out this situation and to do it as quickly as possible. And that job is being performed.[2]

He would broadcast twenty-nine more radio addresses through 1944, speaking about the economy, the New Deal, and the war. These plain-spoken messages, known as fireside chats, usually began with a folksy greeting and ended on an optimistic note of some kind.

In the summer of 1939, my buddies and I were eagerly anticipating our senior year at Phoenix Union High School. We expected our teams to win every championship, set school records, and reclaim the glory for the Red and Black. We couldn't wait for senior class traditions like ditch day and donkey football. We argued about who would take whom to the Girls' League coed dance and who would do better on the comprehensive examination we faced in the spring.

Our summer of high expectations was put on ice soon after school began. On September 1, 1939, Hitler's Nazi army invaded Poland. Two days later, Britain and France declared war on Germany. That evening President Roosevelt spoke to the nation.

> My fellow Americans and my friends:
>
> Tonight my single duty is to speak to the whole of America. Until four-thirty this morning I had hoped against hope that some miracle would prevent a devastating war in Europe and bring to an end the invasion of Poland by Germany. . . .
>
> This nation will remain a neutral nation, but I cannot ask that every American remain neutral in thought as well. Even a neutral has a right to take account of facts. Even a neutral cannot be asked to close his mind or his conscience.
>
> I have said not once, but many times, that I have seen war and that I hate war. I say that again and again.
>
> I hope the United States will keep out of this war. I believe that it will. And I give you assurance and reassurance that every effort of your Government will be directed toward that end.[3]

We were just poor kids in a desert town but we knew enough about history to wonder how long the nation could remain neutral. We also heard plenty of stories from veterans to suspect our youthful rites of passage were about to be hijacked by the war in Europe. Many of them lamented the wantonness of war, pointing out the sad fact that most of the 127 Arizona boys killed in the First World War lost their lives in the last days of battle.[4]

School was business as usual. The games played, the dances held. But the specter of war seeped into our daily lives. The members of the choir felt it when the music they ordered from a London publishing company could not be delivered because of the war. The kids in the German club reacted to it by hanging a "MAKE FRIENDS NOT BATTLESHIPS" sign in their homeroom, referring to the behemoth *Bismarck* launched earlier in the year by the Nazis. Football players were inspired by it when they started calling wins on opponents' turf a

"European." A team from California, the Covina Colts, was besmirched by it when our yell leaders plastered signs in the visitors' locker room that read KILL THE HUNS and DESTROY THE HUNS, using the Colt's horseshoe emblem for the U in Huns.

The second semester of our senior year saw Germany invade France and attack England by air, followed by invasions of Denmark, Norway, Holland, Belgium, and Luxembourg. On May 26, 1940, the president's voice was heard again in living rooms around the country.

> My friends:
>
> At this moment of sadness throughout most of the world, I want to talk with you about a number of subjects that directly affect the future of the United States. We are shocked by the almost incredible eyewitness stories that come to us, stories of what is happening at this moment to the civilian populations of Norway and Holland and Belgium and Luxembourg and France . . .
>
> At this time, when the world—and the world includes our own American Hemisphere—when the world is threatened by forces of destruction, it is my resolve and yours to build up our armed defenses.
>
> We shall build them to whatever heights the future may require.
>
> We shall rebuild them swiftly, as the methods of warfare swiftly change.
>
> For more than three centuries we Americans have been building on this continent a free society, a society in which the promise of the human spirit may find fulfillment. Commingled here are the blood and genius of all the peoples of the world who have sought this promise.[5]

We graduated five days later in an evening ceremony at the school stadium. Dedicated in 1927, it had a seating capacity of 23,000. On the home side of the field, beautifully adorned cupolas were connected by thirty limestone arches rising high above the bleachers. Looking like a Greek temple, it was a house of worship. Adoring football fans filled the seats every home game.

That night, with only a few thousand guests in attendance, the place felt empty. Standing around in caps and gowns, waiting to get started, my classmates and I shared stories about our experiences there. Many of us remembered being in the stadium as kids watching the "Wonder

Team" of 1930. The boys won the state championship that year, going 13–0.

Thelma Nielsen, a cheerleader, said, "I'll remember playing Phoenix Indian School the week of Thanksgiving. Even though we always won, they were good sports, with long memories. They proudly displayed signs and posters that said, 'Remember 1912' or 'We'll always have 1912.'"

"We became a state in 1912. What else happened that year?" someone asked.

"The Braves trounced us 47–6, and we've been playing them ever since at Thanksgiving-time," she said.

I commented, "Speaking of Indians, I met Jim Thorpe here five years ago."

The boys knew who I was talking about; the girls didn't. Simultaneously they said, "Are you kidding?" and "Who's he?"

One of the boys replied, "Only the greatest athlete ever. He was a college All-American at Carlisle Indian School, a pro baseball player, and the gold medal champion in the pentathlon and decathlon in the 1912 Olympics in Sweden."

"I spoke to him right over there," I said, pointing to the end zone. "He was here with his sons for Greenway Field Day."

"Isn't that the year a guy got skewered by a javelin?"

"Yep. The dumb lump wasn't paying attention and walked across the field just as a guy chucked the spear. It put a damper on the track meet but the down time gave me a chance to meet Big Jim."

A girl from the pep club spoke about her times in the rooting section across the field from the spectators. The club's specialty, cross fire syncopated cheers, was a fan favorite. Another girl referred to singing the fight song when the team scored. We joined in a semi-circle with arms slung over shoulders, and sang it right there on the spot.

> *On coyotes, on coyotes,*
> *Break right through that line*
> *Run that ball right down the field*
> *A touchdown's sure this time!*
> *RAH! RAH! RAH!*
> *On coyotes, on coyotes,*
> *Fight on for our fame*

Come on and fight!!
Fellows fight! and
We will win this game

That led to another fond memory. After games the team would gather at the fifty-yard line and face the home side of the field. Then, with arms raised high and while flashing the V for victory sign, the players and fans would sing our alma mater.

At eight o'clock the Girls' Band wearing white sailor caps and navy blouses over skirts and the ROTC Concert Band looking like toy soldiers in red military coats with brass buttons and high-plumed hats began playing *Semper Fidelis March* by John Philip Sousa. My graduating class walked to the beat around the stadium in four columns, taking our seats on the field, facing the stage set up at the ten-yard line. A large American flag about three-quarters the size of the stage served as a backdrop.

Parents in the stands, still weary from the last war and wary of a new one, were more somber than celebratory. Reverend Stott from Garfield Methodist tried to comfort them in his opening prayer. He prayed for peace in the world and a blessing upon the participants in the program. The reverend's prayer was partially answered that night. Peace, though, would have to wait five years.

The first speaker was valedictorian, Catherine Washburn. Her topic: "Training for Democracy."

"It is fitting and right that the Class of 1940 marched into this stadium to the sounds of Sousa's *Semper Fidelis*. It is the music of the United States Marine Corps. More important, *semper fidelis* is the Marine Corps' motto"—she paused briefly, her voice rising an octave or two. "It means always faithful, always loyal!"

The stadium erupted in applause. The place was starting to warm up. Cathy had set the tone.

There would be no speeches given that night like the ones expressed at previous commencement ceremonies. No impassioned pleas to remain true to the ideals taught at PUHS: "PUNCTUALITY, UNITY, HONOR, and SCHOLARSHIP." No reminiscences about kind deeds and loyal friends or tropes about the promise of a brighter future. These were untenable topics for the class of '40. The civilized world had unraveled in the preceding nine months and we saw it happening right before our eyes on newsreels at the picture show.

The salutatorians, John Haynes and Virginia Rehnstrom, spoke about the need for individual training from the male and female perspectives. John spoke of the pride he felt in seeing ROTC cadets in uniform three times a week. Virginia paid tribute to the marksmanship of the Girls' Rifle Team. Both of their remarks were laced with references to duty, honor, and service. Their words were met with cheers, long and loud.

Mel Ormsby, like me, the grandson of Arizona pioneers, talked about "Our Responsibility to the Future." At one point he said, "We will have no future unless the ambitions of despots and dictators are crushed by men willing to die for freedom. That is our responsibility to the future." Everyone stood up, clapping and shouting amens.

The ceremony continued with our 150-member choir, the Oratorio Society, singing a classic piece followed by a popular tune called *Sweethearts*, taken from a Nelson Eddy and Jeanette McDonald movie. The choir sang our alma mater as its grand finale, earnestly and emotionally. Several of the seniors in the choir struggled to get through it, many with bowed heads and slumping shoulders that shook in concert with their sniffles and sobs.

Hail phoenix hail
Of thy glories we sing
Far over the western skies
Our voices now ring.

Before the first line was sung some of my classmates stood and then a few more and a few more until the entire class was standing and singing along with the choir. With arms outstretched, we flashed the victory sign one more time as proud Coyotes while finishing the words of the song.

Our colors sail,
They will never fail;
Our sons will forever be loyal
Hail phoenix hail.

We clapped and cheered for ourselves for what seemed a long time—long enough to be told to sit down. Then it was time to receive our diplomas.

The president of the board of education was to present them to us in a strictly non-speaking role. At the appointed time, he rose from his chair and walked to the podium. Instead of reaching for the stacks of diplomas, we saw him adjust the microphone, and then he began to speak. Needled by his friends for his extemporaneous outburst, he would later claim he was so caught up in the patriotic fervor that he couldn't help himself.

"We are proud of the rich military tradition here at Phoenix Union. Some of you might know that nine of our graduates died in the Great War. We are also proud to be the first high school in the nation to create a Junior Reserve Officers' Training Corps program."

He paused to recognize the ROTC cadets in our graduating class. They stood to thunderous applause. He then asked the Girls' Drill Unit of the ROTC to stand, and they were received similarly.

"Our ROTC program was created a year before the Great War ended. And now just twenty-two years later we are on the precipice of another world war. You, the graduating class of 1940, may be called upon to serve and to sacrifice. Many of you will leave home in the coming months to help our great nation prepare for that possibility. We pray the conflict overseas will soon be over and that you will not be called upon to risk your lives in battle. But if that day should come, rest assured, we, your PUHS family, will be praying for your success, safety, and speedy return."

The crowd clapped politely.

Stepping away from the podium, he gave a serious nod to the teachers posted at the top of the stairs on each side of the stage. They moved to upright microphones and began to read the names of students ascending the steps. We were standing in alphabetical order in two lines on each side of the field, the A to Ms on one side of the stage and the N to Zs on the other. Pockets of family and friends erupted in cheers as their loved one's name was announced. I stood near the back of the line talking to my friends. The guy in front of me turned around and said, "Mitt me, kid. We made it!" I shook his hand. "But what's next?" he asked. The kid behind us leaned forward, "I'm enlisting!" he proclaimed. The bravado was contagious, spreading like a fever.

"Me too," another guy said.

"I'll be ready when the time comes," said the guy behind him.

I joined in the revelry, adding, "You know me, if there's a fight, I'm in!" We inched toward the platform, anticipating our brief moment of glory, the crowning achievement of our past twelve years. Only it didn't seem so grand anymore.

Diplomas in hand, we returned to our seats and Reverend Stott offered the benediction, ending with words both familiar and new: "Yea, even as they walk through the valley of the shadow of death, bless them to fear no evil: for thou art with them; and let thy rod and thy staff sustain them in their days of affliction."[6]

More than nineteen hundred sons of Arizona died in World War II. Five hundred and ninety-five of them were from the Phoenix area. Eleven of them were in my graduating class at Phoenix Union High School.[7]

Notes

1. The epigraphs in Ernest Hemingway's book *The Sun Also Rises* refer to a Gertrude Stein quote ("You are all a lost generation.") and Ecclesiastes 1:4–5 (KJV), from which the title of the book was taken: "One generation passeth away, and another generation cometh; but the earth abideth forever. The sun also ariseth, and the sun goeth down, and hasteth to his place where he arose."

2. "Franklin D. Roosevelt," *Miller Center of Public Affairs*, accessed October 14, 2014, http://millercenter.org/president/fdroosevelt/speeches/speech 3298.

3. Ibid., 3315.

4. "Arizona's War Dead: WWI, WWII, Korea, Vietnam, Southeast Asia," *The World War I Document Archive*, accessed August 24, 2014, http://wwi.lib.byu.edu/index.php /Arizona's_War_Dead:_WWI,_WWII,_Korea,_Vietnam,_Southwest_Asia.

5. "Franklin D. Roosevelt," *Miller Center of Public Affairs*, 3316.

6. Psalms 23:4 (KJV).

7. State Summary of War Casualties from World War II for Navy, Marine Corps, and Coast Guard Personnel from Arizona 1946; Department of the Navy, Bureau of Naval Personnel. (1942–09/18/1947); National Archives Identifier: 305188 World War II Honor List of Dead and Missing Army and Army Air Forces Personnel from Arizona, 1946; War Department, The Adjutant Generals Office. Administrative Services Division, Strength Accounting Branch; National Archives Identifier: 305279.

CHAPTER 2

I enlisted in the Army Air Corps within a month of graduation and served for five years. During that time, I experienced things that will be forever riveted to my soul: days of triumph and failure, witnessing cruelty and kindness, enduring tragedy, finding slivers of light in all that darkness and learning it can never be fully extinguished.

Decades after I returned home from war, my son found my footlocker in the garage and brought it into the house. Time had not been kind to my old friend. Its leather handles were rotted and worn through; its army green paint had faded into a pasty hue; its hardware was rusty. My name and serial number were barely legible, but they were there, stenciled on the top and side of the box: LT. FRANK KIRKLAND/0-680914. As were these words: MISSING IN ACTION.

"Dad, look what I found in the garage," my son hollered. He had seen it before, as a kid, but hadn't shown much interest in its contents. Now there was excitement in his voice, like he had found buried treasure. "This is your footlocker from the war, right? I found it under the workbench covered by that old parachute we used to play with. I've not seen it in years!"

His tone was quite different from the last conversation we had about the war many years before. He was in college then, filled with book learning. He tried to tell me the causes of World War II, suggesting Roosevelt may have provoked Japan into bombing Pearl Harbor.

"You're a fool if you believe that hogwash," I told him. He said there were several books that suggested it may be true. "My experiences fighting in the war trump anything you're learning sitting on your rear end in a classroom!" The conversation got pretty heated after that. Neither of us backed down.

We didn't see eye to eye on a lot of things in the 1960s. He considered me old-fashioned and out-of-touch. I thought his worldview was naive and unrealistic. Fair or not, I couldn't help but think about the responsibilities I shouldered when I was his age and tended to use my wartime achievements as the baseline for measuring his accomplishments. His baseline was thirty, as in "don't trust anyone over thirty," so he felt that my counsel on any subject was unnecessary.

Every generation revolts against its fathers, but the rebellion of the late '60s stands out. Young people engaged in shocking countercultural activities. They shut down college campuses with sit-ins. They marched against the Vietnam War. Many of their protests involved fire: young men burned their draft cards; young women set their brassieres ablaze. Their shifting values were epitomized by a famous rock concert and hippiefest on a 600-acre farm near Woodstock, New York. Four-hundred thousand long-haired, unshaven, barely clothed people crammed into the place for three days, singing, dancing, drugging, and loving, all in the name of peace. Soon a new term was added to the American lexicon to describe them. They were called the Woodstock Generation.

And so, perhaps, it was inevitable that my generation, called the GI Generation, soon after the Second World War would butt heads with the Woodstock Generation. We marched to defend liberty; they marched to advance civil rights. We wanted to preserve the status quo; they passionately tried to change it. We clung to traditional moral values; they exhibited a fondness for "drugs, sex, and rock 'n' roll." There definitely was a gap between us. People called it a generation gap, although I really gave no thought to it back then. It was just the way things were in those days.

My son wasn't a practicing hippie (but wore his hair too long), but there definitely was a gap between us. That day, though, as he opened the trunk, I sensed something had changed for the better. Maybe it was because I was a widower, nearing the end, and he was a middle-aged father, searching for answers. Time had softened both of us, I suppose. I just knew it was time to reach out, close the gap, and attempt to fill in the gouges left over from days when I scratched my way through life. I wanted my grandchildren to know something about me and hoped that my children would understand me better. Strange as it seems, I envisioned many of my fading generation in living rooms and hospitals, at christenings and wakes, some clear-headed and others not so much, doing what I was about to do.

There was nothing inside my footlocker relating to my life after the war. No gold watch given at retirement; no family photos or Father's Day cards. It was bereft of any post-war references to my first wife, whom I met when I was stationed at a base not far from her home, or my second wife, a coworker at the telephone company whom I met a dozen years later. It was filled, instead, with the fading relics from my place in history. It was the tomb of my youthful ambition.

From the pull-out shelf, my son picked up a black-and-white photograph of me, wrench in hand, working on an airplane engine, and another one, aviator cap pulled over my head, straps unbuckled and dangling on each side of my then handsome face. There was a torn yellowed furlough pass with dates, times, and places, signed, "Lt. Bob Vance"; a small gold patch in the shape of a boot; a broken Hamilton wristwatch with a rectangular face and olive green band, the hour and minute hands frozen at two and six; a green woolen side cap with a red felt star loosely sewn onto the front; and a copy of *Stars and Stripes*, containing military news and commentary, with the headline reading "Rescued Flyer Returns Home."

Below the first shelf was a trophy with the figure of a batter at the plate, the top half of the bat broken off. The inscription read, "Most Valuable Player, Northeastern Texas State Championship, 1942." My aviator jacket was also there, a leather patch stitched over the left breast. The patch contained a caricature of a pilot, grinning and strutting, a parachute strapped to his back, with 56th FIGHTER printed to the left of the figure and SQDN to the right. Sticking out of the pocket of the jacket was the patch of the 429th Bomber Squadron, a yellow quatrefoil bearing the image of an Indian shooting a bow and arrow downward from heaven. I never had the inclination to have it sewn on. My old uniform, an olive drab four-pocket coat and trousers, was folded neatly at the bottom of the box. A blue circle patch was sewn on the left sleeve of the coat. It had an inner gold band surrounded by gold wings, a white star with a red circle at the bottom, and the number fifteen in gold stitching near the top. It was the patch of the 15th Air Force. Lifting the uniform out of the locker, my son found something he thought peculiar at the bottom: a colorful Indian blanket.

"What's the blanket doing in here?"

"It was a gift to my grandfather from an Indian chief."[1]

"You've got to be kidding."

"Nope."

"What happened?"

And so I told the story about my grandfather being surrounded by the chief and his gun-toting, lance-wielding, bow-and-arrow-aiming braves, and the trading of Grandfather's cattle and other supplies for his life, and the token gift of the blanket from the chief. I continued with another one of Grandfather's "close-call" stories, this one involving his encounter with Cochise and thirty Apache braves.[2]

Those stories led to another one about Grandfather's run-in with Geronimo; and still another about a confrontation with a one-eyed Apache renegade named Delshay who called my grandfather "Brave Captain."[3] I shifted gears and started in on the exploits of my uncle Jim Roberts who married my father's sister, Permelia. He was a famous gunfighter in the Graham-Tewksbury feud in Pleasant Valley. The feud led to thirty-four deaths, the most casualties in any civilian conflict in US history. Later, Uncle Jim became a legendary lawman in Jerome, a mining town in the Black Hills of Arizona.

"My grandfather died before I was born but I knew Uncle Jim really well. He was known as the best shot around, better than Wyatt Earp. After retiring from police work, he worked as a security guard for a mining company in Clarkdale. In 1928, when he was 70, he was making his rounds when two men stole 40,000 dollars—the mining company's payroll—from the Bank of Arizona. They were about to get away in a car when Uncle Jim came on the scene. One of the robbers fired at him as they sped away. Standing in the middle of the street, he raised his revolver with both hands, as was his custom, and coolly fired a shot through the back window of the car, killing the driver. The old boy thwarted what would have been the richest bank heist in Arizona history."[4]

I started to mention that the famous Western writer Zane Grey based one of his characters on Uncle Jim in his book *To the Last Man*.[5]

"They even made a movie about it: Randolph Scott was in it, Buster Crabbe, even Shirley Temple . . ."

"What about this old war stuff, Dad? Do you remember anything about it?" my son asked, abruptly, as if to say, "Enough of the cowboy and Indian stuff. Let's stay on topic."

As far as I am concerned, the stories about my ancestors and my memories of the war are inseparable. My brothers and I were honor-bound by many of the unwritten rules and traditions of the Old West. Things like "defend yourself whenever necessary," "look out for your own," "don't make a threat without anticipating the consequences," "be courageous—cowards aren't tolerated in any outfit worth its salt,"[6] were hardwired into our Kirkland cores.

All of this came into play one night when I was a teenager, in 1934, about the time Uncle Jim died. Walking through the front door of our home, I found my little brother standing barefoot at the top of the stairs. One end of a rope was slip-knotted loosely around his neck and the other end had been thrown over an open beam and tied off at the rail. Two of my brothers surrounded him, and they were fuming. Strutting back and forth, they were interrogating him like he had committed a capital offense. My presence must have emboldened him some as he spit out a toxic combination of threats and obscenities. The reaction was chemical, stripping the brotherhood from the room.

Fortunately, no one was seriously hurt that night but such episodes were not uncommon among us. We were ferocious rivals, and close friends, and somehow, I believe, the intensity by which we lived together in those early years and the values we were taught inoculated us from the perils we would face in the Second World War. Some of us fought on beaches and in jungles, others in the air or on oceans. And though more than four hundred thousand American servicemen died in the war, all of us managed to return home safely. Some of us were wounded. All of us needed mending.

I responded to my son's question with a question: "Do I remember?"

Of course I remember, I thought to myself. Even things I want to forget, I remember. Memories of war loop through my mind on a continual reel. They have blurred, to be sure, and become brittle over time, but the residue of even the most fractured frames persists.

Walking over to the front window of my home, I looked over to my boy and then up to the cloudless Arizona sky. It was time to tell the stories of war that shaped my life—before it was too late.

I pulled out some of the papers from my footlocker: military orders, my flight log, telegrams. I gave him a wink and a smile and said, "Like it was yesterday, kid; like it was yesterday . . ."

Notes

1.   Vance Wampler, Arizona, *Years of Courage 1832–1910: Based on the Life and Times of William H. Kirkland* (Phoenix: Quail Run Publications, 1984), 58–62.

2.   Ibid., 53–54.

3.   Ibid., 64.

4.   Jim Hutchinson, "Jim Roberts: He died with his boots on," *The Verde Independent*, December 3, 2013, accessed January 20, 2016, http://verdenews.com/main.asp?SectionID=74&ArticleID=57553.

5.   Zane Grey, *To The Last Man: A Story of the Pleasnt Valley War* (New York: Harper & Brothers, 1921).

6.   "The Code of the West," *Legends of America*, accessed January 11, 2013, http://www.legendsofamerica.com/we-codewest.html.

CHAPTER 3

My remarkable wartime journey started with a train ride to a town linked to aviation history. In 1911, during the time of the Mexican Revolution, Charles Hamilton, a private citizen flying a civilian plane out of El Paso, Texas, observed Poncho Villa's rebels advancing in the distance. He landed his plane and warned the authorities of the imminent attack on the American and Mexican troops guarding the border between El Paso and Ciudad Juarez, Mexico. It was the first time an airplane pilot looked down on ground troops in a combat situation.[1] The report was duly noted by the US Army brass, and they began to make plans to take advantage of the airplane as a potential instrument of war. Over the next thirty years they would conceive, design, and construct a master planned series of training grounds, flight schools, and airfields, the crown jewel being Randolph Field, Texas, where I was to report for duty.

My orders were to take the Southern Pacific to El Paso, transfer to a train to San Antonio, and from there catch a bus to Randolph Field. It would be my first time on a train but not my first time leaving the state, if you count the fishing trip I took a couple of days before with my buddy Warren Weems. He was the star athlete at PUHS and had just signed induction papers for the Navy.

We drove his '29 Ford to the Colorado River, camping on the Arizona side. The next morning we crossed over the bridge at Blythe to fish on the California side of the river. We caught a couple of rainbows and were frying them up for breakfast when a fish and game warden moseyed up to our campfire, asking to see our fishing licenses. We explained we were from Phoenix and didn't know we needed a license to fish. He gave us a stern talking-to about obeying the law, respect, and a whole lot of "didn't your parents teach you boys nothin'?"

Throughout the lecture, we could hear the crackle of the oil and the sizzle of the fish. Smoke rose from the pan as the warden began writing us up, slowly, and tore out two tickets, slower still, from his book, each fitted with a one dollar fine. He was aware of what was happening to our breakfast but demanded our full attention, insisting he was "this close" to taking us in. By the time he was through, there were no rainbows left on the trout and no trout left in the pan, only the charred residue of our last boyhood adventure.

We got back into the car and crossed over the bridge to the Arizona side. Warren crumpled the tickets into a ball and threw it at me. My usual instinct was to catch whatever Warren threw, footballs, baseballs, it didn't matter, but I let this one pass by me and watched as it flew out the window. We both laughed and began to speculate where we would be and what we'd be doing on the date we were ordered back to Blythe to pay the fines.

"You'll be peeling bugs off windshields, hah," he suggested.

"You'll be scraping barnacles off of old scows," I countered with a laugh.

We exchanged a few more insults and then grew quiet. As the ticket ball bounced down the road behind us Warren chortled, "What's the game warden going to do about it anyway?" I nodded in silence as we headed back to Phoenix.

On my last night home, I stuffed a few things into a small suitcase for the trip: my glove and the baseball cap I wore in the state championship game, socks, a few tee-shirts, and a few pairs of BVDs. Dad used to joke that in a pinch you could wear the same underwear at least four days: right side out one day, inside out the next, forward one day, backward the next and repeat as long as necessary. He said he lived that way as a young buck hauling freight across the desert in buckboard wagons. While I always laughed at the story, I sincerely hoped I wouldn't have to resort to such measures before getting my government issued gear.

The next morning, my parents drove me to Union Station. Not much was said. Mother handed me a crumpled grocery bag from Mary Lou's market. Inside were packed homemade tortillas wrapped in tin foil, frijoles in a Mason jar, and some oranges.

As we stood on the platform, waiting for the train, a Mexican woman, about fifty years old, approached us.

"Are you Frank Kirkland?" she asked.

Dad and I answered in unison, "Yes."

Looking at my dad, she asked, "Is your father William H. Kirkland?" He nodded affirmatively.

"My mother was Mercedes Quiroz," she said, her eyes searching for some recognition in our faces.

"Yes. How may I help you?"

"My mother's family worked for your father at his lumberyard near the Santa Rita Mountains."

"Many people worked for my father."

"She was kidnapped by Aravaipa Apaches when she was twelve, and your father rescued her.[2] I wouldn't be here today if it weren't for him."

"You're her daughter? Well thank you for introducing yourself, my dear."

He put out his hand to shake hers. She threw her arms around him. He remained ram-rod straight.

It was not unusual for one of us to be stopped in public places, asked if we were Kirklands, and be regaled with a story or two about our grandfather's good deeds. I was waiting for the day someone approached us about the haircut story, wondering how Dad would react to that one. Grandmother had beautiful, long, thick, black hair, a feature Grandfather very much admired. Unfortunately, a doctor cut it all off as a remedy for her chronic headaches. It would be his last medical procedure. Grandfather confronted him in a saloon and shot him dead after the doctor lunged at him with a knife.[3] Criminal charges were not filed. A man had the right to uphold his wife's dignity and self-defense was a time-honored tradition in the west, even if you provoked the fight.

A porter yelled out, "Ten minutes . . . train to El Paso leaving in ten minutes!"

Mother looked over to me, bowed her head, then looked up and stared at me, her deep brown eyes moist. She tried to speak but found it difficult. Finally she said, "Be careful and make me proud."

Dad suggested I may need some money and started to hand me a five-dollar bill. I protested, weakly, showing him the seven dollars in my wallet. I noticed Dad looking at the wallet with a bit of a smile, at least his lips pursed. He expressed admiration for my leatherwork, proudly commenting on the fact that I had carved our initials—FJK—and my Jr. between columns of curlicues into the leather. Eager to impress him further, I was about to show him my custom-made comb holder in the other back pocket when I felt the fiver slipping from my fingers. Apparently, Dad thought the seven bucks would hold me over just fine. As I tried to compose myself after this bit of misdirection, we said our good-byes, shook hands, and parted ways.

I started walking down the platform, looking for my coach car. I passed by some officers and enlisted men, families with small children, and some accompanied by grandparents—recruits like me leaving home for the first time. There were so many people that I had to turn my shoulders this way and that to pass by them, being careful not to hit someone with my bag. The pace was slow, allowing me to overhear snippets of conversations: confessions of love and promises to wait, a man encouraging his wife to be strong until he could send for her, expressions of hope for work in faraway cities, and mothers telling sons to write.

I boarded the train, taking a seat across from a pretty young mother with two small children, a boy and a girl. Sitting next to me was an old man, and next to him, his daughter, a middle-aged woman, nicely dressed. After making our introductions, I learned the young mother was joining her husband, who had found work in El Paso. The old man was a cotton farmer from Buckeye, and his daughter, the widow of a Doughboy killed in France. She had no children, so she devoted her life to caring for her parents. Her mother had recently passed, and they were taking her remains to be interred in Tucumcari, New Mexico.

"Where are you headed, son?" the old man quizzed.

"Randolph Field in Texas, the West Point of the Air!" I said proudly, explaining it was a training base for pilots.

"Do you have a girlfriend?" the young mother asked, joining in the pleasantries.

I nodded in the affirmative and said she was one of the reasons I joined the Army Air Corps.

"How so?" she asked.

"Her name is Helen Norwood," I explained, "but I call her Twee."

Helen lived in a nice neighborhood near the capitol building. A couple of days after graduation, she arranged for me to meet her neighbor, Pat Maguire, an airline pilot, at her house one afternoon. He appeared to be in his forties, wearing slacks, a pin stripe shirt, tasseled cordovan loafers, and aviator sunglasses. He was nice enough at first, sharing his background and experiences: crop duster as a teen, pilot during WWI, flying mostly reconnaissance missions, and then, after the war, landing a job with upstart Trans World Airlines. He had been flying the Phoenix to San Francisco route for a couple of years when I met him.

"Flying is the only thing I have ever wanted to do in my life," I told him. "When I was a little boy I used to crawl under the fence at Sky Harbor Airport to play in an old Jenny parked in the outfield."

"Oh, you liked playing on the Farm?" he asked. "Years ago, I used to have to buzz the airfield to clear off the stray cows before landing." He started to laugh, and Twee joined him. I just nodded my head.

I didn't say so, but I always thought "the Farm" was a crude way to characterize a magical place where people could fly. Even the words "sky harbor" caused my imagination to stir about a wonderful world where flying ships sailed a blue sky stretching beyond oceans I had never seen.

"It was always a game of cat and mouse with the pilots and maintenance men. They would run me off the property, and I always came back," I told him.

"I didn't know that," Twee interjected.

"Sure, I learned the best time to sneak onto the plane was during lunch hour or when other planes were landing. Once inside the cockpit, I was short enough to be somewhat hidden, and when I slid down to reach the braces with my feet, I felt practically invisible. I climbed into the old plane many times, passing the time pushing the stick back and forth, dreaming my dream."

Mr. Maguire interrupted, "It couldn't have been that hard to sneak in. The ground crews seemed pretty inattentive in the old days. I remember trying to land there at night just five or six years ago. They forgot to turn on the beacon, boundary, and obstruction lights. I had to fly low, throttle back the engine, and yell out, 'Lights! Lights!' until someone woke up and turned the darn things on."

Helen laughed. I didn't.

"Well, I was just a kid playing make-believe. I'm pretty sure I'd do things differently now."

"Sure, kid," he said, and then began to quiz me about planes, trying to embarrass me in front of Twee.

"Jenny—what model was she?" he asked.

"Curtiss JN-4 trainer plane."

"Bi-wing or mono?" he asked. It was a stupid question, really. Curtiss didn't build a mono-wing plane until the Robin in 1928. The JN-4 was at least ten years older than that.

"Bi-wing, equipped with a forty-five horsepower motor. In its heyday it could go sixty miles per hour."

"Yes," he said, "that was a great little plane. It's quite simple by today's standards."

"I know what you mean. The instrument panel inside the cockpit just had a basic compass, an altimeter, and a ball bank indicator, used to measure the pitch and roll of the plane. There was no control yoke, the steering mechanism was a simple stick and foot brace system cabled to the rudder and elevators. The pilot controlled the movements of the plane in a synchronized dance with his hands on the stick and his feet under the wood braces."

"Frank, you know everything about airplanes," Helen mused. I gave her a quick wink.

"So Frank, what do you want to ask me? Helen set this meeting up by promising me some cookies or something, if I were nice to you, is the way she put it." Twee blushed and I took her by the hand.

"Well, sir, I want to learn how to fly. I want to get my pilot license."

"My boss at TWA, Jack Frye, received the first commercial pilot license in the state. I am sure we can find you a suitable school."[4]

He suggested several civilian flight schools, including one operating out of the north terminal at Sky Harbor. He told me about college courses I could take. My answer to each recommendation was the same:

"Sounds good, but that costs money and I don't have any."

Growing weary of our conversation, and perhaps my excuses, he said somewhat curtly, "If you really want to fly, join the Army Air Corps!"

And so I did.

I arrived early the next day at the recruiting station downtown and signed induction papers within an hour. The master sergeant told me I could do my basic training in California or Texas. "Texas," I replied. "I've already been to California." That was kind of a whopper but not really. I had stood on California soil, if only for a few hours, and I knew that Texas was the major training hub for Army Air Corps pilots, and that is where I wanted to be.

"So you're going to be a pilot?" the old farmer asked, his raspy voice barely rising above the noise of the lumbering train. "How exciting," his daughter exclaimed.

"Actually, the recruiter said that with just a high school education I couldn't be a pilot, so I signed up to be an airplane mechanic," I rather reluctantly acknowledged.

Except for the little boy and girl, my traveling companions gave me the kind of painful look Mother gave when she caught me in an exaggeration. I tried to explain that I still planned to fly but my words disappeared along with their interest. I wanted them to know that the Air Corps required two years of college in order to take the qualifying exam for flight school, and that I had just finished high school. But after a few "good lucks" and "God bless yous" they returned to their prior preoccupations.

A few hours later I felt, surprisingly, a little low. I was riding on a train with no return ticket and didn't know when or if I would see my friends and family again. I tried to relax by listening to the rhythm of the train. Closing my eyes, I felt the power of the locomotive engine, metal striking metal, as the cars glided across the rails. When I opened my eyes I noticed that the passengers sitting in the forward facing benches were always looking forward, and that those stuck in the rear-facing benches would regularly look over their shoulders to catch a glimpse of what lay ahead. And then it hit me—some would call it a revelation, pushing aside my doubts and fears.

I had many good ideas pop into my head before this one. I conceived of a way to stay cool during hot summer nights with blocks of ice and burlap sacks. I found a sting-proof method to catch scorpions using cheesecloth, tape, and a broom handle. I had implemented many schemes to get the best of my brothers. But those were solutions for simpler times. Now our country was headed for war, and I would have a part in it, at least I hoped so. I tried to recall what Reverend Lane meant when he talked about putting away childish things and seeing through a dark glass, but I couldn't remember his point. *Doesn't matter,* I thought, *I like the sound of my own new testament better anyway: Don't look back!*

As we crossed into New Mexico, I asked the farmer why he was burying his wife in Tucumcari. "She grew up there, 'tho it was called Six Shooting Siding when her parents first settled in," he said, explaining the town had a sordid history of deadly gunfights. The conductor announced we were nearing the station, so the farmer and his daughter prepared to detrain.

I mentioned that my grandparents lived in New Mexico for a couple of years and that my Aunt Elizabeth and Uncle George went to grade school with William Bonney. "You probably remember him as Billy the Kid, the famous gunfighter. I am sure you've heard of him," I suggested. Seeing their eyes rolling again, I simply said good-bye.

My grandparents were William Hudson Kirkland and Missouri Ann Bacon. He passed in 1910, she in 1915. They're buried in the Tempe Double Butte Cemetery, their final resting place a window to their lives. The ground there is hard and has little shade; there are more rocks than grass. They are interred side by side in a gravesite set apart from other graves in the cemetery, its confines marked by a cement enclosure. A tall, broad monument stands over them. Grandmother's name, birth date, and death date are engraved on the east side of the obelisk. Grandfather's inscription is on the other side, appropriately so. His journey ended as it had begun: facing the West.

In 1850, Grandfather left his Missouri home at seventeen in search of California gold. At Independence he bought a stake in some wagons, oxen, and provisions for 125 dollars, nearly all of his life's savings, and headed west with the Chrisman Train, a company of 30 wagons and 150 men, women, and children. After five years in California and having pulled his fair share of gold dust and nuggets from its streams, he decided to return to Missouri to see his family.[5]

Some miners traveled back east aboard steamships out of San Francisco, paying outrageous sums for their tickets. It cost 125 dollars for steerage, 225 dollars for second class, and 275 dollars for first class.[6] Grandfather refused to buy a ticket at those prices, preferring to ride his horse for free. The route home would take him from San Francisco to Los Angeles to the Arizona Territory, passing through Yuma and Tucson, and then on to New Mexico, Texas, and then north onto the Santa Fe trail.

Atop a horse is a good place to think. Grandfather did a lot of it during the long quiet stretches between towns. Restless and ambitious, he pondered what to do with the gold slung over his saddle in pouches. He hadn't gone very far when it dawned on him it was merchants who were getting rich in the gold fields, not common, everyday prospectors like him. If you wanted to work, it cost you eight dollars for a mining pan that had cost fifteen cents before the rush. If you wanted to eat, an egg cost a dollar. Butter was six dollars a pound; a box of sardines, sixteen dollars; flour, fifty dollars a barrel.[7] He would always remember what happens to prices when the demand is greater than the supply. Eventually he would experience the bitter consequences of what happens to prices when the supply is greater than the demand.

At that time Arizona was comprised of land split off from the New Mexico Territory and 45,000 square miles in and around Tucson purchased from Mexico in 1853, in a deal known as the Gadsden Purchase.[8] To maintain law and order before Mexico turned over control of the area to the United States, Mexican troops remained garrisoned at a fort in Tucson—the Presidio San Agustín del Tucson. They were still there when Grandfather arrived in 1856. At the appointed time the soldiers were ordered back to Mexico.

With much pomp and pageantry, the Mexican troops marched out of town in their dress uniforms. As the rear guard reached the end of what is now Washington Street, Grandfather mounted an American flag on the roof of a dry goods store. It was the first time an American flag flew over Arizona. Seeing the flag, twenty Mexican soldiers returned, demanding that it come down until their army was out of sight. Grandfather refused, saying, while holding a Navy Colt revolver in one hand, "Old Glory will never come down unless we're compelled to do so by force, and I don't think you're up to the task, my amigos."[9] The Mexicans swore at him and marched away for the final time.

Sensing an opportunity to sell supplies to the incoming United States Army, Grandfather remained in Tucson. He started a business that sold corn to the Army. Within three years he would parlay his profits from the corn into a logging operation in Madera Canyon and a cattle ranch on the Santa Cruz River. He never made it back to Missouri.[10]

My grandmother's family was from St. Louis. In 1859, they headed west in a wagon train, stopping in Tucson in October.[11] Her father, a Presbyterian minister, determined they would remain there so he could try his hand at preaching. While he looked for the lost sheep of God's fold, my great-grandmother opened the first restaurant in town, and Grandmother helped run the place.

Grandfather met Grandmother there and became a frequent patron. A year later they were married.

Most of their early years together were marked by frequent moves as Grandfather doggedly looked for new business opportunities. The farming, freighting, lumberjacking, ranching, mining dairyman would also become a road builder, irrigationist, and contractor. His friends said the Kirklands moved so often their chickens, at seeing Grandfather return home, fell on their backs and stuck up their feet to be tied with twine, readying themselves for travel in the buckwagon.[12]

The frequent moves were also driven by an innate need to live away from people. It has always puzzled me why he would start a settlement or town and move away just as it was coming on. This wanderlust may have scratched some kind of an itch, but it also made life more dangerous, exposing his family over the years to frequent threats from Apaches, banditos, and marauders. After many years of resistance, Grandfather grew tired of losing his livestock to thieves. Grandmother was even wearier from sleepless nights spent, rifle in hand, protecting their children and home while he tracked down rustlers.

In 1871, with three children to care for and one on the way, they moved to a safer place north of Maricopa Wells in the Salt River Valley, an area that would become the financial center of Phoenix.[13] Glass and steel skyscrapers are now planted where alfalfa and cotton once grew. A twenty-story office building is located on the north side of Washington Avenue, equidistant to Central Street and First Avenue. It sits over the site where Grandfather built their adobe home.

Grandfather quickly became active in civic affairs. He was appointed a member of the first Maricopa County Board of Supervisors. After moving to Tempe, he was appointed justice of the peace and thereafter was known as Judge Kirkland. The year before the move, the Phoenix township awarded him half a city block for "services rendered" as a public servant. Regrettably, he traded the future downtown Phoenix property for a yoke of oxen for his new farm. Of course, downtown lots were selling for around 8 dollars and a yoke of two oxen was worth about a 150 dollars, so it wasn't such a bad deal at the time.

Millions have come to the boom-and-bust state that is Arizona since the old days. My grandfather was a trailblazer to those who made fortunes, as well as to those who lost them. Timber, gold, silver, wheat, cattle, water, real estate—he blazed all of those trails and then flamed out financially. A year before he died, he wrote to an old pioneer friend: "So you see I was about first in everything pertaining to enterprise though the Bible says the first shall be last and last shall be first. That has been my fate."[14]

Notes

1. WPA Texas, *Randolph Field: A History and Guide* (New York: The Devin-Adair Company, 1942), 31.

2. Vance Wampler, *Arizona, Years of Courage 1832–1910: Based on the Life and Times of William H. Kirkland* (Phoenix: Quail Run Publications, 1984), 67–69.

3. Ibid., 29.

4. "Jack Frye," *Wikipedia*, accessed July 28, 2014, http://en.wikipedia.org/wiki /Jack_Frye.

5. Wampler, *Arizona, Years of Courage*, 14–15.

6. Ibid., 29.

7. Ibid., 28.

8. "Gadsden Purchase, 1853–1854," *U.S. Department of State, Office of the Historian*, accessed February 8, 2013, https://history.state.gov/milestones/1830-1860 /gadsden-purchase.

9. Wampler, *Arizona, Years of Courage*, 36–37.

10. Ibid., 50–51.

11. Ibid., 84–85.

12. Ibid., 125.

13. Ibid., 138.

14. Ibid., 212.

CHAPTER 4

Our train chugged along the ancient pass through the Franklin Mountains and into El Paso Union Passenger Depot. I helped the young mother—by then I knew her by name, Catherine—and her two kids off the train and into the care of her husband. My connection to San Antonio didn't leave for a few hours, so I had some time to poke around.

The station was an architectural marvel, with coffered ceilings, arched windows, and a large gabled tower. I walked around looking through display cases of Mexican and Indian artifacts. A map oriented me to the city relative to the Rio Grande River. Old black-and-white photographs of the depot under construction hung on the walls. An inscription posted to the side of the exit door read, "El Paso del Rio del Norte," and in smaller type, "The Pass of the North River." *So that's where the town got its name*, I thought. I amused myself thinking about it. I knew El Paso meant the Pass but I had never thought to ask why. I began to wonder what else I didn't know about the things I knew.

Pushing through the double doors I was briefly blinded by the sun. As the spots faded from my eyes, I noticed ten or so enlistees heading toward International Bridge. On the other side of the river was Ciudad Juarez. Founded in 1659 by Spanish explorers seeking a route through the southern Rockies, the city was originally called Paso del Norte. I ran after the guys, asking about their plans. One of them pointed across the river and another guy blurted, "We're headed to the Papillon Club in Juarez."

"What for?" I asked.

Raising his curled fingers and extended thumb to his mouth, he replied, "Cerveza, lots of cheap, cold cerveza. And women, lots of cheap, hot women!"

Everybody laughed and exchanged nods, shoves, and winks. It seemed like more trouble than I was prepared to take on at the time, so I dropped back from the pack and followed the pathway along the river back to the depot. A hodgepodge of gift shops—some of them selling Mexican trinkets, others turquoise jewelry—and a few cafes, a coffee shop, and taco stands dotted the neighborhood around the station. Hungry, I decided to find a place to eat.

There were several options that appealed to me. The Harvey House, a sit-down-order-your-food-from-a-waitress type place—too expensive; a covered wooden booth in which sweet-smelling onions, peppers, and carne asada were sizzling in oil on open griddles—very tempting; and a taqueria with no front door, one front sliding window, and murals painted on either side of the window of two old Mexican women, one in a yellow dress, the other wearing a coral colored dress, rolling tortillas on a flat stone over a campfire. Above the window in bright blue paint were the words, "We Roll Tortillas Like a Mother." Having already eaten or given away the tortillas packed by my own mother, I chose this place with a smile.

There were no tables or chairs. Instead there was a stand-up arrangement with a long wooden shelf about waist high mounted on the wall around the corner, with a long bar along the bottom on which customers could rest a foot. A canvas awning overhead offered protection from the sun. Four white canisters packed with brown paper napkins were mounted above the shelf every five feet. Food in hand, I searched for a spot along the feeding wall, spotting an opening next to a tall, well-dressed man.

"Excuse me, sir," slightly bumping his arm, disrupting his next bite.

"You're okay, young man. Slide on in here before your food gets cold," he said with a high-pitched voice.

I was startled to see that he was a black man. He must have known what I was thinking and, trying to put me at ease, asked, "What's in the bag, son?" He then chuckled and said, while flashing a broad smile, "Cause I'm still hungry."

I laughed in return, the kind of laugh you have to think about to get out. I had never seen a black man quite like him. In a way he reminded me of my high school superintendent, Dr. Montgomery, without the intimidation factor. I had been in Dr. Montgomery's office a time or two, so I knew the difference.

He was wearing a grey three-piece suit and shiny black wingtip shoes, and his bearing was as crisp as his starched white shirt. You'd have to say he was handsome: hair combed neatly with a part to the side, a thin trimmed mustache under a long, flat nose. He was leaning on the shelf with his other arm, a fedora resting nearby, and a brown leather briefcase was upright at his feet.

I scrunched myself into the opening and in between bites of taco, tried to respond to his questions.

"Where are you from?" he asked.

"Phoenix, Arizona," I said proudly.

"Where are you headed?" he continued, seeming to be genuinely interested in my answers.

"Randolph Field, Texas," I said even more proudly.

"I've just come from Texas. Randolph Field is the West Point of the Air, right? Are you going to . . ."

I cut him off before he could finish the question, still stinging from the first leg of my trip. "Yes, but I enlisted as an airplane mechanic. I'm hoping to be a pilot someday, though!"

"It is good for a man to have big dreams. I hope you'll realize yours. We have something in common, you know."

I couldn't imagine what I had in common with this well-spoken black man but I asked anyway.

"I went to Howard University Law School, called the West Point of Negro Leadership. So in a way we're both West Point men. If you're done eating, let's go down to that bench by the river for a visit. My train to Chicago doesn't leave for another hour."

Making liberal use of the napkins, I wiped the grease from my face and hands, and joined him near the water's edge.

"I am George," he said, while extending his hand.

I shook his hand and introduced myself.

"I know a good deal about Phoenix. Know anybody from Okemah?" he asked.[1]

I nodded yes, while giving no indication how I knew boys from that neighborhood. At the same time, I couldn't help but snicker some, thinking about the fistfights we had. I didn't know there was any more to a cracker than flour and salt until I got tangled up with some black boys from Okemah.

He continued: "My cousin lives in that part of town. Did you know Negroes from Oklahoma named their neighborhood after a Kickapoo Indian chief?"[2]

I didn't know that and shook my head as indication.

"A lot of Negroes moved to Phoenix for work, believing they would be treated fairly. My cousin encouraged me to visit. He sent me a newspaper clipping telling me how wonderful things are there. I've got it right here in my briefcase."

Clicking open the double latches, he quickly retrieved the article. "This is from the Phoenix Tribune."

"Never heard of it," I said.

"It's a Negro paper," he said as he began to read, "'Phoenix is the best city in the USA. . . . the most friendly relations exist between Caucasians and the Colored people. Now and then an antagonistic individual bobs up, but the good overwhelms the bad until you scarcely realize that any bad has been done.'"[3]

"Thanks, I didn't know that," I said, proudly.

"It's bologna," he said matter-of-factly.

He pointed out the obvious—blacks were not permitted to use public restrooms, drinking fountains, swimming pools, or other public accommodations—and the not so obvious.

"Did you know that banks won't loan money to Negroes for homes in white neighborhoods? Or that builders won't sell their homes to Negroes outside of Negro neighborhoods? Even the federal government is in on it. The Home Owners' Loan Corporation created national standards for determining property values, which took into account the ethnicity of nearby residents. In Phoenix, the properties in the northern half of the city exclude the so-called 'detrimental races and nationalities.' Negroes are ranked second from the bottom of that list, one rung above Mexicans," he said.[4]

I didn't know anything about that, but I knew colored children weren't allowed to cross Van Buren and walk through white neighborhoods in the northern part of the city, unless they had some kind of chore to do.

"Do you know where Phoenix Union Colored High School is? How about 9th Avenue Colored School?" George quizzed.

"Of course," I said. "My family has been in Phoenix forever. My grandfather was a trustee of School District One, which opened the first public school in Arizona in 1872."

"How do you feel about Negro children being stuck with discarded equipment and supplies, a bunch of hand-me-downs from white schools?"

"That's just the way things are—equal but separate," I protested, feeling somewhat defensive.

"Really, you are content with the way things are? You think things are equal? How can it be okay when children are separated like that in substandard conditions, no textbooks to read?"

"When you put it that way, it does seem they are at a real disadvantage," I replied.

"In my opinion, Negroes have been at a disadvantage in Arizona since its early days. Did you know there were so many strong ties to the South that Tucson folks entered into an agreement to join the Confederacy when the South seceded from the Union?"

I didn't know that.

"And that Tucson was the western capital of the Confederate Arizona Territory for a time?"[5]

"That sounds like Civil War stuff. My grandparents lived around Tucson during the Civil War years. But, no, I've never heard of that before."

"Not many people have. It only lasted a year or so. Union troops drove the Confederate forces out of Arizona in 1862."

"My grandfather hired many coloreds to work in his mine, paid them a fair wage. He thought they had a gift for finding gold and silver. He hired coloreds to work at his Conoa Ranch too. Some of them were freed slaves. I bet if you asked any of them, they'd tell you William Kirkland treated them right."

"Sounds like he's a good man. There are plenty of good white folks who see things the way I do."

He then told me that thousands of white people around the nation opposed segregation, using former Arizona Governor Kibbey as an example. In 1909, he vetoed a school segregation law enacted by the Territorial Legislature, stating it was unfair to give colored children a less effective education than white students. The legislature overrode his veto within a few days, ensuring that white children would not have to attend school with black kids. A few years after leaving office, Kibbey tried again, filing a petition with the court to enjoin school segregation. He argued that "separate could never be equal." He lost, again.[6]

I didn't know there were men like Governor Kibbey in Arizona or anywhere else, for that matter.

"How do you know so much about such things?" I asked.

"It's my business to know about them. I am sure you've gone to the movies and seen blacks sitting in balconies?"

He was not really asking but just stating the obvious. I nodded in the affirmative, and he continued. "When I was a student at a small college in Pennsylvania, I went to the movies with my friend Goody, intending to sit in the white-only section. We rushed past the ushers who were telling us to sit up in the balcony and we took a bunch of guff from some white folks but we planted ourselves right there the whole movie.[7] You can't believe how good it felt to stand up for ourselves that way. Ever since, I have devoted my life to the cause of civil rights for my people. We're Americans, right? All of us—white and black—deserve equal rights, equal protections, don't you think? Is the US Constitution there to protect the rights of white folks only or does it apply to all Americans?"

He was like an evangelist trying to reshape a sinner's stony heart, the power of persuasion his chisel and his strength of character the mallet. Most everything he said I could see from his point of view, but it conflicted with my upbringing and experience. Sure there was conflict but it was just the order of things in those days. In fact, we learned in high school that Phoenix was downright progressive when it came to colored folks.

Phoenix was one of the few towns that banned *Birth of a Nation* from its movie theaters. The hugely popular 1915 silent movie had a very loud impact on the nation. Set in the Reconstruction period, it glorified the Ku Klux Klan as the righteous force that protected noble white folks from overbearing and sexually aggressive blacks. The newly organized National Association for the Advancement of Colored People decried the movie and tried to have it banned. But the effort was largely ignored in most cities, and even in the nation's capital. After seeing it in the White House screening room, President Wilson was reported to have said, "It is like writing history with lightning, and my only regret is that it is all so terribly true."[8]

The reaction of the general public was predictable. Black audiences shed tears while many white audiences cheered. As the film swept the nation, white-on-black violence broke out in major cities including Boston and Philadelphia, and in small towns such as Lafayette, Indiana, where a black teenage boy was killed.[9]

The Ku Klux Klan successfully used the movie to kick-start an aggressive membership drive, with the clan's numbers peaking afterwards. But the movie promoters were no match for the ladies of the Arizona Federation of Colored Women's Clubs.[10] The ladies of the various groups like the Order of Calanthe, Sisters of the Mysterious Ten, and the Daughters of Tabor joined forces to oppose the movie, and they succeeded in having it banned in Phoenix. When the movie came back around in the 1930s, the ladies of the colored clubs regrouped to keep the most objectionable scenes from being shown.

There were also white folks in town willing to extend a helping hand and there were public places where people coexisted just fine. The Phoenix Americanization Committee, hoping to assimilate immigrants into American culture, established the Friendly House in 1922, a two-room community house on 1st Avenue. Immigrants were taught lessons in English, hygiene, homemaking, and job placement skills.[11]

People of all races patronized Joy Land for picnics, marathon dances, and burlesque shows. Another popular place was the Riverside, an amusement park that included an outdoor ballroom that could hold up to 3,000 people. Thursday was blues night, primarily for Negroes. On Wednesday and Saturday nights, Anglos would dance to the music of Bob Fite and the Western Playboys. Sunday night was Mexican night, featuring Latin bands.[12]

Starting in 1927, Phoenicians of all persuasions joined together in an annual pageant called "The Masque of the Yellow Moon" at Montgomery Stadium.[13] It was inspired by the ancient Indian tradition of giving thanks at the time of the full spring moon. The pageant director, Cordelia Perkins, selected a southwest history theme each year and worked with the students at my high school to create costumes, music, and dance routines for the production. The much anticipated coronation of the annual Queen of the Masque took place during the pageant's intermission.

I told George about all of these things.

"Were Negroes allowed to dance on the same dance floor as whites?" he asked.

I assured him they were.

"The same time as white folks?"

"Most places don't but they can at the Riverside."

"You mean to tell me that Negroes and white folks dance around the dance floor together, at the same time, at the Riverside?"

"Well, no, Negroes dance on their side of the floor, Anglos on the other side."

"That's what I thought. Were Negro children allowed to participate in the Yellow Moon pageant?" he asked.

"They could buy a ticket and watch like everyone else."

"That's not what I mean. Did Negroes get to wear costumes? Did they dance at the pageant?"

"How could they? They don't go to Phoenix Union High School."

"Come on, Frank. Since they can't even go to your school, that doesn't hold any water with me or any right thinking person for that matter! By the way, was the pageant queen ever anything other than a white child?" he asked.

"No."

"So, what were you doing in Texas? Do you have family there too?" I asked, trying to change the subject.

He told me his trip was all business. He worked as a special assistant to Thurgood "Goody" Marshall, lead counsel for the NAACP, and George's friend from college. They had been in a series of meetings with Governor Allred to protest Texas procedures that prevented blacks from serving on juries, and to make it clear that the practice was a violation of Texas law.[14] After the meetings were over, George remained in Texas for a time to see the initiative through to the end.

"Do you think it is fair that black folk can't serve as jurors or blacks accused of crimes don't even have the possibility of a jury of their peers?" He didn't let me answer. "The governor eventually saw it our way and took it one step further, agreeing to order the Texas Rangers to protect black jurors during trials."

He looked at his pocket watch and indicated it was time to catch his train. Placing his hand on my shoulder, he smiled kindly, then turned and walked toward the station. "So long, Frank. Good luck becoming a pilot!" I said good-bye and turned toward the Rio Grande, attracted to the sound of the constant flow of the great river, slipping past grassy shores. I never saw George again, but I did see a picture of Thurgood Marshall on the cover of *Time* magazine about fifteen years later. In a landmark case he won nine Supreme Court converts—white men in black ropes—who ruled that separate was not equal. A seven-year-old black girl named Tina Brown had prevailed over the all-white Topeka, Kansas, Board of Education.[15] It would be the first crack in the wall of segregation.

Standing on the shoreline, I looked up to see a flock of honking geese flying in some semblance of a V formation. The weaker, slower geese were bouncing back and forth near the tail end, trying to fall into the draft line where the flying was easier. It portended things to come for me. I saw similar flight patterns during the war. Flying in formation was the creed and ritual of every American bomber pilot. We were trained to do what those birds did naturally. Before each run the commanding officer would say something like, "Okay boys, keep your planes tucked in tight and you'll make it back alright!" Unfortunately, there were stragglers in our formations too—sometimes it was pilot error, just as likely, fatigue; maybe an electrical malfunction or tuckered out engine; or simply because the plane was shot to pieces, steel shredded, oil spewing, tail torn in two—easy pickings for German fighter pilots.

I gazed northward. A wall of granite had disappeared over time under the constant flow of the Rio Grande. The immovable object had been no match for the unstoppable force. A northern passageway had been carved through rock and stone without hands. I spent a fair amount of time thinking about that and what I had just experienced with George, and then headed back to the train station.

Notes

1. David R. Dean and Jean A. Reynolds, *City of Phoenix: African American Historic Property Survey* (Phoenix: Athenaeum Public History Group, 2004), accessed January 22, 2016, https://www.phoenix.gov/pddsite/Documents/pdd_hp_pdf_00082.pdf.

2. "110 Years Ago: April 22, 1902 Town Opens!," *Okemah Historical Society*, accessed March 18, 2014, http://okemahok.blogspot.com/2012/04/brief-history-of-okemah-oklahoma-110.html.

3.   Dean and Reynolds, *City of Phoenix: African American*, 11.

4.   David R. Dean and Jean A. Reynolds, "Hispanic Property Survey: Migration, Marginalization, and Community Development, 1900–1939," accessed March 18, 2014, https://www.phoenix.gov/pddsite/Documents/pdd_hp_pdf_00045; Dean and Reynolds, *City of Phoenix: African American*, 31.

5.   Thomas D. Gilbert, "Confederate Arizona," accessed March 18, 2014, http://www.civilwarhome.com/confederatearizona.html.

6.   Dean and Reynolds, *City of Phoenix: African American*, 24. See also, *Dameron v. Bayless (1912) 14 Ariz.*, 180.

7.   "Thurgood Marshall," accessed February 8, 2013, influentialamericans.html.

8.   "D.W. Griffith's *The Birth of a Nation* (1915)," PBS.org, accessed February 13, 2013, http://www.pbs.org/wnet/jimcrow/stories_events_birth.html.

9.   Ibid.

10. Dean and Reynolds, *City of Phoenix: African American*, 29.

11. Dean and Reynolds, "Hispanic Property Survey," 49.

12. Ibid., 64.

13. "Masque of the Yellow Moon," *PBS: Arizona Stories*, accessed March 18, 2014, http://www.azpbs.org/arizonastories/yellowmoon.htm.

14. "Thurgood Marshall and the Texas NAACP Connection," *West Texas Tribune*, accessed July 1, 2009, http://westtexastribune.com/thurgood-marshall-and-the-texas-naacp-connection-p759-1.htm.

15. *Brown et al. v Board of Education, 347 U.S. 483* (1954).

CHAPTER 5

There are 550 miles between El Paso and San Antonio. I have no memory of how I passed the time between towns, so consumed was I with the things George talked about. He had made an assumption about me that was only half right. He also assumed I hadn't faced any prejudice, and he was completely wrong about that.

My mother's name was Marie Espinoza. She was fourteen years old when her impoverished Mexican parents sold her to an American man living in Tempe. She escaped when she was nineteen, running away to Tucson. My father started working as a mule skinner when he was thirteen, hauling timber, ore, and equipment in twelve-mule wagons, back and forth to the mines.

My birth certificate lists the "color or race" of my parents. For my father, his color, "white," was noted. When it came to my mother's classification, her race, not color, was given and "Spanish" was listed. That was the polite way to refer to Mexicans in those days. As children, though, we never really talked about the fact that we were half Mexican, or even half Spanish for that matter. It was a reality we learned to ignore in our mostly-white neighborhoods. We were around Mexicans all of the time, though, and briefly lived in an area we called Mexican Town. Mother was very proud of her heritage, but I didn't know much about her family. I never met her mother and saw her father, a mangled-arm fellow named Mocho, only once.

While my early years included plenty of tussles with black toughs, I caught grief from Mexican kids too: "You gringos stole our land!" When I was feeling playful, I usually fired back some shaky reference to "Manifest Destiny," thanks to Dr. Ogle's history class, and said worse things when I was in a foul mood. The Indians could have had a field day on this topic but they generally kept quiet.

Lessons on race relations started early for me, and many came uncomfortably close.

One day when I was about eleven, I was helping Dad at work, grabbing tools, running little errands, keeping his canteen full. It was a parkway project on the other side of town, a make-work operation of the Works Progress Administration, one of the New Deal agencies of the Roosevelt Administration trying to slay the Great Depression. In those days nearly every town had a few WPA projects—bridges, schools, roads—to provide work for men desperate to support their families. They were paid fifty cents per hour for unskilled labor and up to one dollar and twenty-five cents for technical and professional work. Dad was paid somewhere in the middle and was grateful for the work.

At the end of the day he got a little drunk with his crew, so he told me to drive him home. I was barely tall enough to see above the steering wheel and have my foot on the gas at the same time. Engaging the clutch to shift gears made matters worse. With the sun going down, we headed for home. I was straining to reach the gas with one foot and holding myself up by the steering wheel, occasionally dropping one hand to shift gears. I was reluctant to tap the brakes or engage the clutch with my other foot, lest I completely take my eyes of the road. Once I got the Olds into third, things settled down. When the sun set, I could see ahead only as far as the headlights shone in the moonless desert night. The dusty, unpaved road made matters worse. Crossing the road to head east, I hit something and yelled at Dad about what had happened. He quickly poked his head up from the backseat, looked around and said, "It's just an old Indian, keep driving." I begged him to let me stop and check on the man. "Do as you're told," he snarled, and so I kept on driving.

And so I knew more about prejudice than I let on with George back in El Paso. I was the son of a former slave, a poor kid of mixed race. There was much *he* didn't know about *me*. But then, how could he? The color of my skin revealed nothing about my heritage, and my feelings on the matter were tucked tightly away from his view.

I got off the train at the main gate in San Antonio and walked to the Alamo Bus Station, passing a "Colored Waiting Room." There were two ticket windows at the bus station, one for whites, the other for coloreds. Both windows were covered with an ornamental wrought iron lattice with a small crescent opening at the bottom. The line for whites was empty so I brushed past the colored folks and slid a quarter to the cashier for a ticket. Lucky for me I didn't have to wait, since the bus was already out front with its motor running when I got there.

The bus had a shiny green aluminum shell accented with white paint stripes. The words "RANDOLPH FIELD" hung over the large windshield in a wood and glass case. Climbing three steps up, I greeted the driver and surveyed the bus. The seats were covered with thin tissue paper, rolled out like you see on a doctor's examination table. The back half of the bus was full of women wearing aprons, men in overalls, and others in variety of work clothes, all Negroes.

Dozens of cadets sat in the front of the bus, ready to enter basic flight school at Randolph, having completed primary flight school. There were enlistees like me in civilian clothing, a couple of officers, and a handful of females—nurse, clerk, and secretary types—all Anglos. I sat down in the third row behind the bus driver, tossing my suitcase overhead. I didn't have the heart to look behind me a second time. But I knew this much: there would be no Negro enlistees back there. Nor would I see them on the base. The military reflected the social structure of the time, and blacks served in segregated units. Neither would there be any Negro aviation cadets on board the bus. There weren't any in the entire Army Air Corps at the time. It was not until the next summer that aviation cadet training was offered to qualified Negro applicants at Tuskegee Army Airfield in Tuskegee, Alabama.

The straight stretch of road between the bus depot and Randolph Field was flat, but our emotions were up and down. Fifteen miles out, bedlam erupted on the bus. "I sure hope we get to fight!" someone said.

Ten miles to go—mirth. "We're going to kick the 'sour' out of those Krauts!"

Five miles out—apprehension. "Sure hope we can hack it . . ."

Last mile—fear. "Will we make it back alive?"

It was unsettling to see how quickly the flame of our youthful enthusiasm was extinguished.

Admittedly, the guys headed to flight school faced greater danger than ground crew types like me, and that began with their training. They would be training at surrounding airfields named for flyers killed in the line of duty, but none of them wartime casualties. And we were all about to arrive at the field named for Lieutenant William M. Randolph, who entered the army in 1916, served in World War I, became a pilot in 1919, and died in a nearby plane crash in 1928.

When this tradition of honoring dead flyers got started, most Americans knew more about planting cornfields than they did about airfields, or flying machines, for that matter. After all, World War I began just a decade or so after the Wright brothers' first flight at Kitty Hawk. By the start of the Second World War, airplanes were commonplace. Commercial flights were not unusual and military aircraft dotted the sky. By the end of the war there were more than 300 military airfields around the country.[1]

Our bus turned onto the long boulevard leading to Randolph Field. The driver shouted over his shoulder, "Welcome to the Country Club, ladies and gentlemen." We proceeded through the North Circle, passing through two long rows of oak trees. "You're looking at the George Washington Memorial Trees," the driver noted proudly, referring to the 120 oak trees donated by the Daughters of the American Revolution in 1932 to mark the bicentennial of the first president's birth.[2] A few seconds later, he pointed out the window and said, "We are now passing the Taj Mahal," referring to a large building with three archways in the portico. The main part of the building served as the base of a 170-foot, eight-sided observation tower capped with a dome of glazed blue and yellow tile. It was the Post Administration Building. I hadn't been to Randolph Field more than two minutes when I realized there was a nickname for almost everything there.

We drove around the administration building to the west, revealing the stately commanding general's quarters, after which the expansive campus came into view. In all there were 2,300 acres with intersecting roads radiating outward in octagon patterns. The driver pointed ahead to the officers club and the mess hall in the center of the quad. He motioned with his arm back and forth pointing out the officers' quarters, hundreds of them.

The driver continued with the tour. "To the right you see the post garage."

Its wide barn doors were open revealing tools, supplies, and a jeep up on blocks.

"Next, you'll see the quartermasters corps warehouse, the supply depot, and the dope storage warehouse."

That probably requires some explanation. From the days of the Wright Brothers, fabric was used to give an airplane its shape. Airplane dope, a plasticized lacquer, was applied to stiffen the fabric, making it airtight and weatherproof. Although aluminum replaced fabric in the high performance planes of WWII, many of the trainer planes had fabric coverings, and so dope was stored in the warehouse.

The guy next to me shouted, "Where do they work on planes?"

The driver pointed to a sprawling building. "The Air Corps Shop is right over there. It's a substation of the Air Corps Repair Depot over at Duncan Field. Any of you boys going to be airplane mechanics?"

A dozen of us raised our hands.

"If you hang around here, you'll probably be working at the shop or the depot."

He turned left on Fifth Street and pulled to the side of the road. As the engine idled, the driver said, "See the roof over there with the checkerboard pattern? That's one of the airplane hangars. The taller building with the darkened glass is the control tower. There's another set up just like it to the east of the quad."

The driver put the bus in gear and went ahead to West F Street, turning left. "There's the hospital. I hope none of y'all end up in there. That there two-story building next to it is the School of Aviation Medicine."

The School of Aviation Medicine was first established in 1919 at Mitchel Field,[3] Long Island, and had a home at Brooks Field in Texas for a time. The origin of the aviation branch of medical science seems to have started in France in 1910, when the first articles written on the subject were published in scientific journals. Two years later, the US Department of War, headed by Secretary of War Henry Stimson, had the foresight to direct the Army Surgeon General to develop a physical examination for all aviation hopefuls.[4] It took another couple of years before the physical was implemented but the requirements were so rigid that no one passed in the first month, and the standards were lowered.

During the First World War, courage was considered the only essential trait for pilots, and one who possessed it to a high degree was on his way to flying. However, for every one hundred British pilot deaths in the war, only two were the result of combat and eight because of mechanical defects. The other ninety were due to individual deficiencies, sixty of which were attributed to physical defects. The American casualty rate was not any better.[5] After so many needless accidents wiped out hundreds of brave souls with weak constitutions, not to mention the loss of expensive military hardware, serious consideration was given to developing methods to measure flying aptitude.

French, British, and Italian psychologists and physicians developed subjective methods to select and classify aviators. Even though the United States didn't enter the war until 1917, its medical officers were sent overseas at the start of the war to observe the physical effects of combat on Allied pilots. That led to the establishment of the Central Research Laboratory at Hazelnut Field, Long Island, which was the beginning of the School of Aviation Medicine.

During its twenty-year history prior to my arrival at Randolph, physicians and scientists at the school adapted the field of medicine to accommodate evolving Air Corps criteria. Technological advances in aircraft and equipment required equally innovative medical responses. The army developed cutting edge physical examinations and devised special procedures for flight training and pilot testing.[6] Every candidate, cadet, and aviator would be impacted by the work done here. Some of them would wash out; others would advance. But their success or failure would be based on more scientific data and objective measurements than had been done in the past.

With Europe embroiled in war in 1940, the Republican Henry Stimson was asked to serve a second stint as Secretary of War, this time in the wartime cabinet of President Roosevelt, a Democrat.[7] It is extraordinary that the aero-medical developments that took root during his first stewardship twenty years earlier fully ripened during the final season of his service just as America was being drawn into another world war. Equally significant was the fact that he would be in Washington, again, taking on the colossal task of utilizing those innovations and advancements to prepare, in short order, airmen for battle. That job was even more challenging because of the limited number of trained pilots in the Army Air Corps at the time. From 1928 to 1935, only 1,924 aviation cadets graduated from flight school. By the end of World War II there were 250,000 of them.[8]

Notes

1. Scott D. Murdock, "WWII Army Air Fields-Database Summary," *The Use in 1995 of World War II Army Airfields in the United States*, accessed February 25, 2013, http://www.airforcebase.net/aaf/wwiidata.html.

2. WPA Texas, *Randolph Field: A History and Guide* (New York: The Devin-Adair Company, 1942), 109.

3. Ibid., 115–16.

4. Ibid., 115.

5. David R. Jones, "Flying and Dying in WWI: British Aircrew Losses and the Origin of U.S. Military Aviation Medicine," *Ingenta Connect*, February 2008, accessed January 22, 2016, http://www.ingentaconnect.com/content/asma /asem/2008/00000079/00000002/art00011?crawler=true.

6. "Initial Selection of Candidates for Pilot, Bombardier, and Navigator Training," *WWII Sacrifices*, accessed January 24, 2016, 7–20, http://www.wwiiarchives.net/servlet /action/document/index/1556/0.

7. "Henry L. Stimson," *Wikipedia*, accessed August 3, 2013, https://en.wikipedia .org/wiki/Henry_L._Stimson.

8. Bruce A. Ashcroft, *We Wanted Wings: A History of the Aviation Cadet Program*, (Randolph Air Force Base, Texas: HQ Air Education and Training Command, 2005), ii, 1.

CHAPTER 6

Stepping off the bus, we were greeted by an aggressive chorus of "Pile out, you misters! Grab your bags and fall in line at the curb!" The aviation cadets were directed to the front of the Cadet Administration Building for processing, a phalanx of upperclassmen awaiting them. Referred to as "dodos" while in primary flight school, they had to get used to a new appellation: "dum-dums." The upperclassmen started in on the cadets the moment they got over to the administration building. "Stand at attention, you dum-dums!" "Quit slouching, dum-dum!"

The rest of us were told to tag our bags and herded to the back of a large khaki-colored, tarp-covered truck, but I couldn't keep my eyes off the cadets. I felt sick, wanting desperately to learn how to fly. "Eyes straight ahead, mister . . . and keep 'em there," I was told. "Pretty raunchy, mister, but we'll make a soldier out of you yet," some sergeant yelled at me.

One brave soul with a heavy accent asked, "Where we headed, sir?"

A menacing looking corporal shouted, "You grease monkeys are shipping out to Brooks Field."

We bounced our way in the back of the truck over to Brooks, only a few miles from Randolph. Over the next few hours, nearly 1,000 enlisted men arrived, all of them recruited under an Air Corps expansion program charged with turning out more aviation mechanics. The commanding officer, Major Stanford Smith, greeted us, exclaiming, "You are here to learn to do an important job. Our job is to help you succeed. Most of you already have had some manual or mechanical training, and all of you show great promise."[1] After a few more pleasantries, the major administered the oath of office to us: "Gentlemen, raise your right arm to the square and repeat after me."

> I, Frank James Kirkland Jr., a citizen of the United States, do hereby acknowledge to have voluntarily enlisted as a soldier in the Army of the United States of America for the period of four years under the conditions prescribed by law, unless sooner discharged by proper authority; and do also agree to accept from the United States such bounty, pay, rations and clothing as are or may be prescribed by law. And I do solemnly swear that I will bear true faith and allegiance to the United States of America; that I will serve them honestly and faithfully against all their enemies whomsoever; and that I will obey the orders of the President of the United States, and the orders of the officers appointed over me, according to the Rules and Articles of War.[2]

Some parts of the oath became very personal to me. It instilled in me a higher sense of duty and purpose. I felt safe, secure. If I obeyed my superiors, I could count on receiving "bounty, pay, rations, and clothing as prescribed by law." I liked the certainty of this arrangement. But when you pick up one end of the stick, you pick up the other. At a critical juncture of my training, I had to endure bitter disappointment in order to "obey the officers appointed over me," and again while overseas. Later, I was ordered back to the states by "proper authority," contrary to my wishes, in order to preserve military secrets.

The Quartermaster Corps estimated it cost the Army $215.35 a year—59 cents a day—to feed a soldier; $173.70 for clothing; $44.70 for individual equipment; and $31.31 for barracks equipment.[3] My starting pay was 21 dollars per month. These were trifling sums to many people but to me they were a God-send. I had three meals a day and I could eat as much as I wanted. I had money in my pocket. Life was looking up.

Even though my circumstances were improving, no one would confuse Brooks Field for a country club. At first there was no covered place to sleep because the War Department was playing catch up, trying to mobilize for war before training facilities were ready. A month later we moved into pyramidal tents with wood frames and floors. It took another two months to get Army gear. Until then we wore our civilian clothes while soldiering, and my pants, underwear, and shoes were worn through by the time I got any government-issue clothing. Even so, the transition from civilian life to a soldier's life went fairly smoothly for me. It was kind of like crawling into a cold bed. It's a bit uncomfortable at first but you know if you stay in long enough, things will warm up.

After thirty days of drill and instruction—called the "school of the soldier"—we assembled in a large hangar and met the chief mechanic, Sergeant Powers, but everyone called him Chief. He didn't look like a grease monkey. His hands and overalls were clean—no traces of grease anywhere. He stood in the center of a circle of thirty eager would-be airplane mechanics, all of whom were relieved that they had come to the point in their service when they would march less and fix more.

Chief had been in the Army for twenty years, working on planes. Like most guys, though, he had never been in combat and had never even seen a shot-up plane.

"Your duty here is simple: maintain and repair airplanes. Our motto is also simple: 'Keep 'em flying!'"[4]

He went around the circle asking about hometowns and our experience working on airplanes. The first four or five guys he asked had never touched a plane. Some had only seen them flying over their farms.

"Okay," Chief said, "Let me ask it this way: who has worked on something with a motor?"

Hands shot up: tractors, cotton gins, trucks, forklifts, all manner of farm and factory equipment were mentioned. A few guys, like me, mentioned cars.

"You, standing there on the end—the wiry one with the black hair—what's your name?" he asked.

I told him my name.

"Kirkland, tell me about your experience working on cars," he demanded.

"I built a car from scratch with no money or help from anybody. I started the project when I was fourteen. Found a chassis in a junkyard and hauled it home. I kept going back week after week, looking for free parts. I found a carburetor, then a magneto. Piece by piece I found what I needed and eventually, by the time I was seventeen, I had my wheels."

"How did you do it? Use a Chilton's?"

"Yes, sir. Checked it out of the library nearly every month for three years. Come to think of it, it is probably back home somewhere. I forgot to return it."

Chief looked around the hangar as if tracking a sparrow in her wandering,[5] before setting his sights on me.

"You better have your momma return the manual, son. We don't want you arrested on account of an overdue library book." The hangar erupted in laughter, and he added another volley: "So you think your little hobby project means you can fix airplanes? I'm highly skeptical, son, highly skeptical."

Actually my "little project" gave me more than mechanical skills: it increased my confidence. It was not something I lacked before the car. In high school, kids looked up to me because I was a good ballplayer, and some feared me because I was an even better fighter. But those skills came easily to me, and I had come to define myself in terms of wins and losses, batting average, and the guys I could take. Building a car from scratch without any money or help from others required a lot more from me. When high school ended I began to believe my intelligence and mechanical aptitude would lead me to a better life. And as far as I was concerned, they had.

I returned the volley from Chief with a shot of my own, loaded with hubris and wry: "Sergeant, I am sure that with your guidance and my skills I'll be able to fix anything you throw my way in no time."

"Well, if you can fix things half as good as you can talk you may work out just fine," he said as he turned to another guy and started in on him.

My maintenance training came alongside technical sergeants. I watched them work, grabbed wrenches for them, and eventually did the work myself. Elbow deep in engine parts and grease most every day, I went to sleep at night staring at a photograph I clipped from a local newspaper. It was a picture of a graduating class of flying cadets, three rows of leather jackets and garrison caps with smug grins in between.[6] I would tell myself my daily grind in the grease would one day give me an advantage over guys like them. When it was my turn to fly, I would know more about planes than any of them, from the theory of flight to piston pressure. I would not only be able to read the instruments inside the cockpit but also understand the dynamics of the wiring system throughout the plane and how the electrical impulses to the gauges were generated. I would have a better appreciation for the work of the ground crews, and know how to partner with them for the betterment of my plane.

The ground crews were led by an engineer officer who had four assistants. Next in the mechanics' chain of command: the line chief, a master sergeant, and then an assistant line chief who was responsible for three hangars. Each hangar had a chief, an enlisted man with a technical sergeant's rating, and maintenance crews led by a crew chief and an assistant crew chief.[7] These were dedicated men who pored over every detail of each plane on a regular basis. They did daily inspections and rigid checkups after twenty-four hours of flight time. After fifty hours, the plane was taken apart, the power plant was carefully overhauled, and detailed examinations of the ignition system, landing gear, and instrument panel were undertaken. Specialists would carefully inspect the wings, control rods, and cables. All of this work was noted for each plane in a "Form 41" and posted in the hangar. The form would be updated with each hour of flight and every act of maintenance and repair until the plane was taken out of service.

During the war, there were more than half a million mechanics and maintenance technicians servicing aircraft.[8] At first, basic airplane mechanic school lasted thirty-eight weeks, after which the mechanics were expected to be able to service any type of aircraft. They couldn't. Field commanders complained that new mechanics required additional training when they arrived in combat zones. As a result, the old training program was scrapped and new courses specific to aircraft type were created, allowing better-equipped mechanics to enter the field in half the time of the original program.

Some of the mechanics went on to receive additional training, becoming specialists: engine mechanic, airplane machinist, propeller specialist, aircraft welder, instrument specialist, aircraft metalworker, and aircraft electrician.[9] They were following in the footsteps of World War I "airplane mechanicians."[10]

In operational theaters during World War II, each flying squadron was assigned enlisted personnel to serve as its ground crew. Fighter squadrons had about 160 to 175 ground personnel, bomber squads between 180 and 250 men. A ground crew, under the direction of a non-commissioned officer called the crew chief, maintained each plane. He reported to the squadron engineer. Front-line crews handled general maintenance, inspection, and repairs. Specialists assigned to rear area bases repaired planes requiring major replacement parts, or those that had been seriously damaged.[11] The planes shot to pieces and beyond repair were cannibalized for useable parts and towed to aviation boneyards.

Everyone in the service knew aircraft maintenance was an essential component of combat operations. Our superiors often repeated the mantra: "All failure in the air can be directly or indirectly traced to failures on the ground." Despite this important role in the war effort, I was driven to get out of maintenance. Ground crews did not get a lot of recognition. Pilots were the glamour boys, the quarterbacks of their squadrons; mechanics were the unsung heroes, toiling in anonymity.

Notes

1.   Unnamed newspaper clipping dated July 31, 1940, in the WWII files of Frank J. Kirkland Jr.

2.   "The Story of Glen Eldon Seeber," accessed March 6, 2013, http://www.b17tail gunner.com.

3.   "Ardmore Army Air Field, Ardmore, Oklahoma: A Training Base for the U.S. Army Air Forces, WWII," *Bright Net Oklahoma*, accessed March 6, 2013, http://www.brightok.net/~gsimmons/1jogger.html.

4.   WPA Texas, *Randolph Field: A History and Guide* (New York: The Devin-Adair Company, 1942), 22.

5.   Proverbs 26:2 (ASV).

6.   Unnamed and undated newspaper photograph of a graduating cadet class from the WWII files of Frank J. Kirkland Jr.

7.   WPA Texas, *Randolph Field*, 96–98.

8.   "Individual Training in Aircraft Maintenance in AAF," *WWII Archives*, accessed January 24, 2016, 35–74, http://www.wwiiarchives.net/servlet/action/document/index/1525/40.

9.   Ibid., 160.

10. Ibid., 4.

11. Ibid., 2–3.

CHAPTER 7

In February 1941, I transferred to the newly built Goodfellow Field outside of San Angelo, Texas. I believe I was the first soldier assigned to guard duty there. You wouldn't think there would be much to learn about guard duty, but the Army had a regulation for everything. Field Manual 26-5 outlined the types of weapons we were to carry, taught us how to salute an officer, and mandated that we have a whistle and billy club with us at all times. The most challenging rule for me was to not to talk to anyone except in the line of duty.

That summer I was recruited to play softball on a team called the Fighting 49th, representing the 49th Squadron. I was not a member of the squadron but was encouraged to join the team by some of my friends who were. We played at Kiwanis Park against civilian teams, the Junior Sheep Herders, Baily Auto Dodgers, Phillips 66 Gas Station, Findlater Hardware, the Sons of Legion, and the local chapter of the Knights of Pythias.

Our worst game of the year came against the Knights, and a sportswriter for the Standard-Times, Blondy Cross, had something to do with it. Blondy was a funny guy whose easy smile revealed slight gaps between his teeth. He wore glasses, large round lenses with opaque plastic frames. He looked more like a professor than an athlete. One thing we all knew about him was that he liked to needle military teams in his sports columns. It was always good-natured, the kind you would expect from a guy who hung around ballparks and locker rooms, whose life's work was devoted to writing about games.

Blondy came to Goodfellow one day and parked his big Chrysler in front of the 49th Squadron office hut. Some of the enlisted men knew he was coming and planned a surprise for him. Once he was inside the office they quickly jacked up the back of the car just high enough to lift the tires off the ground but not so high to be noticeable. When Blondy got back in his car to leave, he stepped on the gas pedal but the car didn't move. He gave it more gas and the tires whirled ever faster. Perplexed, he got out of the car and kneeled down next to the rear tire on the driver's side. Removing his glasses, he got up close to the tire and discovered the prank. The guys who had been hiding across the street howled with laughter as the snookered sportswriter vowed his revenge. It was all in good fun. The guys lowered his tires to the ground and were exchanging insults with Blondy as he got back in the car, the knees of his white linen trousers still covered with red dirt.

"We Texans know how to handle your kind," he hollered as he drove away laughing, shaking his fist.

When Blondy got back into town, he told the Knights about the prank and encouraged them to teach us a lesson during the game we had with them the next evening.

"Those guys are not treating us right. They're jokesters. . . . They're pranksters. . . . They play them on me. . . . So instead of letting the score be close as usual, let's play a prank on them and beat them by at least 10–0!" he pleaded.[1]

We played the Knights the next night and lost 10–1. We only got 2 hits off their ace, Bill Unger. One of them, a single into center field, was mine.

Blondy walked over to our dugout after the game wearing a white hat with a black band and a big toothy smile. He was joined by one of the Pythian players, his white uniform adorned with *Knights* in black script lettering angled across his chest and an embroidered patch on his sleeve, a triangle surrounding the letters *F*, *C*, and *B*.

"You boys had better not mess with me again or my noble Pythian friends will whip you twice as bad next time," he joked. "Y'all ought to know better than to mess with your commander-in-chief's fraternity brothers," he added with a wink.

"President Roosevelt's a Knight of Pythias?" I asked.[2]

"That's right, boy," he said, then turning to the player on the other team, added, "You sure put the large pajamas to these boys. Now that the 49th has learned a lesson about playing pranks, maybe they'll settle down."[3]

I was still at Goodfellow the next year, working on planes and marching. Still pulling guard duty. One afternoon I was blowing off steam, hitting the speed bag at the makeshift gym we had there. *Bam-bam-bam-bam-slam. Bam-bam-bam-slam.* Over and over, faster and faster, my eyes trained on the recoiling bag.

"Private Kirkland." *Bam-bam-bam-slam.* "Private Kirkland!"

I looked to my left to see who was yelling at me, sweat pouring off my face. It was an officer, so I stopped punching, making a lame attempt at a salute with a gloved right hand.

"I'm Bob Vance," he said with a slight grin.

I knew who he was: Lieutenant Vance, the Commander of the 49th Squadron. He was a well-respected officer and an uncommon leader. My friends from the softball team told me stories about him, how he treated everyone with respect, regardless of rank, and worked right along side his men. He led by doing.

Leon Robert Vance was born in Enid, Oklahoma, in 1916, the son of a middle school principal. An honor student and gifted athlete, he looked, talked, and acted like a model officer and gentlemen.

"How can I help you, sir?" I asked.

"I'm looking for a good middle-weight for my boxing team. I heard about you from some of the officers here. They said you were a tough kid who could fight. They also said you wanted to fly."

"That would be me, sir."

"I was a boxing champ at West Point. I could turn you into a real fighter. Are you interested?" he asked.

"No, sir. I'm saving my brain for flight school."

"If you want to be a flier, what are you doing in that grease monkey suit? How many years of college have you completed?"

"None, but I'll be kite flying soon enough, sir," using the reference to primary aviation school I had picked up, thinking I might impress the lieutenant with my command of Army Air Corps colloquialisms.

He then spoke words never to be forgotten: "Maybe I can help you with that."

"Holy Jack, can you really?" I asked.

Lieutenant Vance told me about a new regulation that replaced the two-year college requirement with the Aviation Cadet Qualifying Examination. By then, the law of supply and demand was in full effect. The nation was officially at war and the need for more pilots was becoming increasingly clear. As a result, the requirements to qualify for flight school shifted from college experience to aptitude and potential, giving guys like me a chance to fly.

"All you have to do is master several subjects like mathematics, English, and science, and you'll be ready to take the exam," he said in a matter of fact kind of way.

"No problem. What do I have to do?" I asked, acting cool as a cucumber, but feeling like a little kid who had found a shiny coin on the sidewalk. I was excited but cautious, fearing someone might come by and take this precious opportunity away from me.

He looked at me quizzically and laughed. "No problem? You're kind of cocky, aren't you, private?" he asked.

I didn't say anything, just looked him square in the eye. He continued after a few seconds of awkward silence.

"You'll need to teach yourself, mostly. On weekends you can go to campus for some tutoring and to take tests. If you pass your classes, you'll be ready to take the ACQE here at Goodfellow. The next test is in June."

"What are my chances of passing the test?"

"That's up to you, don't you think? We don't have much experience with the new test, but historically the passage rate on aptitude exams has been less than forty percent," he replied.

I didn't say "no problem" this time, just shrugged my shoulders and gave the "thumbs up" sign. Inside me, though, a fire was burning. I wanted to fly so badly it hurt. Writers have lifted themselves from poverty by the power of their words; baseball players have done the same with the power of their swing. I was determined to change my life forever, or die trying, at the controls of an airplane.

Within a couple of weeks, Vance had me enrolled at San Angelo Junior College, located a few miles from the base, and signed me up for the classes I needed to prepare for the ACQE: English grammar and composition, United States history, general history, arithmetic, higher algebra, geometry, trigonometry, and elementary physics.[4] I'm not sure where the money came from, but he paid for my tuition and books and set me on an accelerated course acceptable to the college.

He was like that, though. He famously built a hunting lodge at nearby Lake Nasworthy for his Fighting 49th Squadron, and his men loved him for it. They all pitched in money, rounded up donated materials, and worked together on weekends until they had the lodge, an archery range, a softball diamond, horseshoe pits, and a lighted badminton court. They also collected a fleet of fifteen small fishing boats, ten of them with motors.[5] There were a few other improvements that had been planned but were never completed. The war got in the way.

I learned a new word, "autodidact," while teaching myself geometry, trigonometry, and physics. I also had to get reacquainted with algebra and English. I spent every available hour studying. For months it was nothing but soldiering, fixing airplanes, and hitting the books. But it all paid off; I passed my classes and felt ready to take the exam. Only one problem. Just before the test, I was transferred to Perrin Field, near Sherman, Texas. I was sick. After all the hard work, just weeks from getting my ticket punched to aviation school, I got my orders to ship out. "Don't worry, Frank. I will fly you down when the time comes," Vance promised.

I was scheduled to take the test on June 20, 1942. True to his word, Vance sent a plane to pick me up at Perrin Field and return me to Goodfellow Field, having secured a pass for me so I could leave the base. The BT-14 trainer with tandem cockpits had a 420 horsepower engine and a two-way radio so the instructor and cadet could talk to each other during training exercises. I asked a few questions and did a lot of listening during the flight, as the pilot explained the innerworkings of the plane. It was my first time in the air, and I was not disappointed in any way. It felt as though the plane was gliding through heaven, the sun glistening off its bright yellow wings; its blue fuselage rumbling like some kind of a celestial chariot. From my new perch atop endless blue sky and rolling white clouds, I grasped as never before the reason pilots called their planes ships.

I thought about the amazing journey I was on. Soon I would take the written exam and undergo a physical, and then I would be the one flying the plane. It wouldn't be quite that simple, but I kept thinking positive thoughts, trying to clear my mind and steady my nerves, not wanting to throw away this amazing opportunity.

The three-hour aptitude test covered vocabulary, reading comprehension, practical judgment, mathematics, mechanical comprehension, and alertness to recent developments, which focused on aviation, science, and military affairs. One question asked me to identify which of five planes used in the Royal Air Force was not American-made. If only the other questions had been so easy. A few weeks after the test, I received a letter from the Office of Chief of the Army Air Corps:

"We regret to inform you that you failed the Aviation Cadet Qualifying Examination. You are eligible to retake the test in 30 days."

I felt sucker punched, and my disappointment wasn't the worst part. I felt tremendous guilt in having let Vance down. But as anxious as I was to tell him, he was gracious.

"Well, Kirk, you're living life now. When are you going to take it again?" he asked. I decided to get back to the books immediately while the information was still fresh in my mind and build on the foundation of my initial effort.

Notes

1.   Blondy Cross, "Phillips Pops Sons of Legion and the 49th Learns a Lesson," San Angelo Standard-Times, circa Summer 1941.

2.   "Knights of Pythias," *Wikipedia*, accessed December 23, 2013, https://en.wikipedia .org/wiki/Knights_of_Pythias.

3.   Cross, "Phillips Pops Sons of Legion and the 49th Learns a Lesson."

4.   "Initial Selection of Candidates for Pilot, Bombardier, and Navigator Training," *WWII Sacrifices*, accessed January 24, 2016, 7–20, http://www.wwiiarchives.net/servlet /action/document/index/1556/0.

5.   "Fighting 49th Builds a Play Place," San Angelo Standard-Times, June 11, 1941, from the WWII files of Frank J. Kirkland Jr.

CHAPTER 8

If the imprimatur of the President of the United States is any indication, the war's effect on professional baseball was an important public consideration. It was a legitimate question given the precedent set in World War I when the 1918 pro season was canceled. Many fans feared that baseball would be canceled again after Hitler's initial romp through Europe. On January 14, 1941, the commissioner of baseball, Kenesaw Mountain Landis, named for the mountain spot where his father was wounded in the Civil War, inquired of President Roosevelt as to the wartime status of baseball. Apparently the issue was of such import that the president sent his reply the very next day. Known as the "Green Light Letter," President Roosevelt wrote:

"I honestly feel it would be best for the country to keep baseball going. . . . Here is another way of looking at it—if 300 teams use 5,000–6,000 players, these players are a definite recreational asset to at least 20,000,000 of their fellow citizens—and that in my judgment is thoroughly worthwhile."[1]

He also urged the commissioner to encourage the players of military age to serve, and they did, with over 500 major leaguers, including Joe DiMaggio, Stan Musial, and Ted Williams, and 4,000 minor league players enlisted in the service.[2]

"Even if the actual quality of the teams is lowered by the greater use of older players, this will not dampen the popularity of the sport,"[3] the president noted in his letter.

The sport was popular at Randolph and the surrounding airfields. The top brass must have recognized the morale boost baseball gave to the men, and so they authorized the formation of leagues. One of them, the San Antonio Service Baseball League, eventually included major and minor leaguers and drew crowds as large as 4,000.

I was invited to play on a baseball team called the "Perrin Field Officers." We didn't have any pro players on our team, only officers, except me, and I don't know why they asked an enlisted man to join them. Maybe they saw me throwing the ball around. Maybe they overheard me talking about my state championship team. Most of my teammates were flight instructors. Jimmy Denton, our third baseman, was an officer in the Office of the Air Judge Advocate of the Army, meaning he did legal work for the Army Air Corps, sometimes as a prosecutor.

I played catcher on the team, batting third in the line-up. Other teams may have had more accomplished players, but our team was filled with talented pilots. They were in the air every day flying North American BT-9 and BT-14 trainers with their dum-dums. I looked up to them and thought how great it would be to be an instructor. Most of them felt the assignment was a burden because their former classmates were advancing at other airfields and schools through additional training and work. Instructors tried to make up for it by flying their high-powered service planes, which they called "pea shooters," during off-hours, oftentimes at night.

I was always peppering them with questions about planes and flight school, and they mostly chided me about focusing on the game.

"Kirk, we're here to play ball. Give it a break!"

Sometimes it was, "Drive it in the hangar," meaning, shut up, or "Roll up your flaps!"[4]

But I couldn't stop talking about it. We made side agreements, pegging my performance with the time we could spend talking about aviation and pilot training. One game it was "You drive this guy in, and I'll tell you how to do a chandelle." I cracked a single, drove in the run, and spent thirty minutes after the game learning how a plane gains altitude and changes direction at the same time. During other games the deals involved throwing out runners or stealing bases in exchange for other insights into the world of flying, and that information meant the world to me.

We won most of our games that inaugural season and qualified for the Northeastern Texas State Championship game in Gainesville. Our starting pitcher took ill during warm-ups, and I was his reluctant replacement, even though I had not pitched an inning the entire season.

Not to worry, somehow I managed to throw a shutout, leading our team to a 2–0 win and the championship. It felt like the World Series to me, made sweeter by the most valuable player trophy my teammates awarded to me.

After the big game, a corporal named Johnny, a good looking guy from Texas who was equal parts devilish, charming, and dangerous, in a fun sort of way, picked me up in a military jeep. He was my regular driver to the games, having been ordered by one of the officers on my team to see that I got to games on time and returned to Perrin Field on time. When I jumped into the jeep, Johnny headed in the opposite direction of the base.

"We're heading the wrong way! I've got to get back to the base!" I yelled.

Smirking, he replied, "You've got to learn to live a little, have some fun."

"Listen, you've got to take me back to Perrin. I don't have permission to go anywhere else," I protested, worrying about what would happen to me if I were found to be AWOL—away without leave. I was preparing to take the entrance exam again and couldn't let anything jeopardize my chance to fly.

Down shifting to second gear, he said, "Relax, Kirkie-old-boy. We're taking a detour to a little bar just across the Red River, about ten miles up Highway 77. We'll meet up with some of my buddies and a few girls, dance a little, and have a few drinks." By the time he hit third gear, he was woofing about his exploits and escapades involving whiskey and women, and I began to think I was entitled to some fun after my big game.

He stepped on the gas and let out a "yeehaw!" as we sped down the road, the warm summer air breezing over us. Crossing the river, we drove past the "Entering Love County, Oklahoma" sign, prompting Johnny to say, "See, I knew this was going to be a great night!"

A few minutes later we were at the Wolf Hallow, a little weather-beaten place with a few tables and chairs, a jukebox, and tall stools at the bar. An old billiards table stood in the corner, its green felt torn and stained. Large pitchers of beer, most of them empty, and several shot glasses rimmed the rail cushions of the table. The locals were friendly and kind, offering to buy us drinks and expressing appreciation for our service to the country. Some of them got a little fussy with me when I turned down their offers of booze, teasing me for only drinking milk. A cowboy was strumming his guitar in the corner, the song barely audible above the din of the crowd. After about thirty minutes, Johnny suggested we listen to some big band tunes and do some dancing. By this time he had consumed prodigious amounts of whiskey, and was already bombed.

"How about *Humpty Dumpty Heart?*" one of the girls suggested after looking over the title cards behind the glass of an old wooden jukebox. The Glenn Miller song was great for dancing, nice and easy. Someone in our group slid a nickel in the coin slot and the 78 rpm record was lifted up to the needle pointing down from the tone arm. As the needle was notching into the record's spiral groove, we all grabbed a girl, and, holding them close, began to sway and spin to the music, at first to the sound of brass instruments and then clarinets, and then the refrain from the band's crooner, Ray Eberle. In a creamy smooth voice he sang of pick-up lines, grinning faces, romances, and the possibility of it all cracking up. The bar's modest dance floor kept us turning in tight, slow circles, but we didn't mind.

When the song ended someone pushed another nickel into the jukebox and another Glenn Miller song started spinning, and so did we, swing dancing to the upbeat orchestral sound. We were having a grand time, oblivious to the fact that the civilians were getting upset. Soon they were jawing at us to "Slow down!" and "Watch where you're going!" and to "Tone down the racket!"

"What's wrong with you people? The big band sound is the best, and Glenn Miller is the greatest!" shouted one of the guys, a private, who was also blasted by that time. We all laughed and chimed in, "That's right! Better than that old twangy stuff you all call music!"

Miller was not only a great musician; he was a patriot, joining the Army in 1942, and then transfering to the Army Air Corps. Too old for combat at thirty-eight, he organized a fifty-piece military band and toured England, entertaining the troops more than 800 times. Shockingly, his single-engine aircraft disappeared in December 1944 over the English Channel while en route to France to entertain soldiers in Paris. No trace of the plane or its passengers was ever found.[5]

We played another Miller tune and the locals' anger kicked up a notch or two, even as our group was getting progressively louder and drunker. One of the girls overheard the barkeep calling for the military police and warned us. Recognizing the signs of a brewing fight, I sized up the room quickly, looking for a way out.

Soon the MPs were pouring through the front door just as we were running out the back door. We jumped in the jeep and tore out of the place, with the MPs in hot pursuit. Johnny was in no condition to drive but he did anyway, and each time he tried to shift, the gears made a crunching, groaning sound. We hadn't gotten much past the parking lot when we spun out of control and into a cornfield. When the jeep straightened out, Johnny began racing through the field. The green stalks slapped at us as they fell in our wake. Eventually we flew over a cement culvert, tearing the transmission off its mounts and causing major damage to the jeep. The MPs found us easily by following the path of flattened corn stalks. After pulling us out of the jeep, they knocked the stuffing out of us with their batons.

We spent the night in jail, charged with drunk and disorderly conduct, resisting arrest, and malicious destruction of government property, meaning the jeep. The next morning we faced a military judge for arraignment. The prosecutor from the Judge Advocate General's office was none other than Jimmy Denton, my third baseman. "What are you doing here, Kirk? I thought we sent you back to the base last night?" he asked. I told him the whole story—that I had only been drinking milk at the bar—and pleaded with him to get me out of there. Somehow he managed to have the charges against me dropped, and I returned to Perrin Field without any repercussions. One of the officers on the team was waiting for me. "You're lucky we won the game last night, slick. Who knows where you'd be if you hadn't pitched so well," he said in a semi-serious tone. I smiled, thinking baseball had never been so good to me. It was not too long after that I was promoted to sergeant and given a pay raise.

On those rare occasions when I hear Glenn Miller music today, I am transported back to that Oklahoma tavern, as if by a spell. Within a note or two, I see pretty girls dancing and laughing, and soldiers flirting with them. I smell cheap beer and malt whiskey. I feel emotions convulse as we dart through fields of corn. I relive the unspeakable joy of returning to Perrin Field with my service record intact, and I remember with deep gratitude the judge advocate, my teammate, who made it possible.

When it came time for me to take the test again, Vance sent another plane to pick me up at Perrin Field and fly me to Randolph Field, the new location for the testing center. A few weeks later I received a familiar looking envelope. It was the same shape and size as the rejection letter I received before, with the same return address. I was so anxious that I nearly tore it in two. With shaking hands, I quickly scanned the letter looking for the dreaded word—failed. It wasn't there. I then calmed down and read it again from the beginning. I had passed the ACQE and was conditionally admitted into the next class of aviation cadets subject to successfully completing a physical examination. It was the best day of my life.

The physical standards for flying were higher than the requirements necessary to enlist in the Regular Army. In 1939, more than 8,000 applicants who were academically qualified were disqualified from cadet aviation school because of physical defects. It didn't matter. I knew I would easily pass the physical. Over several days, the medical staff thoroughly examined my body, measuring, poking, and prodding. My height was measured at 68¼ inches. I weighed in at 153 pounds and my pulse rate was 72 after two minutes of strenuous exercise. One doctor observed as he was removing a rubber glove from his right hand, "You're a little tight down there, son." I responded as I was pulling up my trousers, "It's the first time anyone has poked around down there, doc, I was a little nervous." He laughed and walked away.

They checked my teeth to make sure I had the minimum requirement of six masticating and six incisor teeth and confirmed that I had at least 20/20 vision. They ran me through various tests to be sure I had unimpaired ocular muscle balance, good respiratory ventilation, perfect hearing, stable equilibrium, and sound cardiovascular and nervous systems. My coordination, reflexes, finger dexterity, and motor skills were also evaluated. Next they put me through a series of tests to detect mental and nervous diseases, including a deeply personal and intrusive psychological examination. They asked about my family history, home life, achievements, and emotional balance. They wanted to know about my sex life—"Do you like girls?"—and they asked about tobacco, alcohol, and drug usage, things they called somatic demands. They inquired about my social needs and whether I had "self-seeking tendencies," whatever that means. Finally they asked about my philosophy of life.

"Don't look back," I said.

"What do you mean by that, sergeant?" asked the man in a white lab coat, holding a clipboard.

"I can't worry about or change the past. There's no time for regrets . . ."

"Yes, go on," the man said earnestly.

"Look, I believe in myself. I know I can become an excellent pilot," I said impulsively.

The man scribbled something down and walked out of the room.

I began to wonder what he wrote down, assuming it had something to do with my confidence, leadership capacity, and strength of character. If those are self-seeking tendencies, I thought, I've got 'em in spades!

I passed the physical examination and qualified for flight school.

Notes

1.   Gary Bedingfield, "Baseball in World War II," *Baseball in Wartime*, accessed March 18, 2013, http://www.baseballinwartime.com/baseball_in_wwii/baseball_in _wwii.htm; Gerald Bazer and Steven Culbertson, "When FDR Said 'Play Ball:' President Called Baseball a Wartime Morale Booster," *National Archives*, accessed March 18, 2013, https://www.archives.gov/publications/prologue/2002/spring/greenlight.html.

2.   Bedingfield, "Baseball in World War II."

3.   Ibid.

4.   WPA Texas, *Randolph Field: A History and Guide* (New York: The Devin-Adair Company, 1942), 130, 133.

5.   "Glenn Miller Biography: Conductor, Songwriter (1904–1944)," accessed February 12, 2014, http://www.biography.com/people/glenn-miller-37990.

CHAPTER 9

The Army Air Corps did not have the capacity to train the thousands of pilots needed for the war, so a decision was made to contract with civilian-owned flight schools to provide the first phase of aviation training, called primary training. Under the plan, the civilian operators of the schools would provide all of the necessary services and facilities, except aircraft, while the Air Corps would control the methods and means of instruction. The government agreed to pay 1,170 dollars for each primary school graduate and 18 dollars per hour for each cadet who washed out.[1] This was a godsend to many of the operators who had suffered through the Depression and a great opportunity for some start-up operations. Sixty-four civilian flight schools trained more than 250,000 cadets over the course of the war.[2] I was one of the 8,000 men who trained at the Wilson & Bonfils Flying School in Chickasha, Oklahoma.[3]

The town is located about fifty miles northwest of Oklahoma City. It was founded in the middle of the Indian Territory, hence the name. Depending on whom you ask, the name of the town is derived from the Choctaw word for "the tribe that left a long time ago" or an Indian word that means "rebel."[4]

Chickasha looked and felt like a lot of the small towns I had been around since leaving home. It was a railroad hub with two train depots. There were banks, businesses, shops, and cafes lining both sides of Main Street, with an assortment of cars and trucks parked diagonally in front of the establishments most of the time. Some of the businesses had canvas awnings for shade in the summer and covers in the winter. Many of them had neon signs that lit up the streets at night, beckoning travelers to slow down, stop in, and drop some coin for sundry items like fresh pie, a hot cup of coffee, or a tank of gas.

In March 1943, a few months after my arrival in Chickasha, the musical *Oklahoma!* premiered on Broadway. It was still running a year later when I arrived in New York from Casablanca, leg in a cast and hobbling around on crutches. The popular production about a white cowboy and his pretty white girlfriend depicted only one slice of life in Oklahoma. There were no "White Only" signs on the set, the kind prominently displayed in both public and private places throughout the state and no less so in Chickasha. And there was no mention of the Jim Crow laws that kept blacks in their "proper" place.

Chickasha's history includes the worst example of human cruelty and the hopeful signs of social progress. In 1930, Henry Argo, a nineteen-year-old black man from Chickasha, was strung up by a mob of white men.[5] His was the last known lynching in Oklahoma. In 1946, a twenty-two-year-old Chickasha resident, Ada Lois Sipuel, was denied admission to the Oklahoma University Law School because she was Negro.[6] She sued the Board of Regents and two years later Thurgood Marshall represented her before the Supreme Court of the United States.[7] The court issued a ruling that entitled her to a legal education at a state institution. It did not, however, rule segregation unconstitutional.[8]

The W & B Flying School was located at the Chickasha Municipal Airport about four miles northwest of downtown, off of Highway 81. My twelve weeks there included 225 hours of ground school instruction. There were twenty-eight rules that were "To Be Read and Thoroughly Understood by Every Student Prior to First Solo."[9] The list of "I understand . . ." and "I will never do . . ." undertakings featured safety rules such as "I understand that stalls, spins, and acrobatics will start at an altitude above 4,500 feet and that chandelles and lazy 8s will be done at an altitude above 3,000 feet . . ." and "I will never enter into clouds or fly within 300 feet of them." Primary training also included ninety-four hours of academic work, fifty-four hours of military training, and sixty-five hours in the air, about half of the time with an instructor.

There were about 600 cadets in my primary class. Mostly we flew Fairchild PT-19A trainers, a low wing 175 horsepower monoplane. We called it a "Cornell." Many guys were more familiar with horses than aircraft and some of them had never even driven a car. We were all used to manual labor, not modern machinery. Nevertheless, we were expected to fly solo after eight hours of dual instruction, which for me happened on December 22, 1942.

It was not "all work and no play." The Oklahoma College for Women was just five miles from W & B's airfield. With no men at the college and the local young men off to war, we had a good thing going with the girls there. We would fly across the campus and drop down over the playing fields, tossing notes wrapped around rocks secured by rubber bands. The notes informed the girls where to meet us for a party or dinner that night. It never failed to attract a crowd of beautiful coeds.

Those who successfully completed primary training were given Civilian Pilot Training wings from W & B. The wings were made of brass and had a blue center crest. We were authorized to wear them on civilian clothes but not on our uniforms. I never did. There were two more phases of training before I would be a bona fide US aviator. As far as I was concerned, being a commissioned officer with silver pilot wings was the only accomplishment worth noting. Anything less was failure, which makes the next part of the story all the more perplexing, even to me.

Cadets were required to sign an oath to remain single during aviation training. But that didn't stop some guys from marrying their girls. At Randolph Field and other bases around Texas, it became an article of faith that cadets would not be drummed out for getting married, so long as they didn't flaunt it. There was even a rumor that some commanding officers would look the other way when brides signed in for visits at the bases, identifying themselves as sisters or aunts.

I met Peggy Bryan when I was still a mechanic at Perrin Field. She worked as a civilian clerk in the office of Perrin's commanding officer. She was a pretty girl, petite, with short brown hair. With an easy smile and a quick wit, she was irresistible to me. Unfortunately, it was unrequited love for a time as she resisted me quite well. I asked her out the first time I met her. She turned me down. She declined my second and third invitations too. I guess I finally won her over, or wore her down, since she agreed to go out with me on my fourth try.

Peggy lived in Denison, a little railroad town not far from the base. She shared a home with her mother on Morgan Street. It was the smallest house in a modest neighborhood, its front-facing wall made of rock. Two large cedar elms stood as sentries between the house and the street. There was a tiny front porch to the left of the door but there were no outdoor chairs. The furniture inside the house was sparse and plain. Peggy, on the other hand, looked bright and beautiful when I picked her up for our first date.

She agreed to bring a picnic lunch and my job was to find a beautiful spot for the picnic. We drove to the Red River and found a cluster of trees and a patch of grass. We spread out a blanket and sat down in the cool shade. A slight breeze was blowing across the water. Before I could say a word, Peg scooted to the edge of the blanket and began to make ready our lunch.

"Slow down there, Peggy. Why don't we talk for a while, get to know each other a bit. Tell me about yourself."

"Well, I just graduated from high school last summer. I live with my mother, and that's about it."

"Come on, at least tell me one thing I didn't know about you before today," I said, giving her a wide-open target since I knew nothing about her.

"Well, did you know General Eisenhower was born in my hometown?"

"That's not what I meant, and you know it," I teased.

"Look, I don't know if I'll ever see you again after today. If I do, maybe I'll share a few more things about me, and then again, maybe I won't," she said.

"Fair enough," I said, sensing it was time to move on to another subject.

"What about you?" she asked. "Where are you from? Tell me about your family."

"Why is that fair? You get to ask me questions, but I don't get to know more about you?"

"Because I'm not going anywhere, and I've had a dozen first dates with guys like you. Who knows where you will be tomorrow or next week. No, I'm not going to open my heart to you today. Besides, if you want a second date, you'll do what I say."

She batted her eyes and smiled coyly, both actions intentionally overdone.

"That's a fair point, and I don't mind talking about myself. Well . . . let's see . . . where do I begin? I'm from Arizona."

"What does your dad do for a living?" she asked.

"He's in construction now but the old boy started working when he was thirteen as a muleskinner in the Tombstone mining area."

"I saw a Randolph Scott movie a couple of years ago about Tombstone. That's where the shoot-out at the O.K. Corral took place, right?"

I nodded.

"But what kind of work is skinning mules? That sounds awful. . . . I never heard of such a thing," she said, kind of shivering.

I raised both hands, palms out, signaling her to slow down.

"Wow, wow, Peggy! You've got the wrong idea. He drove a team of mules. He hauled stuff in a wagon to the mines for people," I explained.

She let out a little laugh and told me of the gruesome picture she had had in her head.

"Do you get along with your dad?" she asked.

"He's the greatest man I know, but he can be hard on me."

"How so?" she said, inching closer to me, concern in her eyes.

"Let's put it this way: he drove those stubborn beasts for more than twenty years and had a few sayings about them. He'd say, 'A good driver has to be more mule-headed than his mules.'"

"He must have been pretty tough, then," she suggested.

I assured her he was and then dropped another one of his favorite lines. "He would also say, 'It is necessary to lead an ass by its nose.'"

"Did he always use such colorful language?"

"He was referring to mules—most of the time, anyway. He liked to remind people that 'You can't drive mules unless you're willing to swear at them—it's the only language they understand.'"

"I didn't know there was so much to know about mules," she said, sounding surprised.

"Actually anybody who knows Dad knows he's not talking about just mules when he says those things, and no one knows it better than me."

"You poor boy, do you want to talk about it?" she replied, inching ever closer to me.

"Not really," I said, taking her hand.

"Okay then, how'd he meet your mom?" she replied, taking back her hand calmly but with conviction.

"Mom was working as a maid in a Tucson hotel when he met her. They had an on-again, off-again courtship. Dad had been on the trail so long it was hard for him to settle down. All that ended a couple of years later. One night he saw her dancing with another man on a crowded raised dance floor in the town square. In telling the story, he said her young, pretty face was 'glowing in the light of luminaria' that were set atop the steps and rails of the platform. Angry and jealous, he rode his horse up the stairs and onto the dance floor, scattering the dancers. With reins in one hand, he reached down and pulled Mother up onto the horse and rode off into the dark desert night. And that was that."

"Sounds like a story right out of Hollywood. What else can you tell me about the Kirkland clan? It's kind of an unusual name. I'm not familiar with it here in Denison."

"My people are originally from Scotland. Our family name came about the same way many names came to be over there. Some names refer to lineage, so the sons of Donald became Donaldson. They could indicate a man's occupation, like Mason or Shepherd. In our case, our family name describes a place of habitation, land near a kirk—the Scot word for church."

"So you Kirklands are a religious lot?" she asked.

"Well, we go to church from time to time but we're more about *facta non verba*—deeds, not words. That's what's written on our Scot family crest. We were raised to believe in that ideal, but I'll admit to you, I did more talking than deeding when I was a boy, if you take out the athletics and fist-fighting."

"I bet. How'd y'all get to Arizona?"

"John Kirkland, my great-great-great-grandfather, left Scotland for America around 1770, settling in Tennessee. From there some Kirklands moved to Virginia, then Missouri, and then my Grandfather came to Arizona, settling much of the old territory. They called him Judge Kirkland."

"You seem very proud of your heritage," she said thoughtfully.

"Well, yes, there are a lot Kirkland firsts in Arizona: first white couple married in the Arizona Territory—my grandparents; first cattle ranch stocked by a white man; first white woman to live in what is now Phoenix; first white child born in Phoenix; first white man to employ white labor; first white settler to discover a prehistoric Indian ruin . . ."

I didn't consider it bragging to talk of such things. First off, it was all true. Second, when you don't have much in the way of worldly possessions, it helps to talk about things nobody else has. Recounting my family's good deeds made me stand a little taller, and I wanted to impress Peg that day.

I must have passed muster. We had a second date, and then another. After that we saw each other as often as possible.

When I shipped out to Chickasha, I was so excited to fly I thought it would be easy to live without her. I was wrong, notwithstanding the easy company of the college coeds.

Peg took a one-day leave of absence from her job at Perrin Field to visit me for a weekend, arriving Saturday afternoon. Before she left Denison, I sent her a telegram: "WILL TRY TO MEET YOU AT TRAIN IF CANT RESERVATION WILL BE AT CHICKASHA HOTEL."[10] Two hours after she arrived, I showed up at her room apologetically with a box of chocolates and a bunch of pansies.

My fly school buddies, who had endured my endless confessions about Peg for weeks, had insisted on meeting her. So the next evening, Peg's last night in town, we met my friends and some college girls in the lobby of the McFarland Hotel. We had dinner in the hotel dining room and then went out for a night of dancing.

Throughout the night, my friends recounted for Peg how miserable I had been without her, begging her to put me out of my misery by marrying me. They suggested it would mean a great deal to them too since they wouldn't have to listen to me anymore on the topic of love. We all laughed about it for a while and then I pulled her away from the crowd, got on my knee, and told her I couldn't stand being apart for one more day. She accepted my proposal and we decided to be married that night, if possible.

We found the address of the justice of the peace in the phone book and the whole gang drove in a procession of cars to his home off Highway 81. We rapped on his door for several minutes until the porch light came on and a sweet old lady answered the door. I was surprised at her reaction as she carefully looked us over, a bunch of guys in uniform and young women bundled in winter coats. We tried to apologize for being so late but she interrupted.

"You're not the first ones to drop by and you won't be the last, at least so long as this war is going on," she whispered.

I knew for a fact we were not the first couple who opted for the certainty of marriage during times of war. Many of my generation were conceived by parents facing the perils of the last war. Like them, we lived with the reality that military orders could separate us at a moment's notice, or that something as mundane as a malfunctioning engine could separate us forever. From the start of the war until it was over, the Army Air Corps lost nearly 15,000 pilots, crewmen, and other personnel and 14,000 planes inside the continental United States.[11] Two-thirds of all pilot deaths during the war were due to training crashes and operational accidents. Only a third of the deaths were due to enemy combat. This meant that a pilot was more likely to die as a result of training runs, mechanical failures, or weather-related collisions than enemy fire. And so, some of us looked at the odds of survival and decided life was to be lived in the moment. There was no time for a long engagement, elaborate wedding plans, a gown, or even a ring.

The judge's wife asked softly, "Who's the lucky bride?" My friends pushed Peg to the front next to me. The old woman looked at me and with a twinkle in her eye said, "Aren't you the lucky one." She then turned around and shouted, "Poppa, we have visitors . . . lovebirds."

The judge walked in to the front room wearing pajamas and slippers, cinching up his bathrobe as he got to the door. We couldn't tell what he was saying at first, but it was clear he was not happy with us, or his wife. "Mother, you have to stop opening the door to strangers," he huffed.

"We owe it to these boys to be kind. Now behave yourself!" she scolded as she stepped behind him, letting him into the threshold.

"Judge, if you don't mind, I'd like to ask you a couple of questions about marriage?" I said.

"Well, if you want to know about the birds and the bees, you better go ask your daddy."

"That's not it."

His wife jumped in. "Poppa, behave yourself."

"Go ahead, young man, I'm listening," he said, ignoring my snickering friends.

"First, is there a waiting period for marriages in Oklahoma?" I asked.

I knew there was a waiting period in some states. In California, it was three days. I knew that because of my days at Sky Harbor. There were people in California, particularly celebrities, who could not abide the three-day waiting period required for a marriage license in the Golden State. Instead, they would fly to Phoenix and get married within an hour, courtesy of the Maricopa County Clerk. The members of the Phoenix Chamber of Commerce wanted to earn some cash, so they built a small open-air wedding chapel north of the landing strip. Made of adobe brick, the mission-style chapel had a bronze bell hanging from an arch.

The plan for quickie fly-in weddings was not a major financial success, but forty California couples were married in the chapel before it was torn down to make room for the war effort. I saw several couples land at the airport and head for the chapel. I was among a crowd of about one hundred, including important-looking people in suits and dresses, to greet Hollywood actor and singer Donald Novis, whom I heard on the radio, and his bride, Dorothy Bradshaw, a Broadway dancer I knew nothing about.

An announcer from radio station KOY was there to comment on the blessed event "sponsored by Nielson Sporting Goods!" He seemed a bit overwrought around the celebrities, earnestly describing their desert vows like it was a coronation, and lavishly praising the background music of the "Spanish orchestra" when it was just a mariachi band with an exuberant tuba player.

"No, son, there is no waiting period here in the Sooner state." Turning to his wife and smiling, he added, "It seems there is no waiting at all. Now, what is your second question?" he asked.

After hearing our story and learning that Peg was headed back to Denison the next day, the judge agreed to meet us at the courthouse at midnight.

Looking at his wife, the judge said, "And the missus can be one of the witnesses and serve as the clerk, if you don't mind her sniffling. She always tears up at weddings."

His wife stepped toward him, placed one hand on his shoulder, and laced the fingers of her other hand through his. She looked at us and smiled brightly.

"Do you know where the courthouse is?" the judge asked, sounding genuinely concerned, more like a parent than a sleep-deprived judge. "It's on Choctaw Avenue and 3rd Street," he instructed, "and I'll see you there in an hour."

We all nodded and laughed some. It didn't take long to know your way around town, and we had just come from the Opera House, a dance hall on Chickasaw Avenue, near the courthouse. It had been a real opera house, the Wagoner Opera House, until 1911. After that it was a movie theater, a pool hall, and by January 1943, a place for soldiers and girls to dance.[12]

And so, on a cold night on January 10, 1943, nineteen days after my first solo, I rushed into a marriage that could have ended my flying career before it got started. Peg returned home the next day and continued to live with her mother while I finished my training at W & B. We would secretly rendezvous again in the coming months as my training continued at other airfields in Texas.

Notes

1. Bruce A. Ashcroft, *We Wanted Wings: A History of the Aviation Cadet Program*, (Randolph Air Force Base, Texas: HQ Air Education and Training Command, 2005); "The Army Air Forces in World War II Volume VI: Men and Planes: Chapter 14," accessed May 13, 2014, http://www.ibiblio.org/hyperwar/AAF/VI/AAF-VI-14.html.

2. Thomas A. Manning, Bruce A. Ashcroft, Richard H. Emmons, Ann K. Hussey, and Joseph L. Mason, *History of Air Education and Training Command*, 1942–2002 (Randolph Air Force Base, Texas: HQ Air Education and Training Command, 2005), accessed January 27, 2016, http://www.aetc.af.mil/Portals/1/documents/history/AFD -061109-022.pdf.

3. "Chickasha Municipal Airport," *Wikipedia*, accessed January 27, 2016, https:// en.wikipedia.org/wiki/Chickasha_Municipal_Airport.

4. Angie Jeffries, "Chickasha," *Encyclopedia of Oklahoma History and Culture*, accessed January 27, 2016, http://www.okhistory.org/publications/enc/entry.php?entry=CH038.

5. Gobe Davis and James M. Fortier, "A Documentary Feature," *American Lynching*, accessed August 27, 2013, http://www.americanlynching.com/main.html.

6. Melvin C. Hall, "Fisher, Ada Lois Sipuel," *Encyclopedia of Oklahoma History and Culture*, accessed August 27, 2013, http://www.okhistory.org/publications/enc/entry .php?entry=FI009.

7. "Ada Lois Sipuel v. Board of Regents University of Oklahoma, 1948–," *Civil Rights Digital Library*, accessed August 27, 2013, http://crdl.usg.edu/collections /sipuel/?Welcome.

8. *Sipuel v. Board of Regents, 332 U.S. 631* (1948).

9. Memorandum from the WWII files of Frank J. Kirkland Jr.

10. Western Union Money Order Notice, No. DAC116, dated January 6, 1943, from the WWII files of Frank J. Kirkland Jr.

11. *Army Air Forces Statistical Digest, World War II* (Office of Statistical Control, 1945), 309–10, accessed January 27, 2016, http://www.dtic.mil/dtic/tr/fulltext/u2/a542518.pdf.

12. "Chickasha Downtown Historic District- 328 W. Chickasha Ave.- Chickasha, OK," *Waymarking*, accessed August 27, 2013, http://www.waymarking.com/waymarks /WMADF1_Chickasha_Downtown_Historic_District_328_W_Chickasha_Ave _Chickasha_OK.

CHAPTER 10

As fate would have it, I was assigned to Enid Airfield for basic flight school, the second phase of my aviation training. It was located just outside of Vance's hometown of Enid, Oklahoma, population 40,000. The town was known as "Oklahoma's Queen Wheat City," and looking down on the landscape from my ship, I could see why. For miles, there was nothing but fields of grain dotted by oil drilling rigs pumping black gold out of the ground. The railroad tracks slicing through the wheat fields looked like sutures holding the earth together. I also saw the schools Vance probably attended and the ball fields where he must have played. I imagined him running around that flat prairie town, a naive boy who became an ambitious young man, with no clue of the dangers he would someday face.

Even though he was just six years older than I was, I wanted Vance to be proud of me. More than a mentor and friend, he was an inspiration. He later became a colonel and then an American hero. During his time as an instructor, he felt enormous frustration as he watched his students and staff learn from him and then go off to war, while he readied the next cadre of cadets to take their places on the battlefront. Two of his clerks at Goodfellow Field, brothers Jack and Mark Mathis, became bombardiers. Both were killed in action over Europe within one month of each other, receiving Air Medals posthumously. The younger brother, Mark, was also awarded the Medal of Honor, the first World War II airman to receive the honor in Europe.[1] The news of the death of these boys was both painful and troubling to Vance. He yearned for the adventure of combat and the glory that would follow, believing he too was destined to be a Medal of Honor recipient.[2]

He seemed to know a lot about the medal, and was fascinated by it. When he found out I was from Phoenix, he asked me if I knew the name of the first pilot to receive the Medal of Honor.

"Frank Luke Jr.," I said.

Vance was amazed. "How'd you know that, Kirk?" he asked.

"My Dad told me about him when I was a kid."

Like many boys in the 1920s, I pretended to be Captain Eddie Rickenbacker, America's most successful pilot in World War I. He was on the radio, featured in newspapers and movie reels, and was the topic of conversation around barbershops everywhere, I presume, but most certainly at Sanchez Barber Shop, where I got clipped. At some point Dad noticed my airplane obsession and told me about hometown hero Frank "Balloon Buster" Luke. Dad was a friend of Luke's father, Frank Sr., who came to town as a German immigrant in 1873. The two of them spoke often of Frank Jr.'s exploits, and when Dad repeated the stories to me, I could tell he was very impressed with the young man, and he was not easily impressed, which made an impression on me.

Born in Phoenix in 1897, Frank Luke Jr. was a good athlete and a tough bare-knuckle fighter.[3] His reputation as a flier took off at Phoenix Union High School when he ran off the roof of the auditorium, hands high over his head while gripping a large umbrella he had filched from a tractor, using it as a parachute. Although he crash-landed and broke his wrist, the legend of the audacious stunt never diminished. The story was still in circulation when I became a student there in 1936. As much as I was amused by it, I tended to focus on his accomplishments after high school, something I thought about often as I walked by the campus memorial dedicated to him by the Class of 1918.

"Luke was fearless," Vance said. "With 18 victories, he was the second-ranking ace behind only Rickenbacker, a remarkable feat considering he flew just ten sorties. Most of his kills were against German observation balloons that were heavily fortified by airplanes and artillery. He maneuvered safely through enemy defenses until the day of his final mission."

"I heard his plane wasn't shot down, but he took a round in the chest from a hillside sniper," I added.

Vance was getting pretty worked up about the story and started talking fast.

"That's right. Even so he still managed to land his plane and took on the German patrol that tracked him down, a revolver in each hand, firing away until the end. Rickenbacker said he was the most daring aviator and the greatest fighter in the entire war."

In December 1943, Vance finally got his chance to prove himself in battle.[4] He became the deputy commander of the 489th Bomb Group, and was given the assignment of preparing B-24 Liberator bomber crews for their missions on D-Day. His time had finally come. Four months later he led his bomb group in a flight over the Atlantic to their new base at Halesworth, England. He named his plane "The Sharon D.," after his one-year-old daughter, Sharon.

On May 30, 1944, Colonel Vance led forty-two B-24s on a raid to bomb the airfield at Oldenburg, Germany. It was the only combat mission he flew in The Sharon D. His second mission was his last one. He was a pilot observer in the Missouri Sue, one of 629 heavy bombers assigned to bomb German coastal defensive installations in France, preparatory to the D-Day invasion. While passing over the target, Vance's plane was hit with intense anti-aircraft fire just as it released its 500-hundred-pound bombs. Shrapnel sliced through the cockpit, killing the pilot instantly. Others were seriously wounded. Three of the bomber's engines were destroyed and a fourth had to be shut down to avoid a stall and to enable the plane to glide back across the English Channel. Vance had been standing behind the pilot when the initial flak hit the plane. While the copilot struggled to keep the plane from going down, Vance lunged at the control panel to hit the switch to the fourth engine, but he seemed to be tied down. He looked back at his foot to see that it had been severed, with only a tendon connecting his leg and foot, which were lodged between the plane's armored plating and the damaged turret. Despite the intense pain, Vance somehow was able to stretch far enough to reach inside the cockpit to shut off engine four.

The plane glided across the channel and all of the crew was able to bail out over British soil. One man landed safely in a minefield. Vance remained in the plane, however, believing that a wounded gunner was still inside. He was not; the crew had strapped him to a parachute and pushed him out of the plane. Vance was also concerned that the remaining bombs on board posed a threat to civilians in the event of a crash landing. So, with his leg still tethered to his foot, Vance stretched himself out to an almost prone position to reach the controls and guided the plane back out over the channel, gently lowering the craft until it began to skid across the water. The impact threw him forward with tremendous force, enough to sever the tendon and free him from his trapped foot. Except for the pilot, all of the crew survived, and Colonel Vance was rescued from the water.

His recovery in a British hospital was difficult, both physically and emotionally. He sorrowed over his lost career and worried over his daughter's reaction to him when he got home. The turning point was an encounter he had with a London lad while walking on crutches down a busy street. The boy saw the American with one foot and said, "Don't worry, Yank, you won't miss it." The boy's mother was mortified, explaining the boy had lost his own foot in a German air raid, and that he was getting along quite well with his prosthetic foot. This brave boy buoyed Vance's spirits, and helped him to face his future with a new sense of optimism.[5]

On July 26, 1944, Vance joined other wounded servicemen on a C-54 Skymaster transport plane for the long journey home.[6] By then, he was joking about his missing foot, lamenting the fact it had not been retrieved from the ocean and mounted as a trophy. He was also making plans to resume his flying career, believing he could still effectively serve in the military. Within a few hours from take-off, the transport plane disappeared somewhere between Iceland and Newfoundland, and like thousands of wives and mothers, Mrs. Vance received word of this tragedy by way of Western Union.

The telegram from Adjutant General, James A. Ulio, read, "*We regret to inform you that your husband . . . has been reported missing . . . the report further states search is continuing . . . your distress during this period of anxiety is fully understood.*"[7]

The transport plane was never found; no bodies were ever recovered. It is difficult for me to comprehend how his torn body could be miraculously rescued from the English Channel only to be inexplicably lost in the North Atlantic Ocean. It is a haunting thought for those of us who have survived such things. Sometimes, even now, the guilt of "Why him?" harrows my soul.

Prior to his departure from England, Vance had been recommended for the Medal of Honor. It was awarded to him posthumously in January 1945, but, at Mrs. Vance's request, was not presented to the family at that time. She wanted her daughter to receive it when she got a little older, which she did in October 1946, at the age of four. After the war, Colonel Vance was honored yet again when Enid Airfield was renamed Vance Air Force Base.[8]

In March 1942 I was ordered back to the country club for additional training. Peg met me in San Antonio the first weekend I was there and a couple of times after that. We were in good company by then. A lot of cadets found their wives during their time at Randolph Field. In fact, there were so many Air Corps-civilian marriages that San Antonio was known as "the mother-in law of the Army."

We spent Saturday evenings through Sunday evenings together, often joining my classmates at the Flying Cadet Club on the third floor of the Gunther Hotel or the Anacacho Room at the Saint Anthony. There was never a shortage of girls for my unmarried friends, some of whom were classified as cadet widows.

A cadet widow was the kind of girl who befriended the cadets of one class, hoping to find a husband, and when that class graduated, moved on to the next class. Many of the girls heard the same stories and "lines" over and over with each wave of cadets, and they became proficient conversationalists about the skills cadets were trying to master. One girl seemed to know more "buzzer"(radio code) than some of the instructors. Her talent was revealed at the expense and embarrassment of two of my buddies who assumed the women could not understand the dah-dah-dit-dah language they were using to discuss their amorous plans for two beautiful girls at the club. To their surprise and my great amusement, the girls' friend, another cadet widow, translated the buzzer for them. The result wasn't what my friends had in mind. Bobby got slapped and old Tom was doused with a drink.

Returning to our table, Tom dried off his face. "I blew it. She was a real *six and twenty tootsie.*"

"What's that?" Peg asked.

"You are, darling," I answered.

Bobby, the guy with the red imprint on his face, chimed in, "A six and twenty tootsie is a gal so alluring that a cadet would risk returning late to the base to spend more time with her. He'll stay out late knowing full well it will mean six demerits and twenty punishment tours."

"What's a punishment tour?" Peg wanted to know.

"The poor shmuck has to walk at a pace of 120 steps per minute back and forth outside his barracks while wearing his dress uniform and white gloves and carrying a bayonet scabbard. He can't talk to anybody unless it is in the line of duty."

It had to be a special girl to risk having to do twenty tours. Most often the punishment tours were meted out on Saturday afternoons, just as the other cadets were going into town for some fun.

"Bobby, do you remember that time you were doing a tour, and the captain checked your rifle?" I asked.

"What happened?" Peg asked.

"There he was, poor old Bobby marching around, paying the price for some dumb thing, when a captain stopped him for an impromptu inspection. Too bad for Bob, the captain found an oil smear on the barrel and gave him another *gig*."

We joked about gigs—demerits—often, but it was no laughing matter. A cadet could be discharged from aviation school if his demerits exceeded sixty while an underclassman, and forty as an upperclassman.

"It seems strange how much trouble you can get into just for carrying a *gig stick*. We're aviators, not soldiers," Bobby concluded.

The consequences of cadet misbehavior were clearly spelled out in the *Flying Cadet Battalion Manual*, a copy of which was in each cadet's room. The most severe punishment was dismissal from the aviation program. This was the penalty for lying, dishonesty, or any vicious, immoral conduct unbecoming an officer and a gentlemen, which implicated those of us clandestinely married.

We were also given a copy of the *Flying Cadet Manual*, which explained the drills we were expected to execute to perfection, and *Compass Headings*, which we called the Cadet Bible. It included regulations regarding saluting, room rules, mess hall manners, and mode of addressing officers, plus a recitation of the honor system at Randolph. We were taught that no cadet could survive a breach of honor and were warned about bragging about one's flying ability.

I will admit to being a little cocky at the time. After all, I was a cadet at the West Point of the Air, and I was really good. We were flying planes that were twice as big and powerful as the ones we flew in primary school, which, by comparison, were like box cars with built-in headwinds. There were also more gauges and instruments to learn and master, altimeters, rate of climb, air pressure, bank indicators, and more. After about five hours with the instructor sitting behind me in the cockpit, I soloed in a BT-9, and eventually had more than seventy hours in the air. This included about six hours of instrument flying instruction, six hours of flying in formation, six hours of daylight navigation and cross-country work, with some occasional night flying. We gradually worked our way up to BT-14s and finally got into real service planes.

At the end of every flight session, cadets were graded on a scale of A to F. You got a white slip if you passed that day's flight instruction, a pink slip if you failed, with a notation of your infraction: "Heavy use of stick and rudder," "Failure to hold sufficient right rudder to counteract torque," or some other form of critique. The flight commander flew with cadets three times during basic training, issuing yellow slips if the flight was satisfactory.

Cadets were ever fearful about washing out. As the time approached for the twenty-hour flight check, everyone grew nervous. Our CO told us not to worry about it, over and over and over.

"We don't want you to fail. Uncle Sam has invested a lot on money in you. Getting *checkitis*[9] won't help you at all, so quit worrying about failure and get your minds right. We're training you to win a war. It's not about you. Never forget it. I am confident in you boys and expect you all will tell your girls back home in your next *sugar report* about your great success after the twenty-hour check."

To pass the twenty-hour progress check, a cadet had to demonstrate a command of flying fundamentals, including how to handle a stall. After forty hours, the cadet was expected to know how to do chandelles, climbing turns, lazy eights, steep turns, and forced landings. The sixty-hour progress check focused on instrument flying, a vital skill when vision is impaired due to heavy snow or fog conditions.

The flight commander was already in the plane when I jumped into the front seat for my sixty-hour flight check.

The commander, trying to put me at ease, said, "Don't let the *washing machine* scare you, Mister Kirkland. We're just going to go up today, nice and easy like. It will be routine stuff for you." Cadets, fearful of washing out, called flight check planes washing machines.

Through the intercom, I responded, "I'm not going to wash out, sir. Not in this ship, not in any ship."

"Don't let pride get in your way, mister. I've seen lots of good men wash out for silly mistakes. You may be an *H.P.* I'll know before too long."

An H.P. was a *Hot Pilot*, and the commander wasn't paying me a compliment. There's a fine line between confidence and cockiness. An H.P. could talk a big game but his skills didn't match his verve.

"Excuse me, sir. I meant no disrespect."

"No sweat, Kirkland. Taxi up and slap on the coal."

When we landed, the commander said, "You're the real deal, mister. Not much chance of you flying the *Gray Ghost*," referring to another term used by cadets. It pointed to the last flight check in the commander's ship. Those who washed out at that stage did so in the Gray Ghost.

"Thank you, sir. I don't expect that I will."

We practiced instrument flying in the air with our canopies shrouded and an instructor in the back of the cockpit, to make sure we didn't crash. Guys who became really good at instrument flying were called *Gadgeteers*. It was said that they could do more things from under the hood than a lot of cadets could do flying with visual contacts. I was a Gadgeteer. We also spent considerable time practicing instrument flying on the ground in a flight simulator known as a Link Trainer, named after its inventor, Ed Link.[10] He was a former organ and nickelodeon builder who used his knowledge of bellows, pumps, and valves to create the 1929 prototype.[11] There were a half-dozen or so Link Trainers at Randolph Field. Cadets called them *jeeps* because of their box-like appearance.

Located in a hangar near the West Flight Line, Link Trainers were highly sophisticated pieces of equipment, but to me they looked like blue carnival cars with stubby yellow wings and tail sections and more Pinewood Derby than Curtiss Condor. They were an electronic marvel, though, recording all the movements that an airplane would make in responding to a pilot at the controls and precisely measuring a cadet's skills, errors, and omissions.

Generally speaking, cadets were not fans of the Link Trainer. They'd get nervous just thinking about the experience, coming down with jeep jitters before even hopping into the thing. After the sessions, you could hear guys complaining about getting *jeepkrieged*, that is, when the link trainer was made to exhibit multiple emergency conditions at the same time. The blasted thing even humbled me one day when I "killed" myself two times in one practice session.

Our ground school training also included twenty hours studying airplane and engine operations, thirty hours on the weather, ten hours on military law, and eight hours on navigation. We spent as many hours as possible studying radio code, doubling up on the subject when bad weather kept us from flying. We were told the more we knew about weather characteristics, the better our chances of survival would be. Likewise, the importance of buzzer class was emphasized by Major Ott, the director of ground training, "Radio code is one of the things you will need very seldom, but when you do need it, it may save your life."[12]

We studied airplane and engine operations in Hangar V, half of which was partitioned into classrooms equipped with working models, cutaways, blueprints, charts, and part panels. A front alcove displayed a collection of obsolete airplane engines, including one of the famous 1918–19 Liberty motors built for the Great War. The production of Liberty motors, intended to power US and Allied airplanes, was full of mystique and lore. Politicians and generals marveled at how quickly the design concepts turned into a finished product, reflecting the very best in Yankee know-how and ingenuity. Ford, Buick, and Lincoln, along with some long-forgotten motor companies, built several thousand Liberty motors before the armistice was signed. Had the war continued, another 100,000 engines were in the pipeline.[13]

The other half of the Hangar V was covered with wings, landing gear, fuselages, and tail assemblies of newer modeled aircraft, which gave cadets an up-close perspective on the various component parts of a plane. Of course, my hands-on experience as a mechanic the previous year put me way ahead of my classmates, and I was often asked by the instructors to help them explain things like carburetion or the electrical system to guys who were having a hard time keeping up. Cadets were not expected to be expert mechanics, but they had to know enough to inspect their planes before take-off and be sufficiently familiar with their operations to fill out the ship's Form 1 log upon their return.

In the mess hall, underclassmen were expected to sit on the front four inches of their chairs, heads held high. If you slouched, you would hear someone yell, "Gain some altitude, mister!" Cadets were permitted to use only one hand when eating, unless they were cutting meat or buttering bread. There was a regimen for serving and eating the food too. Underclassmen sat at the service end of the tables. Waiters placed the food there and the two cadets sitting at very end of the table were designated gunners who were responsible for "shooting" or "gunning" the platters of food up the table. Underclassmen were also expected to fill the coffee mugs of the upperclassmen, passing them up the table, with each man repeating, "a cup of coffee for Mr. Blank," as he pushed the mug along to the next guy until it arrived in front of "Mr. Blank."

These little rituals and traditions were supposed to instill discipline, but they were also a source of hazing and even some fun. A bulletin board hung in the middle of the operations office, which prominently displayed the "Star List," but it had nothing to do with being a star pilot. Quite the contrary, cadets who committed any number of listed infractions were given special recognition on the board, with a red star by their names. A cadet who taxied with the flaps up got a star. He got a star for taxiing too fast, being late for a dual ride, leaving flight equipment out, or parking in the wrong stall. He got at least two red stars for taxiing in such a way that dust or dirt was blown into the flight office. The worst offense, meriting five stars, was a "crack-up."[14]

The cadets were required to affix the stars by their names in front of their classmates, who cheered and jeered the poor fellows as they walked to the front of the room. Stars were also awarded to cadets who got disoriented on cross-country flights or made other miscalculations while flying at night. But those kinds of mistakes also qualified the cadet for the "Stupid Pilot Trophy," a large tin bowl with handles, wrapped with a red ribbon, with the names of all the recipients etched on the side.[15] Special ceremonies were organized to award the trophy to the latest stupid pilot who would have to endure the ridicule of classmates and bear the distinction of being its owner until the next poor sap had a major mishap.

One recipient clipped a hangar with his propeller. Another cadet got the trophy for running into another plane while taxiing along the tarmac. The most famous of the bunch was a guy who flew thirty miles past his assigned destination before recognizing his error. He took possession of the stupid bowl amid a chorus of "Wrong Way Corrigan!" "Wrong Way Corrigan!" "Wrong Way Corrigan!"[16]

The chant was a nod to Doug Corrigan, one of the builders of the *Spirit of St. Louis*, the plane Charles Lindberg flew in 1927 on the first non-stop flight from New York to Paris. In 1938, Corrigan flew his civilian plane from Long Beach, California, to New York, with a planned return trip back to Long Beach. He famously flew to Ireland instead, claiming navigational error due to heavy cloud cover and a defective thirty-year-old compass. Thus he became "Wrong Way Corrigan" in the media.

Notes

1.   "Mark & Jack Mathis: Bombardier Brothers," *Home of Heroes*, accessed February 12, 2013, http://www.homeofheroes.com/wings/part2/05_mathis.html.

2.   "Lieutenant Colonel Leon Bob Vance: Burden of Command," *Home of Heroes*, accessed December 28, 2012, http://www.homeofheroes.com/wings/part2/17_vance .html.

3.   Ibid.

4.   Letter to Mr. Frank James Kirkland Jr. dated October 25, 1988, from Irene L. Beshear, Public Affairs Division, Department of the Air Force, Vance Air Force Base, enclosing "Biographical History, Lieutenant Colonel Leon Robert Vance, Junior," "Sometimes I Can't Believe It" by Carl B. Wall, *True Magazine* (1944), 96–98.

5.   Ibid.

6.   "Lieutenant Colonel Leon Bob Vance," Home of Heroes.

7.   Ibid.

8.   Letter to Mr. Frank James Kirkland Jr. from Irene L. Beshear.

9.   This is slang from Rudolph Field, meaning a cadet who worries about check rides with a Flight Commander; WPA Texas, *Randolph Field: A History and Guide* (New York: The Devin-Adair Company, 1942).

10.   Maurer Maurer, *Aviation in the U.S. Army, 1919–1939* (Washington, DC: Office of Air Force History United States Air Force, 1987), 378–79, accessed January 28, 2016, http://www.afhso.af.mil/shared/media/document/AFD-100923-007.pdf.

11.   "The 1942 Model C-3 Link Trainer," *Western Museum of Flight*, accessed May 21, 2013, http://www.wmof.com/c3link.html.

12.   Memorandum from the WWII files of Frank Kirkland Jr.

13.   Frederick Upham Adams, "How Changes Hurt Our Air Program," *The New York Times*, no. 3 (1918): accessed May 8, 2013, http://query.nytimes.com/mem /archive-free/pdf?res=F30C14FB3B5F1B7A93CBA8178ED85F4C8185F9.

14.   WPA Texas, *Randolph Field: A History and Guide* (New York: The Devin-Adair Company, 1942), 76–77.

15.   Ibid., 81.

16.   Ibid., 82.

CHAPTER 11

At the completion of basic training, the cadets who didn't wash out were sent to advanced flying schools for ten more weeks of training. At this stage we were divided into two groups: cadets who would train in swift pursuit planes to become fighter pilots were assigned to single-engine schools; cadets training to be bomber and transport pilots were assigned to twin-engine schools. In those days single-engine aircraft were called pursuit planes. The "P" in P-38 or P-40 referred to pursuit much like the "F" in today's F-16 refers to fighter.

Most cadets wanted to be fighter pilots but had no say in the matter. The decision was based on the recommendations of our instructors who evaluated and graded each cadet every day. They measured and considered our judgment in the air, temperament, aptitude, and stamina. They looked at our intangibles like attitude, aggressiveness, and determination. Ultimately, they tried to assign guys to do jobs for which they were best suited.

I wanted to fly pursuit aircraft because it would be more fun, and I would have more control over my destiny. My survival depended on being a better pilot than the German pilots, and I thought I would be. Bomber pilots, on the other hand, were required to stay on an undeviating course to complete their bomb-dropping missions while flying through walls of flak and avoiding the cannon fire of enemy aircraft. Statistically, the odds of survival for fighter pilots were very low. But bomber crews had it worse, with a seventy percent chance of being killed before completing the required twenty-five missions. The odds of survival diminished as the requirement for the number of missions increased to thirty-five and then fifty missions.[1] By war's end, the Army

Air Corps had 72,600 casualties: 54,700 men dead, and 17,900 men wounded. This meant that for every man wounded, three would die, leaving us with the expectation that any airman caught in the crosshairs almost always died.[2]

It seemed that luck was as important as skill for bomber pilots, and I didn't want my skill to be wasted. Bomber pilots were dependent on the courage and skills of their gunnery crews. As a fighter pilot, it would be my finger on the trigger, and I was certain I would become a crack shot. Another consideration was the high level of responsibility bomber pilots felt for the safety of their crews. I didn't want my actions to be restricted by concerns about the lives of other men. But the bottom line was I wanted to fly the fastest planes against the best German pilots. I dreamed about engaging them at 20,000 feet and chasing them into the ground. I trained to make that dream come true. I lived for it, and I was prepared to die for it.

I got my wish. I was ordered to report to the single-engine school at Foster Field, located just outside of Victoria, Texas, and assigned to the 6th Fighter Unit, 2nd Training Unit, Class of 43-E.

Foster Field was originally called Victoria Airfield. It was renamed in honor of Lieutenant Arthur Foster, an Army Air Corps instructor from San Antonio who crashed and died at Brooks Field in 1925. The local newspaper, *The Victoria Advocate*, reported that Foster's widow, two young daughters, and twenty-three-year-old son attended the dedication ceremony. The son flew in from Gardner Field in California, where he was receiving his primary school training. I felt great pride that the War Department had made this family reunion possible despite the millions of moving parts in its war machine. In a way, I felt like the government was telling me that each soldier, each wife, every mom and dad, and every boy and girl affected by war was important to Uncle Sam. This feeling was reinforced when more than a coincidence led Arthur L. Foster Jr. back to Foster Field for advanced training and his commission as a second lieutenant in the Army Air Corps.

After a week at Foster, I couldn't believe my good fortune. We were flying the North American AT-6 Texan, an advanced trainer built by North American Aviation, and the Curtiss P-40 Warhawk fighter, a plane that was used extensively by the United States and its Allies during the war. The Texan had a maximum speed of 208 miles per hour and a range of 750 miles, while the Curtiss Warhawk could get up to 360 miles an hour with a range of 650 miles.

One night, when the lights in the barracks were out, most of us couldn't sleep, so thrilled were we to be flying fighters. I remember lying there on my bunk and feeling the excitement and energy tamping down my fatigue. Sleeping was important only because it kept me alert and upright in the cockpit. Otherwise it was a burden, robbing me of precious hours that could be spent in the air or training to fly or hitting the books.

"I can't believe I was flying a Curtiss Warhawk today," I said to no one in particular. "I used to play around on an old Curtiss Jenny back in Phoenix. I would try to imagine what it would be like to fly, but I wasn't even close."

"Holy flaw, Kirkland, at least you'd been in a plane before. I only saw 'em flying overhead. I'd never been close enough to even touch one, until a few months ago," someone said in the dark.

One guy got mad at us for disturbing his sleep. "If you guys are going to be *bunk flying* for a while, I'm going somewhere else to sleep."

He was the same guy who got up before reveille every morning.

"Now you know how we feel in the morning, you *dawn patrolling* idiot!" another cadet shouted, followed by a chorus of cheers.

Everyone was sharing ideas, offering advice. You hear things, pick up sayings—who knows where they come from, but they reinforced good habits and practices, and helped you to stay alive.

From a few bunks down:

Grab plenty of speed before leaving the ground. When you increase your flying speed you decrease your dying speed.

"Very comforting . . ."

"Thanks, I'll sleep better tonight."

Another gem from across the way:

When you turn near the ground keep your eyes on it. If your altimeter is wrong so are you.[3]

"I guess I've got to work on that. The instructor made me shoot landings all afternoon," someone said.

Then more advice:

A ship landing has the right of way. A dead stick may mean a dead aviator, so give him room. His gliding speed is greater than your take-off speed, so if he tags you, you are it.[4]

"What's a dead stick?" someone asked.

"It's a propeller without any power, you dipstick," another cadet said.

This went on for some time and then someone said, "It's getting late. Time for me to *spin off*," as he rolled over to go to sleep.

From Murphy, a guy who read the Bible most days: "I've got one more."

Let not thy familiarity with airplanes breed contempt, lest thou become exceeding careless at a time when great care is necessary to thy wellbeing.[5]

"Amen!"

"Night, y'all."

A few days later I was required to fly solo to a base in Louisiana, land, refuel, and return to Foster Field that night. The exercise was meant to give me more cross-country experience and an opportunity to fly in the dark, using my instruments to get home. On the return flight, I was over the Gulf of Mexico when I got caught in a vicious tropical cyclone. Visually, I couldn't tell which way was up. I tried to relax, trust my training, and trust the instruments. I pointed the nose of the plane up, hoping to pop out of the soup. As I was nosing upward a thought came to me: if you read the instruments wrong, you are actually speeding toward terra firma. Eventually, I got above the storm but I could not see below because of the cloud cover. I flew a while longer and when a break in the clouds revealed lights, and I headed toward them, thinking I had made it home. It was actually Randolph Field. I landed at the wrong base.

I spent the night at Randolph and returned to Foster the next day. Fortunately the "Stupid Pilot Trophy" was not a custom there. Instead I created my own badge as a reminder of my blunder and had it sewn on to the left breast of my aviator's jacket. It bore the likeness of Aviation Cadet Knucklehead, a character in the War Department's weather training manual who would "commit more errors than a bush league third-basemen, and other aviation cadets are expected to profit by his mistakes." He was shown throughout the manual flying recklessly with summary statements telling us what he was doing wrong often punctuated with him saying, "X marks the spot." The last cartoon in the manual shows him straddling a cloud and a halo over his head. When people asked about the patch I told them the whole story, which usually drew a few laughs. It served a higher purpose though. It was like smelling salts. One whiff of that memory helped to clear my mind of all distractions.

We practiced aerial gunnery on ranges over Matagorda Island in the Gulf of Mexico. Large sleeves of canvas were pulled through the air by trainer planes and we would fire paint balls at them from the "guns" on our planes. It was kind of comical to watch this kind of target practice, with paint splashing against the canvas targets at 10,000 feet, but it was considered cutting edge training for fighter pilots at the time.

We also practiced dog fights against each other, using photographs from cameras mounted to our guns to confirm the number of times we "hit" our opponent while racing around the sky. This was competition at its highest level, with the winners being considered the top guns in their outfits, which opened doors for additional training and better opportunities for advancement. I went up one time to engage one of the top pilots in our cadre, the guy I thought was about the best, Vince Jouret. We were at 10,000 feet when he tipped his wings, signaling it was time to separate and come back around at each other—kind of like a gunfighter saying "draw!" Somehow I managed to get behind him and I chased him to 4,000 feet, pounding him the whole way down. My words followed each shot like tracer bullets: I-AM-BET-TER-THA-N -YOU! He didn't land one hit on my plane.

Our competitive juices were still flowing after we landed and began reviewing the photos with our commanding officer, adrenaline pumping through our veins. We were like two fighters circling the ring, not sensing the round was over. Our CO scolded us for being unprofessional and ordered us to sit down, shut up, and learn.

He finished his dressing down with, "You're both exceptional pilots! But you had better learn to keep your emotions in check. In a few months Jerry will be shooting at you, and he won't be using a camera!"

Those strong competitive feelings stayed with us for a long time. I met Vince and his wife many years after the war at a little restaurant in Mesa, just east of Phoenix. We spent some time catching up, talking about kids, work, and grandchildren. We reminisced about our time at Foster Field and spoke about some of our classmates, not knowing if they had survived the war. And yet they were still alive to us, just as we saw them last. We talked about going to the Easter sunrise service together at the Matagorda Island Bombing and Gunnery Range, where the post chaplain encouraged us to let Christ's victory be ours. Noting the strangeness of the subject of the sermon, considering the place it was delivered, we laughed. Just as our conversation started to lag, Vince brought up our fierce dogfight and suggested it had been so long he couldn't remember who won.

I said forcefully, "Vince, you know as well as I do what happened that day. You were all puckered up when I got through with you. I've never forgotten and neither have you!"

He abruptly got up from the table, grabbed his wife by the arm, and left without another word, never to be seen or heard from again.[6] My wife was embarrassed, but I just smiled, remembering those days—days when I lived!

With our training completed, Class 43E enjoyed the pomp and circumstance of graduation. We were the Army's guests at a graduation stag dinner at the cadet mess. We marched in singing the *Army Air Corps March*.[7]

> *Off we go into the wild blue yonder,*
> *Climbing high into the sky;*
> *Here they come ready to meet our thunder,*
> *At 'em boys give 'er the gun . . .*

The song was rousing and sobering, as a line in the last verse informed us how to live a long life.

> *Off we go into the wild sky yonder,*
> *Keep your wings level and true.*
> *If you'd live to be a gray-haired wonder.*
> *Keep your nose out of the blue.*

The truth is, most of us didn't even think about becoming gray-haired. If that were ever to happen, it would come at the far end of a long tunnel that we had yet to enter. We wanted to survive, but our thoughts and focus were on the immediate task at hand; winning the war. We were simple boys, many of us poor and uneducated, who had been turned into fighter pilots. The next day we would become commissioned officers.

As we took our seats at designated tables, we could tell many people had gone to a lot of trouble to make this dinner special for us. There were centerpieces and tablecloths, silverware and crystal glasses. Even the written menu was formal and festive, with the cooks naming their dishes with an Air Corps flavor. "Reveille" shrimp cocktail, "Silver Wings" ham, "Prop-wash" stuffed pork chops, "A-T" creamed cauli-flower, and "High Pitched" carrots and peas. For dessert we enjoyed "First Squadron" apple pie and "Basic" mince pie.[8]

After dinner we marched out singing the *Spirit of the Army Air Corps*, and again we were reminded of our mortality.[9]

We have our hand on the throttle
As we all wait for the nod,
And we will meet them half-way,
Men we will drive 'em to the sod.
Then, when our last flight is over
And we can meet our flyin' Boss
You can bet the air is clear,
Men, from the Orion to the Cross.

Orion is a major constellation and visible throughout the world. The Cross is a reference to one of the smallest constellation in the sky, the Southern Cross. So, as the song goes, if we die we can take comfort knowing we have rid the heavens of the enemy. We can meet God knowing we sent them to their deaths. While I was sure I was on the right side of the war, I couldn't imagine God being real happy about the death and destruction of it all.

The graduation ceremony was the next day and I had the honor of flying one of the lead planes alongside our commanding officer. We flew in formation over the parade route near the east flying line, and in front of a grandstand full of cheering people. I had come full circle from my childhood experiences at Sky Harbor.

The fly-over was followed by marching bands and speeches. After landing, I hustled over to the ceremony to take my seat among the rows of cadets just in time to hear the final speaker, General Frank P. Lahm, known as the "father of Randolph Field,"[10] and until 1941, the commanding officer of the Gulf Coast Air Corps Training Center.[11] He loved Randolph so much that he had his ashes scattered over the airfield upon his death in 1963.[12]

Lahm began his military service in the cavalry after graduating from West Point in 1901.[13] He was among a handful of eager young officers selected to learn how to fly. The group included Lieutenant Henry H.

Arnold, who would become chief of the Air Corps in 1938 and the commanding general of the Army Air Forces in 1942. He became a five-star general in the Army and when the AAF was organized as a separate branch of the US Armed Forces in 1947, he gained the distinction of being the only general to have ever held the five-star rank in two different military services, and the only general in the history of the Air Force with the five-star rank.[14]

In 1908 Lahm received Fédération Aéronautique Internationale Airship Pilot Certificate No. 2, meaning he was the second person licensed to fly by the governing international federation, headquartered in Paris.[15] That same year he was appointed by the Army to oversee the first purchase of military aircraft.

The Army purchased its first airplane from the Wright Brothers for 25,000 dollars and formed the Aviation Section of the Signal Corps. The biplane met the exacting government specifications that included a twenty-five horsepower motor, a two-man 350 pound weight capacity, and top speed of forty miles per hour, with sufficient fuel and oil to fly 125 miles. The airplane came with a set of flying instructions and some initial training and guidance from the Wright brothers.[16]

On September 17, 1908, Orville Wright and his passenger, Lieutenant Thomas Selfridge, took off in the airplane at Fort Myers, Virginia, circling the field three times at about 150 feet in the air. Heading into the fourth circuit of the test flight, the right propeller broke loose, severed a guy-wire connected to the rear vertical rudder, causing the plane to nose dive. The impact of the crash threw Orville into some wires still taut between the struts, resulting in his suffering a damaged hip, a broken leg, and some cracked ribs. Selfridge was thrown into one of the wooden upright braces, and his skull was fractured. He died later that evening after surgery, making him the first person to die in a crash of a motorized airplane and the first Army air fatality.[17] And yes, an airfield was named for him, in 1917, in Michigan.[18]

The Wright Flyer, designated Signal Corps No. 1, was repaired and the remaining cadre of cadets learned how to fly. Lahm became the Army's first certified pilot in 1909, Arnold, its second.[19]

These young pilots were serving honorably during WWI when the Army Aviation Section became the Army Air Service in 1918. They helped mold the Air Service into the Army Air Corps in 1926. They were responsible for advances in pilot training and the development of sophisticated warfare doctrines when the Army Air Corps was reconstituted as the Army Air Forces in 1942.[20]

So, over the span of thirty-four years, Lahm and Arnold went from being pioneer pilots who had to push-start the first military plane into the air to visionary generals who were instrumental in developing plans to dominate the sky. They were the right men to come along at the right time in our nation's history.

Following Lahm's graduation speech, we received our coveted pilot wings, which were fastened to our uniforms above the left breast pocket. We also were given gold bars, which were affixed to our shirt collars, signifying our commissions as second lieutenants. Another benefit was a huge pay raise to 205 dollars a month with living quarters or $245 per month without quarters. Within a year we could be promoted to first lieutenants with starting pay up to 360 dollars a month.[21] I could not believe I was being paid to do what I always dreamed of doing. Even with the life-and-death stakes of war, I would have flown for free.

Notes

1.   Martin W. Bowman, *USAAF Handbook, 1939–1945* (Mechanicsburg, Pennsylvania: Stackpole Books, 1997), 227–30.

2.   John C. McManus, *Deadly Sky: The American Combat Airman in World War II* (Novato, California: Presidio Press, 1965), 190.

3.   WPA Texas, *Randolph Field: A History and Guide* (New York: The Devin-Adair Company, 1942), 129–38; "Aerial Rules for Aerial Fools," *The Portal to Texas History*, accessed February 1, 2016, http://texashistory.unt.edu/ark:/67531/metapth379961 /m1/12/?q=when%20you.

4.   WPA Texas, *Randolph Field*, 129–38.

5.   Ibid; "Ye Book of Rules for Flying Fools," *Popular Aviation* 8, no. 5 (1931), 16, https://books.google.com/books?id=Jx9Yg9LSkAgC&pg=PA16&lpg=PA16&dq= Let+not+thy+familiarity+with+airplanes+breed+contempt&source=bl&ots=oeiVQF hNlm&sig=JSYS2HgE7Oau6rEp_U_T0BCdi20&hl=en&sa=X&ved=0ahUKEwj- mtWkoKXKAhVU_WMKHeQPC5EQ6AEIHDAA#v=onepage&q=Let%20 not%20thy%20familiarity%20with%20airplanes%20breed%20contempt&f=false.

6.   William Vincent Jouret died when he was 90 years old in Scottsdale, Arizona, in 2007. His obituary states he "served in WWII, retired from the Air Force, earning

the Distinguished Flying Cross." National Memorial Cemetery, William V. Jouret, The Arizona Republic (December 2, 2007).

7.   Printed in the program entitled "Graduation Stag Dinner, Class 43E," WWII files of Frank Kirkland Jr.

8.   Ibid.

9.   Ibid.

10.   WPA Texas, *Randolph Field*, 28.

11.   Frank Purdy Lahm Collection, 3, *National Air and Space Archives*, (Washington, DC: Smithsonian Institution, 1991); WPA Texas, *Randolph Field*, 28.

12.   Frank Purdy Lahm Collection, 2, *National Air and Space Archives*.

13.   Ibid.

14.   C .Peter Chen, "Henry Arnold," *World War II Database*, accessed February 1, 2016, http://ww2db.com/person_bio.php?person_id=321.

15.   Frank Purdy Lahm Collection, 1, *National Air and Space Archives*, (Washington, DC: Smithsonian Institution, 1991); WPA Texas, *Randolph Field*, 28.

16.   WPA Texas, *Randolph Field*, 28.

17.   "Fatal Fall of Wright Airship," *New York Times* (1908), accessed February 1, 2016, http://query.nytimes.com/mem/archive-free/pdf?res=9E00E6DA133EE233A2575B C1A96F9C946997D6CF; "Thomas Selfridge," *Wikipedia*, accessed February 20, 2013, https://en.wikipedia.org/wiki/Thomas_Selfridge; WPA Texas, *Randolph Field*, 29.

18.   "Selfridge Air National Guard Base," *Wikipedia*, accessed February 20, 2013, https://en.wikipedia.org/wiki/Selfridge_Air_National_Guard_Base.

19.   "Aeronautical Division, U.S. Signal Corps," *Wikipedia*, accessed February 20, 2013, https://en.wikipedia.org/wiki/Aeronautical_Division,_U.S._Signal_Corps.

20.   C .Peter Chen, "Henry Arnold," *World War II Database*, accessed February 1, 2016; Frank Purdy Lahm Collection, 1; WPA Texas, *Randolph Field*, 38–41.

21.   Martin W. Bowman, *USAAF Handbook, 1939–1945*, (Mechanicsburg, Pennsylvania: Stackpole Books, 1997), 152.

CHAPTER 12

The epic battles of history have been studied by generations of soldiers hoping to gain an advantage in the next war. At first it was ground battles that were analyzed, then warfare ventured onto the water and naval battles came under review. As World War II approached, however, there were no historical reference points for the kind of warfare that would be waged in the air, although German planes got a bit of a dress rehearsal in 1936 in the Spanish Civil War while some US planes had a pretty good try-out in the Sino-Japanese conflict in 1937.[1]

Horses, around six million of them, were still being used by the cavalries of the combatants in World War I.[2] Trenches dug seven feet into the earth and filled with men and rifles had more impact on the war than the airplanes that flew thousands of feet above it. Pilots engaged in random dogfights, knocked observation balloons and blimps out of the sky, flew reconnaissance missions to determine troop location or provide range data for the artillery, and toward the end of the war flew rudimentary bombing missions. But the planes simply did not have the capacity to deliver a strategic advantage by destroying factories, military installations, or cities.

Brigadier General Billy Mitchell was an early advocate of using concentrated levels of air force to cripple the enemy. After the war he led an effort to decrease the number of observation units and increase the number of pursuit units. His top priority, though, was to significantly add to the number of bombardment groups. While many in the Army agreed that strategic bombing would have a major role in future wars, they had to compete with the other branches of the military to get a larger slice of the funding pie which was shrinking along with the economy of the 1930s.[3] The admirals of the fleet argued that a bomber plane could not sink a battleship, so it would be foolish to divert Navy resources to pay for more planes.

In 1921 Mitchell orchestrated a bombing demonstration involving the *Ostfriesland*, Germany's largest battleship, widely believed to be unsinkable. It had been captured during World War I and was anchored off the Capes of Virginia. Mitchell sent eight Martin MB-2s to bomb the great ship and two others anchored nearby. It took just seven bombs to sink all three of them. The experiment continued two years later with the same result. Two more obsolete battleships were sent to the ocean floor, solidifying the status of bomber planes as a key strategic element in the arsenal of the United States Armed Forces.[4]

During the 1930s US military planners came to believe that tight formations of heavily armed bombers could penetrate enemy air defenses without an escort of pursuit planes to protect them from enemy fighters.[5] This theory may have been one of those chicken and egg ideas since the United States didn't have any pursuit planes that had the fuel capacity to escort heavy bombers on long-range missions to Berlin, and neither did the British. When World War II broke out, the British bombers were getting annihilated on the way to Germany by the Luftwaffe's Messerschmitt 109s and 110s. The German pilots would simply wait for the Spitfires to turn around after escorting the bombers across the English Channel, before swooping down on the bombers. The Royal Air Force countered by performing its bombing raids at night, which reduced casualties but also decreased the effectiveness of the bombing missions. When the United States got into the war, the generals insisted on conducting unescorted daytime bombing missions. This increased the effectiveness of the missions but also increased the number of casualties. The significant losses of airmen and airplanes simply could not be sustained if the Allies were to win the war.

From 1934 through 1939, the US Army worked with private aviation companies for the design and development of a new multi-engine bomber. Boeing designed the plane that would become the workhorse in the US strategic bombing plan, the B-17 bomber. But most of them, along with B-24, B-25, B-26, A-20, and P-40 aircraft, were sent to Great Britain, which was already at war with Germany.[6] The sale of these planes was good for the US economy but further delayed President Roosevelt's plan to strengthen US air power. In June 1939 the Army still had twelve horse regiments of 790 horses each while the Air Corps had only thirteen operational B-17 bombers.[7]

The number of US planes dramatically increased from 1940 through 1942. There were also significant advancements in both pursuit planes and bombers just as I was completing my advanced single engine school in Texas. Bombers were fitted with the Norden bombsight that permitted precision bombing from 25,000 feet. The key was a top-secret mechanical computer system.[8] It measured the trajectory of bombs based on the flight conditions of the plane, automatically calibrating to take into account changes in wind, speed, and other factors as detected from the plane's autopilot system. Experienced bombardiers joked they could drop a bomb into a pickle barrel using the Norden bombsight.[9] That was not too far from the truth. Tests of the Norden system on bombing ranges in the Mojave Desert demonstrated the bombsight enabled planes to consistently drop bombs within seventy-five feet of their target, a remarkable achievement for that era, although the margin of error increased significantly during wartime conditions.[10] Still the Norden bombsite was a game changer.

The P-51 Mustang was another game changer, *the* game changer, according to Hermann Goering, the commander-in-chief of the Luftwaffe.[11] A World War I ace, Goering was the last commander of the Flying Circus, the German fighter wing once led by Manfred von Richthofen, the "Red Baron." After World War II and sometime between his conviction as a war criminal at the Nuremberg Trials and the day he took his own life, Goering was asked when he knew Germany was going to lose the war. He responded, "When they came with fighter escort to Berlin."[12] That was March 4, 1944, which marked the first time a squadron of P-51s escorted bombers to Berlin. Coincidently, my last mission would be exactly one week later.

Bartow Field in Florida was originally planned as a bomber command training station. It was converted to train fighter pilots, opening November 30, 1942. The 56th and 57th Fighter Squadrons of the 54th Fighter Group, equipped with P-51 Mustangs, began training there as an Operational Training Unit in early 1943. The summer before, the 54th FG had been in Alaska fighting Japanese forces that invaded the Aleutian Islands and was awarded the Distinguished Unit Citation for its efforts there.[13]

In May 1943, three hundred fifty men from the various single engine schools were considered for fifteen open slots with Operational Training Units in Florida, and I was selected to fly with the 439th Fighter Squadron. Once there, I was reassigned to the 56th Fighter Squadron of the 54th Fighter Group at Bartow Field for P-51 tactical training.[14]

This was an indescribable privilege and opportunity for me. When my training was completed at Bartow, I would be one of the first US pilots to fly P-51s in combat overseas. There was nothing more fulfilling to me than flying the mighty Mustang, and nothing before or since has made me happier. It was as if the hand of Providence swept aside every obstacle and opened every door to make the impossible happen for me.

The P-51 came about through a British-American partnership that started in 1938, when the British recognized they were heading to war with Germany without the industrial capacity to meet all of their anticipated wartime needs. A delegation of the British Purchasing Commission was sent to the United States to secure contracts for the production of aircraft, starting with two hundred Hudson bombers made by Lockheed and two hundred Harvard advanced trainers made by North American Aviation.[15]

When Germany invaded Poland, the British looked to the Americans for fighter aircraft, hoping to secure production of Curtiss P-40 Warhawks. When Curtiss was unable to commit to the needed delivery schedule, the British turned to North American Aviation to see if it would manufacture P-40s under license from Curtiss. The president of NAA, Dutch Kindelberger, suggested NAA could build an even better aircraft, using the same Allison motor employed in P-40s. The NAA design team worked through that night, and the next morning Kindelberger presented a plan to produce a plane with better performance, firepower, and range. On May 29, 1940, the British ordered 320 of the aircraft at a cost of about 50,000 dollars per plane, while NAA committed to having a prototype ready in eight months. It was done in 120 days.[16]

The lead designer was a German immigrant named Edgar Schmued who oversaw a number of innovations that made the P-51 so special.[17] In terms of design, the laminar flow wing, with its unique angle, gave the plane a maneuvering advantage that could not be matched by German planes. From 1940 through 1944, the plane was retooled with additional improvements. Each generation of the plane was designated with the next letter in the alphabet, starting with P-51A in 1940 until we got the P-51D in the spring of 1944.[18]

The British are the ones who gave the plane its iconic name, Mustang, and also were the inspiration for the improvement that transformed the plane from a nice fighter aircraft and into an escort plane with sufficient range to accompany heavy bombers into Germany.

The P-51 originally carried an Allison V-1710 engine. It did not function well at high altitudes. At first, the British limited P-51s to tactical and reconnaissance missions. A Royal Air Force pilot had the idea of dropping a Rolls Royce Merlin engine into the ship to give it more speed, range, and altitude. It worked.[19] The Mustang was able to fly up to 40,000 feet, allowing it to compete with German aircraft.[20]

The British experience altered North American's production of the P-51 back in the states. The Packard Motor Car Company began building a two-staged two-speed super charged engine called the Packer V-1650, which North American Aviation installed in the P-51B. The improved planes could fly at 440 miles per hour, nearly 100 miles per hour faster than the P-51A.[21] By the end of the war, the Mustang destroyed 4,950 German aircraft in the air, more than any other fighter plane in Europe.[22] The P-51D arrived in Europe in large numbers in the spring of 1944, and the long-range heavy bombing campaign over Berlin began.

We flew P-51As at Bartow. They were built at North American's Inglewood, California, plant and then flown to Florida by female pilots of the Women's Auxiliary Ferrying Squadron, called WAFS.[23] Female pilots completed 12,650 ferry operations over 9,224,000 miles during the course of the war.[24] This was an important service, allowing more male pilots to train for combat overseas. In addition to ferrying operations, female pilots towed targets at gunnery schools and served as flight instructors. Another organization performing the same type of services was the Women's Flying Training Detachment. The WAFS and the WFTD merged shortly after my time at Bartow to form the Women Air Force Service Pilots, known as WASP. More than 25,000 women applied for positions with WASP, but only 1,830 were accepted, and of that number only 1,074 became pilots.[25]

The first director of WASP was an amazing woman named Jacqueline Cochran. By the time WASP was organized in August 1943, Cochran was a well-known pilot whose fame as a record-holding, race-winning pilot equaled that of Amelia Earhart.[26] She was also exceedingly wealthy. Her glamorous lifestyle, though, masked an early life of hardship and sadness.

She was born in 1906 in the Florida Panhandle and given the name Bessie Lee Pittman. At the age of fourteen, Cochran married an airplane mechanic and gave birth to a son the next year. She divorced her husband four years later and then tragedy struck. Her five-year-old son accidently set his clothes on fire and died. Over the next fifteen years, she would become a hairdresser at Saks Fifth Avenue, start a cosmetics business, meet and marry one of the ten richest men in the world, and take up flying, becoming a licensed commercial pilot in the early 1930s. By the start of the war, her fame and fortune gave her high-level access to General Arnold and, with the support of Eleanor Roosevelt, she was eventually able to convince him of the wisdom of using women pilots in the Army Air Corps.[27]

In 2004, what had been the Thermal Airport in Indio, California, was renamed the Jacqueline Cochran Regional Airport.[28] During the war, the airport, located in the Mojave Desert, was used as an air support command base as part of the Desert Training Center. The training center was under the command of General George Patton.[29] Its mission was to train soldiers for Operation Torch, the invasion of North Africa, which would become a pivotal moment in the history of the war. But for me personally the preparation for the invasion was the first skip of a flat stone across a wide pond. It touched down on politicians and generals and soldiers and also me, the weight of the stone taking me down to the bottom.

Notes

1.   Martin W. Bowman, *USAAF Handbook, 1939-1945* (Mechanicsburg, Pennsylvania: Stackpole Books, 1997), 10.

2.   "Horses in World War I," *Wikipedia*, accessed February 1, 2016, https://en.wikipedia.org/wiki/Horses_in_World_War_I.

3.   Martin W. Bowman, *USAAF Handbook*, 3.

4.   Ibid., 4.

5.   Ibid., 7.

6.   Ibid., 10–11, 144–46.

7. "Horses in World War II," *Wikipedia*, accessed November 6, 2014, https://en.wikipedia.org/wiki/Horses_in_World_War_II; Martin W. Bowman, *USAAF Handbook*, 10.

8. Martin W. Bowman, *USAAF Handbook*, 194–97.

9. Ibid., 12.

10. Ibid., 198.

11. Raymond Helminiak, "When They Came With Fighter Escort," *The Milwaukee Journal*, in Gardner N. Hatch and Frank H. Winter, *P-51 Mustang* (Paducah, Kentucky: Turner Publishing Company, 1993), 61.

12. Ibid.

13. "Bartow Air Base," *Wikipedia*, accessed June 12, 2013, https://en.wikipedia.org/wiki/Bartow_Air_Base.

14. Special Orders No. 38, 3, Fighter Command, (Tallahassee, Florida: Dale Mabry Field, June 8, 1943), from the WWII files of Frank J. Kirkland Jr.; Special Orders No. 73, 54th Fighter Group, (Army Air Forces, Office of the Commanding Officer, June 10, 1943), from the WWII files of Frank J. Kirkland Jr.

15. Stephen Sherman, "North American P-51 Mustang," *Acepilots*, accessed February 1, 2016, http://acepilots.com/planes/p51_mustang.html.

16. Ibid.

17. Ibid.

18. "P-51 Mustang Production: North American Aviation P-51 Production," *Mustangs*, accessed September 16, 2013, http://www.mustangsmustangs.net/p-51/p51production.shtml.

19. Sherman, "North American P-51 Mustang."

20. Brent Erickson, Neil Stirling, and Mike Williams, "P-51 Mustang Performance," *WWII Aircraft Performance*, accessed June 15, 2013, http://www.wwiiaircraftperformance.org/mustang/mustangtest.html.

21. Ibid.

22. C.N. Trueman, "P51 Mustang," *The History Learning Site*, accessed February 1, 2016, http://www.historylearningsite.co.uk/world-war-two/weapons-of-world-war-two/p51-mustang/.

23. "Women Airforce Service Pilots," *Wikipedia*, accessed July 10, 2013, https://en.wikipedia.org/wiki/Women_Airforce_Service_Pilots; "Archive: WASP," *This Day in Aviation*, accessed July 10, 2013, http://www.thisdayinaviation.com/tag/wasp/.

24. Martin W. Bowman, *USAAF Handbook*, 158–59.

25. Ibid.

26. "Jacqueline Cochran and the Women's Airforce Service Pilots (WASPs)," *Eisenhower Presidential Library, Museum & Boyhood Home*, accessed July 10, 2013, https://www.eisenhower.archives.gov/research/online_documents/jacqueline_cochran.html.

27. "Jacqueline Cochran," *Wikipedia*, accessed July 10, 2013, https://en.wikipedia.org/wiki/Jacqueline_Cochran.

28. "Jacqueline Cochran Regional Airport," *Wikipedia*, accessed September 16, 2013, https://en.wikipedia.org/wiki/Jacqueline_Cochran_Regional_Airport.

29. "World War II Desert Training Center, California-Arizona Maneuver Area," *Bureau of Land Management*, accessed September 16, 2013, http://www.blm.gov/ca/st/en/fo/needles/patton.html.

CHAPTER 13

I logged only ten hours in the P-51 while stationed in Florida. The plane was experiencing some "teething problems" during our training exercises. The guns jammed often, the engine cooling system was unreliable, and the skin of the plane occasionally folded away from the frame, especially around the tail section. In the month of June 1943, thirteen P-51s crashed at training fields in Florida, resulting in several severe injuries and two deaths. Five of the accidents happened at Bartow Field and two of those guys involved were from my group, Sheftall Coleman and Bill Belton, both of whom survived.[1]

On July 8, 1943, thirty-five of us were assigned to Dale Mabry Air Base in Tallahassee, Florida. The order indicated it was a permanent change of station for us. In the same order, sixteen pilots from the 439th Fighter Squadron were reassigned to the 383rd Bomb Group (Heavy), Geiger Field, Spokane, Washington.[2] A week later I was one of seventy-four fighter pilots ordered to Walla Walla Air Base in Washington. We were given no information about the new assignment. I assumed it was a temporary transfer until the problems with the P-51s were resolved. I was wrong.

A year earlier, President Roosevelt and Prime Minister Churchill had met at Hyde Park, Roosevelt's residence in New York.[3] The tide of the war was tipping in favor of Germany. The Russians were teetering on the eastern front. Hitler's advance on Stalingrad would lead to the death of more than two million soldiers and civilians. So the Allies needed to open a second front in the war to force Germany to divert troops and equipment away from the eastern front, taking pressure off the Russian Army.[4]

The American and British leaders discussed the options for a second front. Churchill favored an invasion of North Africa. Germany had the momentum there too and was close to gaining control of the Eastern Mediterranean. Roosevelt's military advisors favored an invasion of northwestern France, although not until the spring of 1943. An invasion of France from Britain was much more feasible since it required the movement of men and equipment over only a couple of hundred miles. North Africa was 4,000 miles away from the east coast of the United States. Transporting the troops and equipment over the Atlantic Ocean was a risky proposition since the ships would be exposed to German torpedoes for much of the way.[5]

After ten days of meetings, the Allies decided to invade North Africa and Operation Torch was hatched.[6] On November 8, 1942, more than 100,000 American and British troops took the beaches of Casablanca, Oran, and Algiers. Within a few weeks, the Allies had the bridgehead needed to root Germany out of North Africa and from there, Italy. On January 14, 1943, Roosevelt and Churchill met again, this time in Casablanca, Morocco.[7] With the initial success of Operation Torch, the second series of meetings set the stage for the beginning of the end of the war. Part of the strategy was to secure airfields in Italy from which daylight strategic bombing missions to southern Europe and into Germany could be launched. England's weather was unpredictable. It was anticipated that better winter weather conditions in Italy would allow bombers to operate twice as often against German industrial targets than the 8th Air Force could in England. A new division of the Air Force, the 15th Air Force, was created for this purpose.[8]

The 15th Air Force would be activated on November 1, 1943, with headquarters initially in Tunis, Tunisia. A month later, its headquarters would be moved to Bari, Italy, and remain there until the end of the war. Eleven combat units would be transferred from the 12th Air Force to the 15th, including six heavy bomb groups, four of which were exclusively B-17s. The 5th Bomb Wing and its four B-17 groups were added, as were the 42nd and 47th Bomb Wings.[9]

And so, even as I was in the verge of becoming a fighter pilot, the Army Air Corps was in the middle of a reorganization that required more bomber pilots. Unfortunately, there was no time to wait for the aviation schools to train them for the 15th Air Force, and so fighter pilots would be reassigned to bomb groups to fill the immediate need.

Of course I didn't know any of this when I arrived at Walla Walla Air Base. I should have suspected something since I had a copy of Special Orders No. 189 that sent fighter pilots to the 383rd Bomb Group in Spokane.[10]

Located in the southeastern part of the state, Walla Walla, the city so nice they named it twice, had a population of about 18,000, with another 6,000 military personnel at the base.[11] It was the home of the 88th Bombardment Group, an operational training unit equipped with B-17 bombers. Upon our arrival we met with Lt. Colonel Hewitt Wheless, the commanding officer, in the mess hall.

Wheless was a well-known bomber pilot who fought the Japanese in the Philippines. A week after the attack on Pearl Harbor, he flew one of six B-17s that bombed a Japanese stronghold on the island. After dropping his bombs, eighteen Zero fighters raced up to engage him. His crew fought them off, destroying several of them. Somehow he was able to make an emergency landing at a nearby airfield, his plane riddled with more than 1,200 holes, and most of the control cables severed.[12] He received the Distinguished Flying Cross for his actions and his exploits were chronicled by President Roosevelt in one of his fireside chats on the radio. A film based upon Wheless's experience, *Beyond the Line of Duty*, narrated by Ronald Reagan, won the Academy Award in 1943 for best short subject, which was ironic since his nickname was "Shorty."[13]

As he stood before us, all five foot six of him, he seemed quite old for a thirty-year-old man. Speaking perfect Texan, he introduced himself and then added, "Welcome to the 88th BG, gentlemen. We know you are all outstanding single-engine pilots. We plan to turn you into great four-engine pilots, ready to lead B-17 crews into combat. By 0700 tomorrow you will receive orders assigning you to one of four squadrons, the 316th, the 317th, the 318th, or the 399th. Until then, you should go into town to find a place to stay. We don't have any open bunks for you here. Be ready to come to work in the morning at 0730. That is all."

I couldn't believe what I was hearing. I blurted out, "Colonel, there must be some kind of mistake. I'm training to fly P-51s in Florida!"

"Very impressive, but you're not in fighters anymore. We'll see you here tomorrow, lieutenant," he said firmly and walked out the door, ignoring the ensuing cacophony coming from those who were still able to speak.

I stood there in shock, trying to absorb the information. My ambition propelled me to become a top fighter pilot. I attributed my good fortune to a combination of skill and destiny. My pride led me to believe I was in charge of my life. In less than five minutes I learned that was not true. It is strange to think, though, that during my entire training to become an aviator, from primary through advanced schools, decisions were being made to accomplish political and military objectives that destroyed my singular goal of becoming a fighter pilot. I did not react well, and I have never gotten over it, something I cannot explain.

About thirty of us went into Walla Walla, finding our way to the Marcus Whitman Hotel. We checked into our rooms and ate dinner in the hotel dining room. Guys knocked down some drinks, a lot of drinks, and we talked, and the more we talked, the angrier we became.

"They can't do this to us! We're no bomb jockeys," and so it went.

We arrived at the base the next morning and began to congregate in the officers' hall. At 0730, Brigadier General Walter Peck, commanding officer of the 17th Bombardment Training Wing, walked in. Apparently our rumblings about our plight had come to his attention. We all arose from our seats and stood at attention. He was a large, imposing figure, with bushy eyebrows, a mustache, and a receding hairline dissected by a peninsula of black combed-back hair. Any notion that we had the upper hand or were in a position to negotiate was dispelled quickly.

The general spoke in a booming voice. "You are officers of the United States Army Air Corps. You've sworn an oath to obey the orders of the President of the United States and the orders of the officers appointed over you. Today, gentlemen, I represent the president and all officers at Walla Walla who have authority over you. It has come to my attention that you're refusing to fly bombers. Is that true?" he demanded.

He continued, taking on a folksy, kind of friendly manner. "We understand your disappointment, and if you don't want to fly bombers, I will give you another option. You can give up your commissions, grab a rifle, and we will send you to the Western front. Infantry or bombers—be prepared to declare your preference in the next five minutes. After that it is shape up or ship out."

And that is how I became a bomber pilot. My group of fighter-pilots-turned-bomber-pilots became part of the Swah Provisional

Group, named after our commanding officer, Captain Samuel Denver Swah.

I was assigned to the 399th Bombardment (Heavy) Squadron and learned to fly B-17s. My first time up close to one was a quick how-do-you-do, a brief inspection lead by the squadron's crew chief. It started with a walk around the outside of the plane.

"Gentlemen, you are being entrusted with the most expensive plane in the world. I don't have to ask but I'll ask it anyway, have any of you ever seen 220,000 dollars?"

"Take four zeroes off of that, sarge, and you'll be closer to reality for these scrubs," someone hollered.

"Well then, you all get my point. Uncle Sam is putting into your hands a machine that is worth a quarter of a million dollars. You are just a bunch of kids to me and from the looks of you, I wouldn't trust you to drive my car. But you must have something going for yourselves or you wouldn't be here, set to fly this big bird. Any questions so far?" he asked.

"What can you tell us about the engines?" someone asked.

"She's got four 1000 horsepower Wright Cyclone engines, a significant upgrade over the earlier versions that were powered by 750 horsepower engines. She's fast for a heavy bomber and has great range. She's tough, able to fly on just one engine if need be."

We walked below and around the plane. The chief pointed out each of the twelve fifty-caliber machine guns mounted along the sides, top, bottom, and tail of the plane.

"That's why they're called Flying Fortresses, right?" someone asked.

"That's what people call them, or simply Forts, but the guns are only part of the reason for the name. Originally the name was a reference to its mission in the late '30s. Like brick and mortar fortresses of old, the Flying Fortress was meant to protect US coastlines from enemy navies.[14] It's now an offensive juggernaut. Don't forget that all this fire power is not there to protect you so much as it is to ensure your ability to flatten the Germans and get you back to base so you can do it again."

We climbed aboard, peeked into the cockpit, and then turned right to inspect the rear of the plane, walking across the catwalk, above the bomb bay. The chief told us to look down at the space below.

"That's where your precious cargo is stored. Soon enough you'll be practicing over bomb ranges and this area will be filled with 500-pound bombs."

We walked through to the back, passing by the waist guns on each side. We were told to climb into the ball turrets to get an appreciation for the cramped space in which turret gunners must operate, and to get a sense for the effectiveness of the rotating turret, which allowed the gunner to swing his gun around to track enemy aircraft. We then hopped out the back and returned to the front of the plane. We were then put into pairs and told to return to the cockpit, each pair taking a turn inside.

There were two seats in the cockpit. The chief told us it didn't matter which seat we sat in for now.

"The pilot sits in the left seat and generally handles the plane during take offs, formation flying, and landings. As the ship's commander, he is responsible for the crew and everything that happens on and off the aircraft. The copilot sits in the right seat. He shares the flying duties and also acts as the executive officer, supervising the work of the other eight members of the crew. The copilot has to understand the duties and responsibilities of each one: the navigator, the bombardier, the engineer, the radio operator, and the gunners."

I didn't care if I was a pilot or copilot. I had no ambition to be one or the other. At the time I felt bomber pilots were just glorified truck drivers, carrying a load from one place, dropping it off at another. If I couldn't be in a fighter, it didn't matter which seat I was in. As it turned out, it didn't matter to the Army Air Corps either. For the Swah Group, anyway, pilots were selected randomly. They just lined us up and on a one-two-one-two basis, pilots and copilots were selected. I was a two: a copilot.

I was assigned to Crew No. 12. Our pilot, Joe Senta, a Minnesotan, was a second lieutenant, like me, meaning we both were newly commissioned officers. Joe did a fine job as commander, though, instilling discipline while remaining approachable. Unlike the regular Army that insisted on strict lines of authority and protocol, the Army Air Corps encouraged bomber commanders to be a little less formal with their crews, leveling the rank and instilling camaraderie. Our first conversation was anything but friendly, though, the chip on my shoulder getting between us.

"Kirk, we're partners on this plane. I look at you and I see a pilot with exceptional skills, maybe better than mine. I am sorry you got thrown into the copilot's chair," he began.

In my anger and disappointment, I replied coldly, "I could care less about being a bomber pilot, a commander, or any other job on the Fort. I belong to the Army and that means I belong to you. Let's get on with it."

Patiently, he continued, "I can see that you are disappointed, but we've got a job to do. You can't look back and think 'what if?' or 'why me?' I need your absolute best. Our crew deserves nothing less from you."

I knew he was right, but I couldn't help myself when I said, "Listen, Joe, I don't need a sermon from you. I know what we have to do. Just don't expect me to like it."

"Fair enough," he replied. "Let's go over your duties on this ship." He began to tell me what he expected. Since he didn't know any more than I did about flying bombers, he pulled out the *B-17 Pilot Training Manual* and repeatedly looked up at me and then down at the manual, saying, "I expect you to be able to fly the plane in all kinds of conditions—day or night—fog, snow, rain. You have to be an expert on the operation of the engines, and know instinctively how to keep her flying even if she's shot to pieces. You're expected to log the cruise control information and performance data for each flight."[15]

Joe paused, looked down at the manual and continued, "You've got to work closely with the crew and know their duties. Even though we have a navigator, I expect you to be able to navigate, day or night, by pilotage, dead reckoning, and by use of radio aids. Finally, but maybe most importantly, you've got to be proficient flying in formation. Our survival depends on it. If I'm at the controls, you gotta be on top of the instruments, especially if the formation is climbing through the soup. Maintaining our speed and distance in formation is critical so prepare to make engine adjustments as necessary."

Joe hesitated for a moment, smiled and looked up from the manual. I grinned too, telling him, "I am glad you've got an instruction book there, skipper, since we are flying the most expensive ship in the Army Air Corps."

Our navigator, George Lund, from Brooklyn, and bombardier, Tony La Chiusa, were also second lieutenants, and had just finished their advanced training in Texas. La Chiusa was a fast-talking New Yorker with movie star good looks. It wasn't fair really, Chuchie in uniform. Women flocked to him wherever we went, stateside and overseas. As many hearts as he may have broken during the war, it cannot compare to the number of guys who went broke trying to beat him in a hand of poker or a roll of the dice. He had an uncanny ability to beat the odds, and that good luck followed him into combat.

Our engineer, Richard "Red" Rivers, and radio operator, Frank Knoble, were staff sergeants. They also manned two of the guns on board. The remaining crewmen were gunnery specialists, Ercole DeLorenzo, Bill Dreste, and Carl "Andy" Anderson—all staff sergeants—and Hugo Boroch, a sergeant.

These men became my brothers over the next four months of training. Working closely with Joe, I began to appreciate each man on the crew and what he brought to the team. It became important to me to really understand them, their idiosyncrasies, their capabilities, and their limitations. Slowly I came to realize how much we needed each other to carry out our missions and to survive.

We flew across the Western skies, oftentimes at night, sorting out our duties and perfecting our formation flying. We worked closely with our navigator, setting coordinates and ensuring we were following the proper flight plan. We practiced with the bombardier, releasing control of the plane to him through the automatic pilot system, letting him make adjustments to the speed and pitch of the plane before yelling, "Bombs away!" over practice ranges just outside of Arlington, Ephrata, and Moses Lake.

The chip really never left my shoulder, but I worked hard not to let it interfere with my work.

Notes

1.   "AAIR Search Result for Aircraft Type: P-51," *Aviation Archaeology Investigation & Research*, accessed June 11, 2013, http://www.aviationarchaeology.com/src/dbaat .asp?theAT=P-51&Submit3=Go&offset=900; "Action Codes," *Aviation Archaeology Investigation & Research*, accessed June 11, 2013, http://www.aviationarchaeology. com/src/help.htm#ACTION; "Unit Roster A-F," *354th Fighter Group*, accessed September 16, 2013, http://www.354thpmfg.com/unit_roster_a-f.html.

2.   Special Orders No. 189, (Tallahassee, Florida: Dale Mabry Air Base Command, July 8, 1943), from the WWII files of Frank J. Kirkland Jr.

3.   Meredith Hindley, "Friends and Allies: The Second Washington Conference," *Humanities: The Magazine of the National Endowment for the Humanities* 33, no. 3 (2012), http://www.neh.gov/humanities/2012/mayjune/feature/friends-and-allies.

4.   "Air Phase of the North African Invasion," *U.S. Air Force Historical Study No. 105,* November 1944, accessed February 1, 2016, http://www.afhra.af.mil/shared/media/document/AFD-090522-041.pdf.

5.   Hindley, "Friends and Allies."

6.   "Air Phase of the North African Invasion," *U.S. Air Force Historical Study No. 105,* November 1944, accessed February 1, 2016.

7.   "Roosevelt and Churchill begin Casablanca Conference," *History.com,* accessed September 18, 2013, http://www.history.com/this-day-in-history/roosevelt -and-churchill-begin-casablanca-conference.

8.   Barrett Tillman, "The Forgotten Fifteenth," *Air Force Magazine* (2012), accessed March 21, 2014, http://www.airforcemag.com/MagazineArchive/Pages/2012 /September%202012/0912fifteenth.aspx.

9.   Kenn C. Rust, Fifteenth Air Force Story . . . in World War II (Temple City, California: Historical Aviation Album, 1976), 5.

10.   Special Orders No. 189, (Tallahassee, Florida: Dale Mabry Air Base, July 8, 1943), from the WWII files of Frank J. Kirkland Jr. A week before fifteen fighter pilots from the 439th Fighter Squadron at Mabry were reassigned to the 383rd Bomb Group at Geiger Field in Spokane, Washington.

11.   "Walla Walla, Washington," *Wikipedia,* accessed September 17, 2013, https:// en.wikipedia.org/wiki/Walla_Walla,_Washington; "Walla Walla Regional Airport," *Wikipedia,* accessed September 17, 2013, https://en.wikipedia.org/wiki/Walla _Walla_Regional_Airport.

12.   "Hewitt T. 'Shorty' Wheless and Boyd T. 'Buzz' Wagner: World War II Fighter Pilots," *History Net,* June 12, 2006, accessed September 19, 2013, http://www.historynet .com/hewitt-t-shorty-wheless-and-boyd-t-buzz-wagner-world-war-ii-fighter-pilots .htm.

13.   "Beyond the Line of Duty," *Wikipedia,* accessed September 19, 2013, https:// en.wikipedia.org/wiki/Beyond_the_Line_of_Duty.

14.   Martin W. Bowman, *USAAF Handbook, 1939–1945* (Mechanicsburg, Pennsylvania: Stackpole Books, 1997), 9.

15.   "Duties and Responsibilities of The Airplane Commander," *303rd Bomb Group,* accessed September 27, 2013, http://www.303rdbg.com/crew-duties.html.

CHAPTER 14

The next stop for the Swah Provisional Group was Herington Field, Kansas. It was our final staging area before we were deployed to Italy. Under the direction of the 21st Bombardment Wing, ground crews and other support staff worked around the clock to get us ready for combat. On average they processed over eighty-six crews and seventy-six aircraft each month.[1]

Processing of crews entailed a final audit of our personal records. I still had a balance on my account for the Hamilton watch, two pairs of trousers, six undershirts, and six drawers I purchased in Florida, and I had to pay up. We were also asked to make decisions about the disposition of our wages and to name the beneficiaries of our 10,000 dollars death benefit. We were given form wills with boxes to check and blanks to fill in. I designated Peg as the recipient of my wages, death benefit, and whatever else I had, with Mother and Dad next in line.

We sat through a prisoner of war lecture and reviewed a document called the *Geneva Convention relative to the Treatment of Prisoners of War*. Next we were taught how to write letters home, that is, what we could say and what we were not permitted to say. They reminded us of enemy spy operations and that unauthorized disclosures could lead to untold deaths and mission failures. We were introduced to Victory mail, known as V-mail. Letters written through the V-mail system were written on sheets of 7 × 9 inch paper, and reduced on microfilm to about the size of a thumbnail. When they reached their destination, the microfilm image of each letter was blown up to about 60 percent of its original size and delivered, postage free, in 3½ × 4½ inch envelopes marked "War & Navy Departments, V-mail Service."

V-mail helped the military reduce the fuel needed to ship letters and opened up cargo space for equipment and supplies. It took thirty-seven mailbags to move 150,000 letters, weighing about 2,500 pounds, but only one 45-pound bag for the V-mail microfilm containing the same number of letters.[2] My letters to Peg were sent this way. Her letters to me were sent to a military post office in New York, where they were microfilmed and shipped overseas.

The next step at Herington involved a final physical fitness examination and an inspection of our clothing and equipment. A team of inspectors, civilian and military, looked over our things.

"What do we need, sergeant?" Joe asked the one in charge.

"Your crew seems to have everything you need . . . if you're headed to the Pacific."

"We're not."

"I know. You boys are going to freeze your butts off if you don't get warmer stuff. You're heading into winter in Europe and your plane will get around 30 to 50 below at 35,000 feet."

"Sergeant, I don't mean to be impertinent, but that is why we are here. Most of these men got their gear in Florida and Texas this past summer. We've been cold enough just flying around the Pacific Northwest. Tell us where to go to get winter gear," Joe said politely.

"Roger that, lieutenant. Take your crew down to the depot to get suited up properly."

Fortunately things had changed quite a bit since the early years of flight. In the beginning stages, pilots focused solely on the goal of mechanically leaving the earth. Little consideration was given to the flesh and bone questions that separate man and bird. Slowly, as engineering, science, and medicine began to catch up with man's determination to fly, improvements were made to take into account the physiological responses to high altitudes, cold temperatures, and gravity's pull. The Army established an Aviation Clothing Board in 1917 and the Air Service Engineering Division was established shortly after that.[3] They immediately began to develop electrically heated flight suits, but they were unreliable, sometimes catching fire. The development of electrified suits continued during World War II, but I never wore one. The planes I flew were stripped of any excess weight in order to carry more bombs, and that included the heating elements for the electric suits.

In addition to keeping pilots and crews warm, the suits also had to be practical. Pilot movements and vision could not be impaired. Bombardiers and navigators had to be able to access their equipment and instruments. The crew had to be able to move to do their jobs, most especially gunners who had to climb inside small turrets and other tight places. Bulky suits could be just as dangerous as the cold temperatures if the men could not do their jobs without interference from their clothing.

The depot was filled with clothing and gear. Goggles, helmets, mittens, armor, jackets, pants, you name it, and it was there. Behind the long counter stood several women who, except for their uniforms, could have been mistaken for sales clerks. Only nothing was for sale. Their job was to match us up with suitable gear for our assignment. A large woman, her hair in a tight bun, greeted us.

"Welcome, gentlemen. I know just what you need. You are free to choose anything here but let me give you some advice. Some of the suits that look the warmest are left over from the Great War. Stay away from the B-1 suits. They are lined with Nuchwang dog fur imported from China.[4] They look good because the big buttons and belts are easy to deploy with gloves on but some crews have reported problems with the fur. It has a tendency to shed. Some of the fur was apparently infested with vermin, but you can't tell 'til you wear the suits for a while. Then they begin to stink. I doubt any of you gentlemen want to stink like a Chinese dog. I suggest you look at the B-2s. They hold up well and they have those big front pockets that come in handy."

Red Rivers was already trying on a B-2 suit. "Hey, this feels like it would be real warm. What's the lining made out of?"

"Nutria," she replied. "It's the fur of a South American rodent. Lots of crews swear by it."[5]

"You got anything better than rat?" Rivers asked.

"There are a few old suits in here lined with calfskin, a couple with Alaskan reindeer. The B-3s are lined with sheep shearling," she said, pointing to a row of suits. "Once you get your jacket and trousers, make sure you pick up some warm gloves, boots, and a good, lined helmet. Frostbite is a constant hazard for bomber crews. There are many casualty reports from Europe noting frozen fingers, noses, and toes," she instructed.

I ended up getting a B-3 jacket and type A-4 trousers and then went looking for gloves, boots, and a helmet.

Most bomber crews left Herington in their own aircraft. Others were transported to ports of embarkation by the Air Transport Command. Our group was ordered to travel by train to Camp Patrick Henry in Virginia and from there board a merchant ship at Newport News, Virginia.

We spent two days at Camp Henry waiting for our ship to arrive. It turned into a forty-eight-hour party. The last night ended with a drinking contest at the Last Chance Night Club between our group of flyboys and some soldiers who were waiting for the same ship. Hundreds of opened bottles of cold beer were set up on a wooden table. The men from the Regular Army lined up on one end of the table; we flyboys stood ready on the other side with the two guys at the head of the lines facing off. The object was to get a bottle of beer in your mouth without using your hands and chug the beer down before the other guy. Then on to the next guy in line who would run to the table, root around for a bottle, then chug-a-lug, and on to the next guy. It was like bobbing for apples, sort of. The first side to get all of its guys through the line won.

Chuchie was first in line for us. A young nurse signaled the start of the game with a crash of a hammer into the shiny lid of a trashcan. As smooth as ever, Chuchie downed his beer. Hugo was next and then another guy and then another. I was near the end of the line, and took my turn. When it was going right, the brew went down fast; when it wasn't, there was broken glass and chipped teeth. If you broke a bottle you stayed in until you got a full bottle of beer down. We won four out of five rounds before the GIs surrendered. With hundreds of empty bottles rolling around the ground, we tiptoed out of the club. The GIs stumbled in one direction, and we went the other way, singing about the wild blue yonder and yelling, "Nothing can stop the Army Air Corps!"

Early on Friday morning, November 12, 1943, we shipped out unescorted on the *USS Alfred Moore*, named for a former US Supreme Court Justice and captain in the Revolutionary War.[6] There were 2,700 nearly identical merchant ships built in the United States between 1941 and 1945.[7] The first one was called the *USS Patrick Henry*, which was a nod to the patriot's famous line, "Give me Liberty or give me death," and the ships following her off the production line became known as Liberty ships.

President Roosevelt called them "ugly ducklings." They were 441.5 feet long and 57 feet wide, with a cargo capacity of 9,146 tons, strictly utilitarian. But the methods and means of production were revolutionary. Henry Kaiser, dubbed "Sir Launchalot," introduced prefabrication methods, borrowed from Henry Ford, which cut the time for construction from six months to ten days. American ship builders said they "built the ships by the mile and chopped them off by the yard."[8]

During the first couple of years, German U-boats sank British merchant ships faster than they could be produced, keeping vital supplies from the front and the English people. The onslaught of the Liberties changed all of that.

At a cost of about 1.6 million dollars, the government calculated one round-trip by a Liberty would pay for itself. In that case, the *Moore* was a bargain. During the eight months before we boarded her, she berthed in ports in England, Australia, Malta, Algiers, Italy, and Morocco, and she continued to ply the Atlantic throughout the war.[9]

Stepping off the gangplank, I was struck by the number of trucks, tanks, and aircraft parts lashed onto the top deck, squeezed into every open slot of space. A cannon and anti-aircraft gun were mounted on the stern, another cannon on the bow. Four .50-caliber and two .30-caliber machine guns were also on deck. Racks of depth charges and anti-submarine devices that looked like big ash cans were bolted down on each side of the ship and were, in fact, called ash cans. Below the deck, five holds separated by watertight bulkheads stored munitions, machinery, food, and housed troops.

The ship was powered by a massive steam engine, twenty-one feet long and nineteen feet high, weighing 237,000 pounds.[10] It was manned by forty-four Merchant Marines. The weapons were under the control of twenty or so Naval Armed Guards, but many on the crew also knew how to use them. We were strictly passengers, however, which made the journey long and tedious.

Our destination was Casablanca, Morocco, a distance of 3,852 miles. The trip across the Atlantic to North Africa was supposed to take twelve days; it took eighteen. The delay was the result of all of the zigging and zagging we did to avoid German submarines that were stalking us. It's a helpless feeling, lumbering along at eleven miles per hour. Surrounded by water, there was no place to hide and nothing to do but sit and hope for the best.

The German's called their submarines U-boot, short for *Unterseeboot*, which means undersea boat. The Allies called them U-boats, and they wreaked havoc, sinking hundreds of Allied combat ships and more than 2,000 Allied merchant ships, many of them en route to England.[11]

The heavy losses caused Churchill to reflect, "The only thing that really frightened me during the war was the U-boat peril."[12] Almost 200 Liberties were among those lost, one right off the coast of North Carolina, another one as it approached Casablanca, and still others were sunk en route to other ports in Africa.

We were tracked by three U-boats en route to Casablanca. At least that is how many we saw during the crossing. Many nights the skipper dumped trash into the water in a kind of reverse Hansel and Gretel move. When it worked, the U-boat captains followed the trash floating in one direction, and we would tack in another direction. One day a U-boat got very close to us. The Navy guards dropped a load of ash cans into the ocean, each one equipped with a detonator set to explode at a certain depth. The shock waves, not the explosion, destroyed the sub, sending her to the bottom and oil and debris to the surface. We all cheered as the shattered pieces of what was left bobbed around the water, not even thinking of the men who had just died. We were still alive and that was all that mattered.

Because of the delays, we spent Thanksgiving at sea. The Navy provided a feast for its crew. The Army had a nice dinner for the soldiers. But no provision was made for the Air Corps guys since we had been scheduled to arrive in Casablanca on November 24, and it was anticipated that we would have a traditional Thanksgiving meal the next day on land. My group decided to make the best of it. We broke into the food supply room in hold no. 3, searching for suitable Thanksgiving fare. All we could find were C-rations, meals in a can. But that was as good as it was going to get, so we scooped up a load of cans and took them into the engine room. Hot steam pipes were everywhere and soon our dinner was warming up on them.

Returning to our quarters, someone said grace over our meal, thanking God for our safe journey, and then it was time to eat. We opened the hot cans with P-38 can openers, spooning out their contents into dozens of mess kits. Each can contained some kind of meat, like pork or beef, coupled with vegetables, beans, or potato hash; others contained spaghetti. We also found some B-unit cans filled with bread and desserts, and a powdered lemon drink, which we mixed with sea water made drinkable by a distillation system on board.

Known as "the Army's best invention," P-38 can openers were not much bigger than a fifty-cent piece. Since a hole was punched into the top of the can opener, a lot of soldiers in the field wore them around their necks with their dog tags, using them for other things—like screwdrivers, fingernail cleaners, and scissors. The name of the device referred to the fact that it took 38 punctures to open a C-ration can, and from the claim that they were as fast as a P-38 Lightning aircraft. While opening cans for my buddies, my mind wandered into dangerous territory; thinking about P-38 fighters led to thoughts of P-51s and my glorious time in Florida, then to the events at Walla Walla. I was still seething, still holding on to my dream of flying fighters.

With our bellies full, our conversations turned to home, and my frustration turned into melancholy. My wife was back in Denison, spending Thanksgiving, her first one as a married woman, alone with her mother. I wrote a letter to her just as the sun was rising in the morning, apologizing for being away on such a day. "With any luck, the war will end soon, and I will be home with you, my darling," I wrote.

My parents were also alone that Thanksgiving. All of their sons were gone, training or fighting far away from home. At least I was able to see them before I left, thanks to Colonel Wheless, who gave the Swah Group a nine-day pass. We could go anywhere we wanted so long as we reported to Herington Field, Kansas, by noon on October 25, 1943.

I spent the first six days of my leave with Peg, seeing the sites around Washington. It was the first time we were able to spend more than two consecutive days together, and we loved every minute of it. We spent hours just talking, getting to know each other better. We promised not to talk about the war, and for the most part, we didn't. I did manage to carve up and purge every morsel of my bitterness over flying bombers instead of fighters.

"Kirk, why are you so upset?" she asked. "Why is it so important to you to be a fighter pilot?"

"Because, since the time I was a kid, it is all that I have ever wanted to do. I've been hanging around airports all of my life, dreaming about it. And there I was at the very top, flying P-51s—the best fighter aircraft ever made . . . ," I started to explain.

"You remind me of a bird I found when I was a little girl. Its wing was broken. When I scooped it up, I could feel its little heart beating so fast. It was scared."

"So you think I'm scared?" I asked, not understanding her point and feeling a bit defensive.

"No. Let me finish. I took the bird to the vet. He was so nice. He straightened out the broken wing and, using a tongue depressor as a splint, set the wing in place with tape. He told me how to feed and care for the bird. I fed that bird every day and watched as it regained its strength. After a few weeks, I removed the splint. The poor little creature tried to fly but its wing didn't work right. It could never get higher than the hedge and never beyond the yard. No matter how hard he flapped, or squawked, he never returned to the sky. Within a day of the cast coming off, the bird stopped eating, and then it died. It was like it couldn't live unless it could fly like before."

"Peg, nothin's broken. I can fly as good as ever," I told her.

"Yes," she said, "but how's your appetite?"

Birds? Appetite? What was my bride talking about? I asked myself.

"What's my appetite got to do with it? I'm ready to eat if that's what you mean!"

"I'm talking about your will to live! I don't want you going off to war hating your job. I want you to be so passionate about our future that you'll do whatever you have to do to get home, even if it means flying bombers."

"I'm not crazy or suicidal. I'm just madder than a hornet that I'm out of fighters," I explained, trying to stay calm, trying to avoid our first fight.

Peg must have been thinking the same thing.

"Let's change the subject. I don't want to fight. Tell me what it was like when you were a boy. I've seen this side of your dream. Tell me how it all started," she said.

"It all started at the Sky Harbor Airport dedication on Labor Day 1929. I was there with my dad. He worked for the construction company that built the one-runway airport for Scenic View Airlines. We were so proud to have an airport in Phoenix. The next month SVA went out of business after the stock market crashed."

"I've heard of Sky Harbor. My boss says aviation cadets are still flying trainers out of there," Peg said.

"They were, up until a couple of years ago when an old Army air-field was reconditioned and renamed in honor of Frank Luke Jr., the first pilot to receive the Congressional Medal of Honor. He went to my high school before the First War."

"What I am saying is, Sky Harbor recovered after the stock market crashed, right?" she asked.

"Oh sure, it was remarkable to watch it expand, and I grew up along with it," I said, remembering the transformation from a dusty landing field to a modern airport.

"I remember when American Airlines started flying there in the early '30s. I was there in 1935 when the city renamed it Phoenix Sky Harbor.[13] They had a big shebang for it. There were all kinds of dedicatory festivities. They had a dance at the Western Ho. There were a lot of speeches. The mayor spoke and he introduced the US Superintendent of Air-Mail Service, Charles P. Graddick.[14] Have you heard of the Army's Rainbow Division during The Great War? Graddick was a captain in the division."

"Anyway, I was leaning against the side of the rostrum, semi-conscious in the shade—there's only so much pomposity a teenage boy can absorb before he starts to doze—when Captain Graddick concluded his speech by slamming his open hand on the podium. 'Let us never forget the sacrifices of our fathers, and may we always remember this day of dedication in the Valley of Sun!' He kind of woke me up, and I will always be grateful. Otherwise I may have missed the moment the sound of 10,000 people clapping politely was overcome by the roar of airplane engines, as barnstormers flying brightly colored bi-planes performed barrel rolls, spins, dives, and loop-the-loops. I went from glazed to crazed in a matter of seconds, jumping up and down, giving the thumbs-up sign to the passing pilots, and they tipping their wings at me, or so it seemed. The adults called it a flying circus. I called it the best day of my life."

"What a great memory," Peg said.

"It was the best day of my life until I jumped into a fighter, took her up to 20,000 feet at 400 hundred miles per hour, and put her into some spins and snap rolls. I felt free, truly free. Nothing was going to stop me; nothing could," I shared with her, hoping my love of flying and my pride in my accomplishments were not getting in the way of an otherwise wonderful day.

Ignoring my unfortunate choice of words—"best day of my life"—and the fact that we had been married before I made it into fighters, Peg said, "I won't feel free until you come home to me. We'll build a life together neither of us thought possible. I won't feel truly free until you're home."

My time with Peg ended too soon and we parted company at a train station in Spokane. She was going home to Texas and I to Arizona. After a long kiss and a lingering embrace, I stepped back slowly and said good-bye to my bride. She continued to hold my hands and for the first time, tears began to roll down her sweet, young face.

"Don't say good-bye, Kirk," Peg urged. "That sounds so final, as if we'll never see each other again. Just say so long."

"Alright, Peg. No good-byes," I said. Drawing her back into my arms, I whispered "So long, my love." She quickly turned from me and climbed onto the train.

Standing on the platform, I watched through the windows as she took her seat. She was still crying. An old woman reached across the aisle to comfort her, handing her a handkerchief. I could not hear their words but I knew what each was saying, and I was grateful for the woman's kindness. I stood there watching until she was gone. An hour later I was on my way home too.

I spent the better part of two days with my folks. My younger brother Ed joined us the morning of the second day, but the circumstances were not ideal. He was in the Navy, stationed in San Diego at the time. He asked his commanding officer for a pass so he could join me at home, explaining that I was heading overseas, and that this would be his last chance to see me. The request was denied. Ed came anyway. He hitchhiked through the night to get home, riding in the back of a fruit truck to Yuma and from there in the cab of a freight truck all the way to Phoenix. The old driver was so touched by this act of brotherly love he dropped Ed off in front of our home on Apache Street.

Ed walked into the house wearing a Navy work uniform, denim pants and a chambray shirt, with a white "Dixie Cup" on his head. Grinning ear-to-ear, looking kind of sheepish, he said, " Hank, it's so good to see you."[15] It had been almost three years. I was surprised to see him but not shocked by his actions. Ed was full of life, his laugh contagious. He's the kind of guy who can't finish a story without busting a gut, delighting in his own humor, and people loved him for it.

We spent a couple of hours trading stories and laughing, all the while knowing it could be the last time we saw each other.

"You've got to get back, Ed. They're likely to lock you up,"

"Don't matter. I had to see you. The Navy brass should understand that," he said.

"You don't have time to thumb your way back. I'm putting you on the bus," I told him.

I drove him to the Greyhound terminal and bought him a ticket.

"Are you nervous, Hank?" Ed asked.

"Not as nervous as you should be. Your CO's going to kill you. I just hope you get out of the brig before the war is over."

"In all seriousness, Hank, I want you to be safe. Don't take unnecessary chances," Ed said.

"I'm not afraid to die. I'd rather be in the game and lose than cheer from the sidelines, wondering the rest of my life if I was good enough to play. That would be worse than dying! If I go down, just know it will be worth it to me. I'll be grateful I got the chance to fly."

Ed got on the bus and I watched as it rolled away. He stuck his head out the window, waved, and then saluted. I returned the salute, standing at attention until I could no longer see him.

He reported to his commanding officer the next morning, letting him know he was prepared to face the consequences. Soon the military police arrived and escorted him to the brig, where he spent the next five days. He also lost his job as radioman and ventral gunner on an Avenger, a torpedo bomber used by the Navy. It was his dream job, but he never expressed any regrets over losing it, at least not to me.

Having seen Peg and my family so recently made it harder, not easier, that Thanksgiving Day aboard the *Moore*. Time and distance combined with military discipline and purpose had crowded out thoughts of family and home for a long time. But thinking about Peg's optimism about our future together filled me with hope. Remembering Ed's escapades to see me for just a couple hours filled me with pride. To be married to such a woman, to have such a brother, what could be better? When you are far from home and facing war, you think about things like that. You hold on to the good memories, take comfort in them. If you're lucky, bad memories melt away, like a block of ice on a hot day. The cold, hard facts vaporized over time, transformed into something you can sometimes feel but no longer have to carry.

Looking for some fresh air, I climbed up to the ship's deck and leaned against a jeep. The weather conditions fit my mood. The white-capped sea churned angrily; the cold wind was laden with heavy ocean spray. Remembering the good times only served to remind me how much I missed Peg, my brothers, everyone.

Joe was up top with me and sensed something was wrong. "Everything okay, Kirk?" he asked.

"Everything's jake, skipper—just too much time on this boat."

Just then a few soldiers we knew from the beer game at Camp Henry walked by and gave us a hard time about our meager dinner while recounting in excruciating detail their sumptuous meal.

Their sarcasm put me back in the right frame of mind.

"Don't worry about us," I said. "We'll fly our missions and be home next Thanksgiving enjoying a nice feast. And you dogfaces will be the ones eating C-rations, somewhere between Rome and Berlin."

I was back in fighting mode.

Notes

1.   "Herington Army Airfield," *Wikipedia*, accessed October 8, 2013, https://en.wikipedia.org/wiki/Herington_Army_Airfield.

2.   "V-mail," *Wikipedia*, accessed October 29, 2013, https://en.wikipedia.org/wiki/V-mail.

3.   C.G. Sweeting, Combat Flying Clothing (Washington, DC: Smithsonian Institution Press, 1984), 1–2.

4.   Ibid., 24.

5.   Ibid., 24–26.

6.   "Alfred Moore," *Wikipedia*, accessed November 2, 2013, https://en.wikipedia.org/wiki/Alfred_Moore.

7.   "Liberty Ships built by the United States Maritime Commission in World War II," *USMM*, accessed November 2, 2013, http://www.usmm.org/libertyships.html; "Building Liberty Ships in Brunswick," *Galileo, Digital Library of Georgia*, accessed November 2, 2013, http://dlg.galileo.usg.edu/liberty_ships/BuildingLibertyShips/?Welcome&Welcome; Kennedy Hickman, "World War II: The Liberty Ship Program," updated May 26, 2015, accessed November 2, 2013, http://militaryhistory.about.com/od/industrialmobilization/p/libertyships.htm.

8. "Vessel Type EC2: The Liberty Ship," *Skylighters*, accessed November 5, 2013, http://www.skylighters.org/troopships/libertyships.html.

9. Movement Card of the SS Alfred Moore from March 5, 1943 to October 3, 1944, US Navy.

10. "Liberty Ships built by the United States"; "Building Liberty Ships in Brunswick"; Hickman, "World War II."

11. "U-boat," *Wikipedia*, accessed October 2, 2013, https://en.wikipedia.org/wiki/U-boat.

12. Ibid.

13. "1935 and the Farm—Sky Harbor's Early Years and Memories," *Phoenix Sky Harbor International Airport*, accessed July 28, 2014, https://skyharbor.com/About/Information/History/75Years/TheEarlyYears.

14. "Biographies of Lamar County Georgia," *Georgia Genealogy Trails*, accessed July 28, 2014, http://genealogytrails.com/geo/lamar/bios.htm.

15. Frank's brothers called him Hank; others in the military called him Kirk.

CHAPTER 15

We arrived at the Port of Casablanca on December 1, 1943. The waters were calm and the city and surrounding territory were solidly under the control of Allied forces. Walking down the gangplank we were pleasantly surprised by the sounds of a small military band. We were to bivouac at Camp Don B. Passage, about three miles southeast of the city. We marched to the cadence of *The Field Artillery Song* until we could no longer hear it. The music seemed to fade from our ears as the sights, sounds, and smells of this exotic place flooded our senses.

Burrowed in the hills, the camp was a half-mile square, enclosed by barbed wire meant to keep supplies in and thieves out. It was a tranquil place, beautiful really, with its view of Casablanca and the shimmering sea.

A year earlier, however, the scene was anything but tranquil. It had been a war zone. In fact, the camp was named after the first American soldier killed in the invasion of North Africa.[1]

France surrendered to Germany in 1940 and was technically neutral up to that point in the war. Implicit in the treaty between the two countries was the Nazi's expectation that France's Vichy government would resist Allied efforts to seize strategic French territory that could be used against Germany. Morocco, a French colony at the time, was just such a place.[2]

Casablanca was France's most important remaining port, the Germans having taken control of France's other ports, including its strategic centerpiece at Toulon, a target I would bomb in the coming months. Casablanca was a large man-made facility with a long stone breakwater separating port and sea. The water surface and wharf structures exceeded 300,000 acres, an ideal location for shipments of men and equipment. Consequently its capture became a key component in Operation Torch.

The port was also home to a Vichy naval base. On November 8, 1942, the French Navy engaged the lead elements of a convoy of US ships charged with the transportation and protection of the invasion task force of 35,000 American soldiers. The naval battle off the Moroccan coast lasted five days. The French lost a cruiser, four destroyers, and five submarines, along with the lives of 460 men. A couple of US destroyers and a battleship were pranged in the conflict but there were no major American casualties until the last two days. By then two U-boats arrived on the scene, sinking four transport ships and killing 174 servicemen.[3]

Operation Torch was a complete success, though, pushing the Axis forces out of North Africa and then driving them from Sicily. The 15th Air Force was activated on November 1, 1943, with headquarters at Tunis, Tunisia. It provided air support as the campaign continued up the toe of the Boot of Italy and further north, capturing strategic airfields in and around Bari, Italy. The 15th moved its headquarters there the day we arrived at Casablanca.

We boarded a train that crossed over Morocco and Algeria, and then to Tunis. The rolling stock came in all shapes and sizes, some transporting equipment, others supplies such as fuel and oil. They were all in various stages of disrepair, showing the effects of war. We boarded wooden boxcars 20½ feet long and 8½ feet wide that had been used by the French in World War I. Stenciled on the outside of the boxcars were the words, *40 hommes et 8 chevaux*—forty men and eight horses—which gives you an idea of the accommodations. Drinking water was available from a fifty-gallon canvas bag suspended from the ceiling. C-rations were available but cold. There were no seats. No beds. No toilets. At night there wasn't a lot of room for a comfortable night's rest. And our mummy bags could not shield us from the sharp ridges of the buckled floor, its wooden slats swollen and curled up at the edges.

There were regular stops along the way in small towns, villages, and makeshift canteens and rest stations in the middle of nowhere. As we got off the train, locals would crowd us to barter their food and drink for anything American: money, Army surplus, cigarettes, chocolate. We picked up several B-17 crews from Bizerte Airfield at some point after crossing into Tunisia. They were part of the 2nd Bombardment Group of the 12th Air Force and were on their way to form up with the 15th Air Force in Italy, as were we. Naturally, we wanted to hear about their missions and combat experiences. They were more interested in telling us things you wouldn't read about in the newspapers.

Alcohol was a favorite topic. There were stories of B-17s flying to London to pick up cases of free booze from generous distilleries in the UK. Another fellow told of a beer run to Marrakech. Since there was no ice available to cool the beer down, the pilot climbed to 35,000 feet, which nearly froze the beer. By the time he landed, the beer was ice-cold and slaked the thirst of dozens of men.

When beer was not available, troops had ample access to cokes. In June 1943, General Eisenhower sent an urgent telegram to Coca-Cola, asking for an immediate shipment of three million bottles of coke and the parts and equipment for ten bottling plants.[4] It was thought the soda pop would be good for morale. The company responded by building a plant in Algiers and sixty-three other plants across the European and Pacific war zones, distributing more than five billion bottles to military personnel. This fulfilled the directive given by Coca-Cola's president, Robert Woodruff, at the beginning of the war. He wanted "to see that every man in uniform gets a bottle of Coca-Cola for 5 cents, wherever he is and whatever it costs the company."[5]

Their stories shifted to another favorite topic: women. Only they didn't speak of wives and girlfriends back home. With wide eyes they regaled us with vivid and somewhat lurid stories of prostitutes who followed the camps of the troops across the desert. Some were pros; others were just poor women—even wives and mothers—trying to put food on the table for their families. This really wasn't much of a shock to us. Such stories were as old as war itself.

We received stateside training that encouraged us to avoid ladies of the night and were given pamphlets to read as we crossed the Atlantic. Artistic posters of beautiful women cautioned soldiers about disease-carrying "procurable women"; others reminded men, "Self-Control is Self-Preservation." It may have been for more than morality's sake, however, that the military was motivated to encourage caution and stress chastity. The generals took notice of the fact that during World War I the Army lost nearly 7 million man-days and discharged more than 10,000 men because of sexually transmitted diseases.[6] To limit the reduction of the fighting force in World War II, the Army set up treatment centers for a series of penicillin shots, wryly referred to as "Casanova Camps."

At some point, we arrived in Tunis, the largest city in Tunisia. Situated on the Mediterranean Sea, the ancient city lay in the shadow of the rugged Djebel Ressas—the Mountain of Lead. The buildings and structures were a mishmash of ancient and modern architecture, comfortably interwoven like a pair of clasped hands. Tall office buildings, white-plastered apartments, and weathered warehouses and shops stretched down to the water's edge.

We boarded an LST waiting for us at the harbor and crossed over to Naples. From there we took a train to Bari, arriving late in the evening. This was not the most direct route we could have taken. Bari, a port city, was a key logistics hub during the war. Dozens of supply ships were regularly in and out of the port, delivering munitions, fuel, and supplies. We could have sailed directly to the Port of Bari except for the fact that it was devastated by German bombers on December 2, 1943, in a raid known as "Little Pearl Harbor."[7]

The German strike force consisted of 105 twin-engine Junker Ju 88s. They were not equipped for heavy-duty bombing, but the element of surprise made up for it. Bari and its port were under the control of the British military. Its commanders had determined that the Luftwaffe was so depleted in Italy that it posed virtually no threat to Bari, and they gave a press conference to that effect just hours before the attack. Consequently, the air defenses were practically non-existent there. No fighter squadrons were based there and those within range had offensive, not defensive, responsibilities.

The Allies let their guard down in another way. They were preoccupied with getting the headquarters of the 15th Air Force set up. Housing and offices for General Jimmy Doolittle and his staff of more than 200 officers, 50 civilian technicians, and hundreds of enlisted men had to be arranged. Communications systems had to be set up between headquarters and airfields for heavy bomber units at Foggia, Manduria, Castellucio, Spinazolla, and Cerignola, and fighter units at Torremaggiore and Fano.[8]

Around 7:30 p.m., the Germans dumped chaff, thin strips of tinfoil, into the night air at 10,000 feet. They were a radar countermeasure, meant to confuse the Allied radar operators, or, as they were collectively known, Mickey. The chaff, called *Duppell* by the Germans, would register as aircraft on radar screens as they floated around, cloud-like, while the bombers descended below the limits of the radar, hitting the city of 250,000 people first, and then attacking the port. It was all over within twenty minutes.

Bright lights lit up the port to expedite the off-loading of supplies, making it an easy target. More than forty Allied ships were moored in the port, mostly Liberty ships, many of them loaded with aviation fuel designated for the 15th Air Force. They were stacked together like a brick of firecrackers. Some ships took direct hits, igniting fuel and munitions, resulting in horrible explosions. Others ships caught fire when the fuel floating on the water ignited. Twenty-seven ships were sunk in the raid; twelve others were severely damaged. The raid completely shut down the port for three weeks and shipping operations were not fully restored until February.[9]

When we arrived in Bari, wisps of smoke were rising from smoldering ruins and acrid fumes lingered in the air. Ash and soot occasionally fell from treetops and building ledges, getting into our eyes. We billeted there, enjoying warm showers and real food. It was a luxury to sleep on cots in warm tents. No rolling sea; no thump, thump of rail cars. Sleep came easily, until some orderlies from the hospital corps rousted us out of bed in the middle of the night.

"What do you think you're doing?" I demanded.

"Sorry, sir, we've been ordered to commandeer your cots," the corpsman responded.

"Listen, you bedpan commando, we've not had a decent night's sleep for weeks. Come back in the morning and you can have them," I told him.

He explained the raid resulted in more than a thousand military and merchant marine casualties and another thousand civilian casualties, with more people pouring into hospitals every day. Our cots were being taken to help care for them.

Some of the casualties complained of respiratory problems and "gritty" eyes, their skin burned and blistered. Doctors suspected some kind of chemical agent was involved and believed the Germans had resorted to chemical warfare. The truth was not widely known until after the war. One of the Liberty ships, the *John Henry*, was carrying

2,000 bombs containing mustard gas.[10] The secret cargo was meant to be used in the event Germany followed through on its threats to use mustard gas in Italy. The bombs exploded when the ship caught fire, spewing mustard gas into the water and atmosphere. Some of the victims who had been thrown into the bay swallowed the gas floating on the water; others came in contact with the fumes wafting over the city. There were 628 mustard gas casualties; 69 of them died within two weeks. Some of them could have been saved had the doctors known the truth. However, Churchill insisted that information about the mustard gas remain a secret. Even so, word leaked out through unofficial channels. Axis Sally, the German propaganda broadcaster heard about it. She taunted us over the radio with, "I see you boys are getting gassed by your own poison gas. Are you sure Uncle Sam is looking out for you?"[11]

While in Bari, I ran into Major Phil Cochran. He was the inspiration for Flip Corkin, a character in *Terry and the Pirates*, a daily comic strip read by millions of people.[12] Phil was America's most experienced fighter pilot at the time, known for his exploits flying P-40s in the North African campaign and made famous through the funny pages. He was a creative genius when it came to mayhem and destruction. One time he skipped a bomb into the German headquarters in Tunisia. On another occasion he dragged a lead weight from his ship to rip out German telephone lines. He trained his unit—he called it the Joker squadron—to fight in ways that were unconventional at the time, using superior tactics to make up for inferior planes. When he returned to the states, he made it his mission to pass along his practical combat experience to pilots training to fly fighters. That is how I first met him, when I was training in Florida.

He was the first pilot I had ever talked to with combat experience not gained in World War I. It was the same for all of the guys I was staging with, and true for most trainees at the time. Many of the new instructors came from the ranks of recent graduates of Air Corps flight schools. Others were civilians with no military experience. As a result the training was, for the most part, strictly by the book.

Cochran stayed with us a few days, eating and drinking with us. He also flew with us, matched us up in dogfights, and mentored us. He was determined to pass on what he knew about combat, helping us to learn practical strategies for low altitude fighting. He insisted that we become proficient with our guns, suggesting that we would use them a lot more than we had been told in school.

It was a surprise, then, to see him in Bari. He embraced me like we were old friends.

"Kirk, how's tricks?" he asked. "What are you flying, P-47s or 38s? Which fighter group are you with?" he continued.

"I'm number 2 in a B-17, assigned to the 2nd Bomb Group," I replied.

He couldn't believe it. "That can't be—you were born to fly fighters," he enthused. Making matters worse, he added, "I couldn't do it. Fly bombers, there's no way."

I tried to shake it off, telling myself it didn't matter anymore. I asked him what he was doing in Bari.

"I'm meeting with General Doolittle and then it's on my way to London, flying with my old buddy Zemke and the 56th Fighter Group. I'm finally rested up from North Africa and can't wait to get back to the real deal," he said.

My mind was racing as he was talking. *What the heck*, I thought, *no harm in asking*: "Any chance you could take me with you? I've got to get back into fighters."

He slapped me on the back the way guys do. "If you can get your CO to reassign you, I'd take you in a second, partner," he assured me.

I was about to get reacquainted with my destiny, I thought, as I started tracking down Major Kutschera, commanding officer of the 429th, my newly assigned squadron. When I found him, I explained my situation, briefly, and he referred me to Colonel Rice, commander of the 2nd Bomb Group. He listened to my complaints, allowed me to vent and mourn about the events in Florida, P-51s, and Walla Walla. I told him about the offer from Phil Cochran, and then he replied, "I think you got things backwards in your mind, lieutenant. Bombers, not fighters, are going to win this war. Fighters exist to support bombers, not the other way around. You've got a remarkable opportunity to be part of something special. Do you have any idea what we are going to do together in the next year?"

I replied, "No sir, but I . . ."

He cut me off and began to describe the objectives of the 15th Air Force with the enthusiasm of a boy anticipating Christmas.

"We're going to destroy the German Air Force in the air and on the ground. We're going to destroy their fighter plants, their ball bearing plants, their oil refineries and rubber plants; we're going to take out their submarine pens and bases. We'll finish the job driving them out of Italy, then the Balkans, and, eventually, France.[13] We are going to flatten them all the way to Berlin and then the war will be over. You're a part of that great mission, lieutenant. What do you say?"

"I can't get fighters out of my system. I belong in a fighter, please give me permission to join Major Cochran in England," I begged.

He wouldn't do it but promised that he would recommend a transfer to fighters after I completed twenty-five bombing missions, half of the required missions in the MTO. I informed Major Cochran of the decision and he said he would see me in London.

Notes

1.   Carl J. Hartstern, *World War II: Memoirs Of a Dogface Soldier* (Bloomington, Indiana: Xlibris, 2011).

2.   "Naval Battle of Casablanca," *Wikipedia*, accessed November 21, 2013, https://en.wikipedia.org/wiki/Naval_Battle_of_Casablanca.

3.   Ibid.

4.   "Coca-Cola: The Pause that Refreshed," *The National WWII Museum*, New Orleans, accessed May 24, 2013, http://www.nww2m.com/2011/08/coca-cola-the-pause-that-refreshed-2/.

5.   Journey Staff, "The Chronicle of Coca-Cola: A Symbol of Friendship," *Coca-Cola Journey*, January 1, 2012, accessed May 24, 2013, http://www.coca-colacompany.com/stories/the-chronicle-of-coca-cola-a-symbol-of-friendship/.

6.   Mark S. Rasnake, Nicholas G. Conger, C. Kenneth McAllister, King K. Holmes, and Edmond C. Tramont, "History of U.S. Military Contributions to the Study of Sexually Transmitted Diseases," *Military Medicine* 170, no. 4S (2005), 61–65, accessed February 2, 2016, http://publications.amsus.org/doi/pdf/10.7205/MILMED.170.4S.61.

7.   "World War II: German Raid on Bari," *History Net*, accessed November 4, 2013, http://www.historynet.com/world-war-ii-german-raid-on-bari.htm.

8.   Ibid.

9.   Ibid.

10.   Ibid.

11.   Ibid.

12.   John Allison, "Phil Cochran: The Most Unforgettable Character I've Met!," *Air Commando Association*, accessed March 19, 2014, http://www.specialoperations.net /ColCochran.htm.

13.   Kenn C. Rust, Fifteenth Air Force Story . . . in World War II (Temple City, California: Historical Aviation Album, 1976), 6–7.

CHAPTER 16

The Office of Strategic Services, the predecessor to the CIA, was also setting up shop in Bari when I arrived. The OSS had been conducting espionage missions behind enemy lines in Europe for some time. Using the most sophisticated spying instruments of the time, they infiltrated the Nazi government, destroyed communication lines and transportation systems, and plotted the deaths of Nazi spies, scientists, generals, and even Hitler. They had special weapons like concealed knifes in both men and women shoes, explosives that looked like chunks of coal, an explosive powder that looked, baked, and tasted like flour, pens that turned into bombs, coins that turned into knives, and devices that attached to trains and exploded when a sensor detected the train passing through a tunnel. They had all manner of portable radio devices, some of which they carried in ordinary-looking suitcases. Agents parachuting into occupied countries could wear SOE camouflaged jumpsuits, designed to be worn over civilian clothing and easily shed upon landing. After landing they whisked away quickly on Welbikes, small, collapsible motorcycles that fit into a parachute container.[1]

One OSS operative was Moe Berg, who played catcher for the Chicago White Sox and Boston Red Sox before the war. Berg was also extremely bright. He spoke ten languages and was a graduate of Columbia Law School. In 1939, he became known for his performances on the radio quiz show, *Information, Please*. The Commissioner of Major League Baseball, Kennesaw Mountain Landis, told him after one show, "Berg, in just thirty minutes, you've done more for baseball than I've done the entire time I have been commissioner."[2]

In September 1943, Berg was assigned to the OSS Balkans desk. By then, Yugoslavia's borders had been carved up by Nazi Germany, Fascist Italy, Hungary, and Bulgaria. They created a Nazi puppet state called the Independent State of Croatia, which was controlled by a fascist organization called Ustashi.[3] The Ustashi were responsible for the slaughter of hundreds of thousands of Serbs, Gypsies, and Jews in Yugoslavia during the war.[4]

Berg parachuted into Yugoslavia to evaluate the capacity of the resistance groups operating against the Nazis and Ustashi.[5] One group, the Chetniks, led by Draža Mihailović, supported the exiled government of King Peter. Another group, the Partisans, led by Josip Tito, had ambitions to create a post-war communist state. The tension between these groups over the conflicting visions of the future of Yugoslavia was compounded by the region's age-old bugaboos: ethnic and religious conflicts. Tito was a Croat and Mihailović was a Serb. Most Croats were Catholic while Serbs, for the most part, belonged to the Orthodox Church. There was also tension with the Muslim population of the region. In many ways there was a civil war within the world war in Yugoslavia.[6] None of that mattered much to the Allies, though. They just wanted to know which side was better at killing Nazis.[7] It was Berg's job to make that assessment so the politicians and generals could determine the amount of aid—guns, ammunition, food, and supplies—to be given to each group.

The OSS office in Bari was also tasked with the mission of rescuing pilots and crews shot down over the Balkans. The control agent there was George Vujnovich,[8] a son of Yugoslavian immigrants who left America in the '30s to study at a University in Belgrade. While there he met and married Mirjana, whose father had been jailed years before on suspicion he was connected to the assassination of Archduke Ferdinand, the often-cited precursor to World War I.[9] In 1939, Germany invaded Yugoslavia and George and Mirjana spent the next two years trying to escape from Nazi occupied-territories.[10] When they returned to the states, George was commissioned a second lieutenant and eventually recruited by the OSS.

OSS agents parachuted into Yugoslavia to establish underground networks for the escape and evacuation of American airmen. The British Secret Intelligence Service, known as MI6, also had agents working undercover in the Balkans. One of its agents was Sir Fitzroy Maclean who lived in the mountains with Tito and his Partisans.[11] Maclean is believed to be the inspiration for the James Bond character in the books written by Ian Fleming, who was a British Naval intelligence officer during the war and the head of 30 Assault Unit, a commando unit that operated in the Mediterranean. [12]

This is all very interesting to think about now, but back then the situation created uncertainty for those of us preparing for missions over and around the Balkans. During our early morning briefings we would be told our targets, informed about the weather conditions, and warned about flak zones and the degree of anticipated enemy aircraft, referred to as E/A, as in, "expect about fifty E/As coming in from the West." We were also instructed about contingency plans in the event we had to bail out. Unfortunately, there were often conflicting intelligence reports from American and British sources, some suggesting it best to be picked up by Partisans and others favoring the efforts of Chetniks. Still other reports said you couldn't trust the Chetniks because they were in cahoots with the Axis while other opinions expressed suspicion about the Communist Partisans. After so many ambiguous briefings, I didn't know whom to trust.

Our last leg of the trip was from Bari to Foggia. We rode in a convoy of trucks, rumbling down pockmarked roads. The closer we got, the worse things looked, mirroring my apprehension of the job I was trained to do. When I first got into Forts, practice over bombing ranges meant puffs of dirt erupting skyward, looking like a cherry bomb in an anthill. In North Africa, I saw a few scarred and broken buildings and the carcasses of formerly mechanized equipment, charred, some covered with sand. In Bari, I witnessed the aftermath of not even a half an hour's worth of bombing.

And then there was Foggia. Nineteen hundred years in the making, it was largely destroyed in nine Allied raids that began in May and ended in September 1943.[13] More than 19,000 civilians were killed, ciphers to war planners and unseen by bomb crews at 18,500 feet. But their demise was evident to us on the ground. Dozens of buildings, crumbling and listing, many with exterior walls ripped off, stood empty. Entire city blocks: gone. Splintered timber and mutilated stone mounded in rows where thousands of homes once stood.

Anxious black-haired children wearing ragged woolen clothes stared at us from both sides of the road, their coal black eyes listless.

Mingled among the horde were obsidian-eyed seraphs with bearings that cursed to hell all the evil that had been poured out on them. They too were staring, but intently, waiting for one of the trucks to slam into a pothole, halting the procession. Providence was on their side that day and they pressed in on us, hands outstretched. We gave them what we had and minutes later our truck lurched forward in sync with the others. The children darted back to the roadside. I watched them as if through a kaleidoscope. The strong and mighty sharing their bounty with the weak and disconsolate ones, their sad and misshapen faces transformed in that moment of relief.

War became real to me that day, ugly and brutal, but not faceless.

We would come to know many of the survivors of the Foggia air raids, young and old; kids who scavenged for food around our camps, metal bowls and cups in hand; grown men who picked through dump-sites, looking for anything of value that could be sold or used to help their families; and women, many widowed, who washed our clothes for a little money. These were desperate times for all of them, and we did what we could to help them. We handed over American cigarettes to the grown-ups who would sell or trade them. We were generous with our food, often filling the bowls and cups of the little ones. On Christmas day, dozens of children, many of them orphans, joined us for a traditional holiday dinner of turkey, mashed potatoes, and pie. They trundled home with wrapped packages, boxes of candy, and matches. Kids were always asking for matches.

Despite these efforts to ease their suffering, poverty drove a few locals to exchange information with German agents for cash. Data about the number of operational planes we had or the physical condition of pilots was easily observable by locals with access to our bases. Occasionally our radio codes seeped out, even though they were changed daily. As a result, security tightened and cottage industries, like laundry pick-up service, were terminated.

The Foggia airfield complex, a series of aerodromes within a 25-mile radius of the city, was originally home to the Royal Italian Air Force and at some point was seized by the Luftwaffe. It was the grand prize in the Allied invasion of Italy. Securing the complex would give the 15th Air Force the platform to fulfill its objectives, and so the airfields were hit even harder than the city.

The Allies also targeted the railroad yards and road systems in the Foggia Province that supported Italian and German troops fighting in Sicily and southern Italy. The bomb raids continued, even after Italy's surrender, until the German army retreated to the north and its air force abandoned the airfields. The Army Corps of Engineers repaired the bombed-out airfields and built new semi-permanent runways and satellite airfields, making way for heavy bombardment missions over Italy, France, Yugoslavia, Austria, Hungary, Poland, Romania, and Germany.

The 15th Air Force had nearly 2,000 aircraft, two-thirds of them bombers, the rest, fighters.

They were distributed among five bomb wings and a single fighter wing. The 5th Bomb Wing consisted of Flying Fortresses, and all of them were located in the Foggia airfield complex. My group, the 2nd BG, and the 97th BG were assigned to Amendola Airfield, located twelve miles from the City of Foggia.

The 15th had four other bomb wings in the Foggia complex. They consisted of bomb groups, all of them flying B-24s.

I paid attention to the fighter groups. There were four of them when I got there, three flying P-38s, one flying P-47s. Three more fighter groups would be added in the spring of 1944. They all flew P-51 Mustangs, and I should have been flying with them.

Today most of the old airfields are like many of us who once fought there: broken-down and returned to the earth.

As the American war machine began to ramp up in 1939, it was the hope of many blacks that the newly constituted Army Air Corps would not adhere to the regular Army's tradition of segregated troops and that it would eschew the Army's practice of relegating blacks to non-combat roles. There was significant resistance to both notions by Army heads—after all, segregated units had been part of the Army since 1863. The Army was not, they argued, the proper place for social experiments. Civil rights leaders persisted, adopting the Double V Campaign at home—victory against fascism abroad and discrimination at home.[14]

For his part, President Roosevelt tried to accommodate both sides of the argument privately but after much debate the White House issued a formal statement. The number of blacks that would be accepted in the Army would be equal to their proportion in the national population, about 10 percent. Army units would continue to be segregated.

Blacks would be permitted to serve in the Army Air Corps as soon as pilots and ground crews could be trained.[15]

Black leaders turned up the heat on the administration. Roosevelt, facing a tough reelection against noted civil rights champion, Wendell Wilkie, attempted to appease his critics by appointing three black men to important positions in the war effort. Colonel Benjamin O. Davis was promoted to brigadier general, the first black general in the regular Army. The commander of reserve officer training at Howard University, Colonel Campbell Johnson, was appointed Special Aide to the Director of Selective Service. And from the West Point of Negro Leadership, Howard University Law School, its dean, Judge William Hastie, was named the Civilian Aide to the Secretary of War Henry Stimson.[16]

The debate continued in Washington. Secretary of War Stimson urged President Roosevelt not to place "too much responsibility on a race which had not shown much initiative in battle."[17] Army Chief of Staff General George Marshall believed blacks were inferior and should be withheld from combat. Still others pointed to low test scores by most blacks on the Army General Classification Test as affirmation of the policy to segregate units and keep black soldiers in non-combat roles. When it came to the Air Corps, they posited, it was inconceivable that white enlisted men in ground crews would take orders from a black pilot, who would be their superior officer.[18]

Hastie bore in with three powerful arguments. First, segregation makes black soldiers feel like second class citizens even as they are being trained to fight with pride and act with dignity. He asserted, "Most white persons are unable to appreciate the rancor and bitterness which the Negro, as a matter of self-preservation, has learned to hide beneath a smile, a joke, or merely, an impassive face."[19] Second, segregation wasted the military's most valuable asset, manpower. Finally, he argued, separating white and black soldiers while fighting to preserve democracy was hypocritical.[20]

On January 15, 1943, Hastie resigned his influential position in response to racially segregated training facilities at Tuskegee Airfield, inadequate training for black pilots, and the backseat role they would play in air operations.[21] The controversy continued in Washington throughout 1943. Studies were made and reports issued sizing up the skills and capacity, mental and emotional, of black air units. One high level report suggested that black pilots were incapable of performing at the level needed to fly combat missions.

Meanwhile the all-black 99th Squadron gained experience in North Africa and practical combat training from Major Cochran,[22] and then moved on to Italy. They were followed by the all-black 332nd Fighter Group and its 100th, 301st, and 302nd Fighter Squadrons, and the all-black 96th Air Service Group.[23]

When they first got to Italy, the black airmen played a limited role in the war, providing close air support for Allied ground troops and targeting enemy shipping lines and ammunition dumps, but they wanted to do more. They wanted to escort bomber planes on bombing missions like the white fighter groups were doing, and eventually they did. Known as the Redtails because the tail sections of their fighter planes were painted red, the Tuskegee Airmen claimed the distinction of never having lost a bomber to an enemy aircraft.[24]

If you want to know the skill level of black squadrons, I suppose you could look up the number of sorties flown or E/As shot down. You could count the medals earned and citations awarded. But the way I see it, a better gauge is the type of aircraft they flew. The Tuskegee Airmen started out flying worn out P-40 Warhawks, more or less hand-me-downs from white squadrons. They ended up in P-51 Mustangs, the best fighter plane we had, the plane I dreamed of flying. Black pilots wouldn't have gotten close to the mighty Mustangs unless they could really fly.

Notes

1. "Resistance," *Museum of World War I, Boston*, accessed January 17, 2014, http://museumofworldwarii.org/resistance.html.

2. "Moe Berg," *Wikipedia*, accessed January 17, 2014, https://en.wikipedia.org/wiki/Moe_Berg.

3. Jasa Romano, *Jews of Yugoslavia 1941–1945: Victims of Genocide and Freedom Fighters* (Belgrade, Serbia: Federation of Jewish Communities of Yugoslavia, 1980), http://www.afhso.af.mil/shared/media/document/AFD-100923-007.pdf.

4. Ibid.

5. "'Moe' Berg: Sportsman, Scholar, Spy," *Central Intelligence Agency*, accessed February 12, 2013, https://www.cia.gov/news-information/featured-story-archive/2013-featured-story-archive/moe-berg.html.

6. Gregory A. Freeman, *The Forgotten 500: The Untold Story of the Men Who Risked All for the Greatest Rescue Mission of World War II* (New York: NAL Caliber, 2007), 127.

7. Harris Gaylord Warren, *Special Operations: AAF Aid to European Resistance Movements 1943–1945* (Washington, DC: Air Historical Office Headquarters, Army Air Forces, 1947) 4–6, 12–13, accessed February 3, 2016, https://ia601700.us.archive.org/5/items/SpecialOperationsAAF/SpecialOperationsAAF.pdf.

8. Freeman, *The Forgotten 500*, 84–85, 138.

9. Ibid., 89.

10. Ibid., 106–38.

11. "First Fitzroy Maclean, 1st Baronet," *Wikipedia*, accessed January 15, 2014, https://en.wikipedia.org/wiki/Sir_Fitzroy_Maclean,_1st_Baronet.

12. "No. 30 Commando," *Wikipedia*, accessed January 15, 2014, https://en.wikipedia.org/wiki/No._30_Commando.

13. "Bombing of Foggia," *Wikipedia*, accessed January 17, 2014, https://en.wikipedia.org/wiki/Bombing_of_Foggia.

14. "A Campaign for Freedom," *The History Engine*, accessed February 3, 2016, https://historyengine.richmond.edu/episodes/view/4682.

15. Ibid.

16. Stanley Sandler, *Segregated Skies: All-Black Combat Squadrons of WWII* (Washington, DC: The Smithsonian Institute Press, 1996), 14.

17. "A Campaign for Freedom."

18. Ibid.

19. Ibid.

20. Ibid.

21. Sandler, *Segregated Skies*, 40.

22. Ibid., 44.

23. Daniel L. Haulman and Air Force Historical Research Agency, *Tuskegee Airmen Chronology* (Charleston, North Carolina: CreateSpace Independent Publishing Platform, 2012).

24. "The Tuskegee Airmen Heritage-History & Legacy," *Red Tail Reborn*, accessed January 22, 2014, http://www.redtailreborn.com/Red_Tail_Reborn/History.html; "Tuskegee Airmen Broke Barriers, Changed Future of the U.S. Military," *American Battle Monuments Commission*, accessed February 26, 2015, http://www.abmc.gov/news-events/news/tuskegee-airmen-broke-barriers-changed-future-us-military#.VrI7RBgrJxM.

CHAPTER 17

Amendola Airfield was located on farmland between Foggia and Manfredonia, a small town near the Adriatic Sea. Local lore had it that New York's Mayor La Guardia trained in the same fields during World War I as an aviator in the US Army Air Service. While most of us attributed the rumor to national pride in the son of Italian immigrants, it turned out to be true.

The conditions at Amendola were raw. There were no brick and mortar improvements like air towers or hangars, mess halls or barracks, hospitals or officer clubs. There was no infrastructure either, no drains, sewer systems, electrical conduit, water mains, asphalt roads, brick infields, or concrete aprons.

It was a boot-shaped dirt field trimmed by dirt taxiways and dispersal points. When they weren't in the air, the Forts were parked nose facing nose on either side of the taxiways on dirt hardstands designated for each squadron. The runway was made out of pierced steel planking called Marsden matting. Each plank was ten feet long and more than a foot wide, weighing about 65 pounds. Engineering crews using hand tools linked the planks together to form the runway, which was about 3,200 feet long and 200 feet wide.

The infield and living areas were covered in ryegrass and clumps of scrub brush. Hillocks rising to the west revealed weathered rocks and boulders jutting up like bad teeth. Gnarled olive trees, witnesses to earlier wars to be sure, were scattered around the hills and fields.

A large farmhouse served as our group headquarters. A small chapel was converted to a medical dispensary. We annexed caves in the hillsides for various uses, calling them the "catacombs." One became a briefing room, another, a clubhouse for enlisted men. Movies were shown in a third cave, and God was worshipped in another.

Historical photographs of the living conditions at Amendola Airfield depict an order and precision I never saw there. They show neat rows of rounded, tall tents with wooden doors, some with brick siding. When I was there we lived in 16 x 16 tents, olive drab in color. Cords strung from the four corners and sides were hitched to wooden stakes, giving tents their shape. (Wooden stakes were used because metal was in short supply.) They were pitched in random places, many of them near olive trees, which provided additional shelter from the wind. At first there were no floors, only dirt. After a few weeks I found some scraps of wood that kept us off the ground.

Officers lived in one area, enlisted men in another. We slept on cots and mattress covers that we stuffed with straw gathered from the fields. A single lightbulb turned on by the tug of a chain gave light. There were no stoves or heaters provided with the tents making cold nights longer. An Arizona boy like me couldn't live that way, so I took matters into my own hands by building a makeshift heater.

First, I stripped the gas line from a Focke-Wulf that had been shot down nearby and attached it to a metal barrel sitting twenty-five feet from our tent. The line was run underground to another metal barrel inside our tent. Both barrels were fitted with a pit spigot. When we wanted to warm up the tent, we poured a small amount of aviation fuel in the outside barrel and then opened the spigot to allow the fuel to enter the line. Then the spigot inside the tent was opened, allowing a few drops of the fuel to empty into the inside barrel. One of us would stand a few feet away and throw a match in the barrel and ka-boom, flames would swirl about and flash heat the barrel. The red hot barrel heated the tent for a good night's sleep. Occasionally, bits of the hot metal would break off the barrel during the eruptions and launch skyward, hitting the top panel and burning small holes into the canvas. We didn't notice the holes until it rained.

A large tent served as our mess hall. It was situated at the base of the hill, between our quarters and the briefing room. It had a stove that provided warmth to passersby and therapeutic relief to returning, half-frozen flight crews.

Heavy rain and strong winds were regular visitors at Amendola that winter. Tents leaked often. Several were uprooted and scattered by cyclonic gusts. Outside, fields turned into bogs under the weight of heavy equipment. Men went knee deep in the mud at times and struggled to keep boots on their feet and out of the grasp of slurping muck. Ground crews laid down sacks of cement to create revetments on which to park the planes when conditions got really bad.

The 2nd Bomb Group was called the Defenders of Liberty. Its patch was a shield-shaped insignia of gold and green, with four blue bombs angling downward, and the words *Libertatem Defendimus* written below. Each squadron was distinguished by a unique emblem. Many of them were created and passed down from earlier years, some dating back to World War I. The 20th Bomb Squad's emblem was a pirate tossing a bomb. The 49th BS had a menacing black wolf, teeth bared and drooling. The 96th displayed a grinning red devil thumbing his nose with one hand and tossing a bomb with the other. My squadron, the 429th, had an arrow-shooting Indian, three red feathers sticking up like a cowlick in need of butch wax. These emblems were worn on jackets to promote pride and unity, signaling one's clan.

Planes also had distinctive markings, but they weren't for show. They made it possible for otherwise identical planes to form up in proper order after take-off. Squadrons of the 2nd Bomb Group were identified with a black Y inside a black ring. The insignia was painted on both sides of the tail section, as were the aircraft identification numbers. Unique squadron tail marks were painted below the numbers. The 49th had a black chevron. The 96th had a T. Our mark was the top half of a black split arrow.

Each squadron had twelve planes. A typical mission included seven to nine of the squadron's planes, if available, and they were divided into elements of up to three aircraft. When planes from the 429th reached altitude, we began looking for the Y and split arrow, and then dropped into place, holding the pattern until each element was in formation, then we would look to join the group, consisting of three other squadrons, and then the wing, each phase accomplished within a designated staging area of thirty to forty miles.

Formations varied, depending on the mission but the point was to fly in a tight protective box, wing to wing but staggered. In a way, the gun-laden Flying Fortresses replaced the gun filled trenches of World War I. Enemy fighters trying to breach the formation faced fifty-caliber guns pointing in almost every direction.

The Germans tried various strategies to break up formations, including ramming their planes into ours. They even tried to get above us and drop bombs on us. But their tried and true practice was to try to knock out planes flying on the edges of the formation, especially those in the rear. We called that spot "tail-end Charlie." On the other hand, the planes in front of the formation typically had the worst end of it when it came to flying through flak.

Life at Amendola was calm until it wasn't, like a fire station until the alarm sounds. Our call to action came during early morning briefing sessions. Walking into the cave you would see a large chalkboard and map covered by a curtain at the other end of the cave, above a small wooden platform. From there the CO announced the crews flying that day, which always drew a reaction: nervous energy for some, sighs of relief from others. An S-2 intelligence officer would rise and remove the covering from the map and we could see a ribbon stretched from Amendola to the target, which drew a louder reaction, the old hands jawing especially loud if it was going to be a tough ride. Then the S-2 briefed us on the target and provided information about the anticipated locations and levels of flak and enemy fighters. Another officer would provide details about the mission, the formation to be flown, and the IP, the initial point of the bombing run, usually about twenty miles out. A weather officer would usually rise and give a weather report and trending weather patterns. Finally, Father St. John or some other chaplain would offer words of hope and encouragement, ending with a prayer in our behalf.

After the briefing we jumped into six-by-six trucks for a ride to the airfield, stopping at the supply shack for our flight gear—Mae Wests, parachutes, and survival packs, which contained crackers and chocolate, some money, a compass, and maps. Another standard issue item was a Colt .45 revolver, which I kept in a shoulder holster. Some guys did not carry them because they added to the bulkiness of the flight gear, and others felt they would be better off if they were captured without a weapon.

The first time the alarm went off for my crew was January 17, 1944. Thirty heavies armed with 500-pound bombs flew to the Tuscany region that day. Our targets were the railroad marshalling yards and adjacent industrial buildings located between Prato and the Monte Retaia northwest of the city. We didn't encounter any resistance on the way to the targets and faced only a little flak on the return flight. It was a milk run.

We had three more missions over the next seven days: two milk runs and then a stiff ride to Rome. On January 24, 1944, I sent Peg a V-mail.[1]

> My darling,
>
> Just a little lonesome tonight, dear. I know my letters must seem awfully dull to you. It is because we never do much to talk about here. What we do we can't write about. You know how that is. I can tell you that I have been over Rome, Palermo, Naples, and a few more large cities in Italy.

I couldn't tell her about the carpet of flak we flew through to get to the Ciampino Aerodrome or the dozen or so Forts that got nicked up, their skins showing significant rug burns. I didn't write about my fears, and it wasn't because I didn't want to worry her. I just considered our missions high-intensity experiences. I was not consumed by fear. The joke was, "too scared to protest, too proud to admit it, and too dumb to quit." What I really felt may have been even more alarming to Peg: how absolutely alive I felt. Primal instincts sharpened with a surfeit of adrenaline elevated my senses. I was among the hunted, focused on avoiding the blast that could end my life.

We flew three more missions in four days. We hit an aerodrome in Lavariano with fragmentation bombs, then another one outside of Udine. We flew another mission two days later to Budapest, Hungary, getting as far as Yugoslavia before being ordered back to camp because of 10/10 cloud cover over the target, an industrial complex. We didn't get credit for that one.

After only two weeks of combat I saw planes shot up and shot down. I saw cockpits aflame and plane parts strewn across the sky, bits and pieces torn off by cannon fire or flak and condemned by heat and gravity. Worse yet were the sounds over the radio, the cries of anguished men, desperation in their voices, flesh singeing, blood hemorrhaging, spiraling to their deaths, alive one second, extinguished the next.

These were excruciating sounds, and I can still hear them. It happens most often when I am with family, enjoying time with my children and grandchildren. Their laughter is like a stethoscope, amplifying internal noises muted by time. Beating against the present, the indelible sounds of the war replenish my gratitude for having lived.

Returning from missions was a relief, but also eerie when there were casualties. Someone had to remove the possessions of downed crews from their tents and make room for replacement crews. For guys who did not return but were not confirmed dead, their things were stored in their footlockers on which "Missing in Action" was stenciled. The lockers were stored somewhere out of sight and out of mind.

You didn't need a report to know that someone had been killed in action. A guy wearing a new cap or donning new sunglasses was a walking obituary about the former owners. A sudden poker game with a large supply of foraged booze was a postmortem ritual. Stacks of clothes left at the base gate by local laundresses sloughed by the wayside like forgotten tombstones. Articles of unclaimed clothing tumbled across open fields sometimes getting trapped in the boughs of trees, flagging death.

Dozens of my friends died on missions from which I safely returned. They died in raids over Lavariano, Udine, Albano, Campoleone, Anzio, and Padua, Italy; many perished over Steyr, Austria; and still others were lost over Regensburg, Germany, and Toulon, France. They became persona non grata to those of us who survived—a strange, but necessary reaction. Talking about them was bad luck, a sure fire way to catch what they got. Given our slim chances of survival, the practice did not seem irrational at the time.

And then there was the reaction of ground crews. They were extremely attentive to the Forts, giving extraordinary care and consideration to every mechanical detail. It was not unusual to see them crying at empty hardstands, mourning the loss of their planes and crews. For those of us who did return, our own ground crews could become strangely aloof, not wanting to get too friendly because chances were high we would soon be gone too.

Notes

1. From the WWII files of Frank J. Kirkland Jr.

CHAPTER 18

A few of us went back to Bari for a day of R & R. The cobblestone streets were busy with locals trying to reestablish their lives and livelihoods. Brits and Yanks had money but very few places to spend it. The USO had a club there, nothing fancy, sandwiches, soda pop, and hot chocolate. But it was warm and comfortable, a place to relax and listen to music.

We found a café in the old part of town. It was a mom-and-pop operation that served a few dishes, mostly pasta. The wooden tables and chairs didn't match and were badly chewed up, looking as though they had been pulled from the rubble of fallen buildings.

We were enjoying our time away from flying, sharing a family-style meal, when three black pilots walked in, taking a table near us. The place grew quiet. The Italians had probably never seen black men before and we had never been in a restaurant with them. I was intrigued thinking about the difference a few thousand miles can make, and perhaps stared too long in their direction.

"Is there a problem, lieutenant?" one of them, a captain, asked.

"There's no problem," I responded.

"No problem, what, lieutenant?" he demanded.

He may have been in a segregated unit but that unit was still part of the Army Air Corps, and he was my superior officer.

"No problem, sir!"

I added, "In fact, why don't you pull up a chair and join us?"

Chui and Joe didn't say a word as the black officers pushed back their chairs and walked toward us. The colonel was first to speak after sitting down, introducing himself, and then his friends, both captains.

Looking over to me, the colonel said, "Lieutenant, don't mind Robert here. He's a little on edge, having just arrived from Camp Henry." But it was more than that, as we were about to learn.

We let them know we had been at Camp Henry too, and reminisced about the good times there, the parties, the dances. Soberly, one of the captains said blacks were not allowed in the clubs, so there were no dances for them. We tried to brighten the mood by giving a play-by-play description of the drinking game the night before we left, Chui standing up to reenact the scene. They listened and smiled, amused by his antics. They countered with another story, about having to sit in a roped off section at the movie theater on base and not being able to use the bathrooms there.

When they were at Camp Selfridge in Michigan, local government officials balked at the notion of black aviators training there. White women were escorted around the base by white military police. Later there was a near riot at Selfridge because black officers were refused entrance in the officers' club.[1] I don't remember much else that was said. But the rawness with which they spoke caught me off guard. I was seeing things more clearly, like a near-sighted man putting on glasses for the first time.

Things changed for the better for the Tuskegee Airmen when they got to Italy. They formed great friendships and strong bonds with white pilots. Many of them socialized together and race became less of an issue, for some. They were doing their jobs effectively and were respected for it, especially by bomb crews whose bacon they saved many times. That mostly changed when they returned from war, and it happened as soon as they set foot on US soil.

Some of the Tuskegee Airmen came home on Liberty ships, arriving at New York Harbor. They passed by the great symbol of democracy, the Statue of Liberty. Sailing forward they could see the red, white, and blue of flags festooned on outbuildings. As the ship nestled near the dock, they looked down on people waving American flags, waiting anxiously for their heroes' arrival. Walking down the gangplank in anticipation of their glorious return, the black airmen were confronted by a young white private standing at the bottom, directing traffic.[2] "Whites to the right, Negroes to the left," he barked.

We were back in the air the next day, one of thirty Forts flying to Toulon Harbor in southern France. Toulon was one of the largest and oldest harbors in Europe and home to German battleships and submarines. Approaching the IP, we encountered heavy flak. Shock waves from the ack ack shots crashed into our ship and concussive explosions rang in our ears as puffs of black smoke filled the sky.

Flak could rip through fuselages like a can opener and sever exposed control cables and electrical wires, and men from their limbs, in an instant. Most crews wore steel helmets and metal flak jackets for protection. Some gunners preferred to stand on their flak jackets to guard against blasts from below.

Joe asked me to fly that day so I was at the controls during the raid, flying tail end Charlie. A couple dozen Me-109s and Fw-90s, some of Goring's Yellow Nose Boys, hit us hard. We maintained a tight formation and made it to the harbor, hitting it with 90 tons of 500-pound general-purpose bombs, and destroying ships, docks, and rolling stock. We also knocked down at least six of their fighters while they managed to shoot down five Forts, all of them in my element, killing my friends Ford Bingham and Dab Lea, and their entire crew, and leaving our plane exposed to unimpeded attacks.

Two German fighters circled back around for us. We were out of the formation's cocoon with no fighter escort. I attempted to keep up with the other planes and merge into the protective cover of another element but I couldn't quite get there. Our plane was full of holes and fire erupted from the nacelles of engine nos. 1 and 3. Joe hit the red AFCE buttons to suppress the fires. It worked but the engines failed.

The plane was holding steady on two engines. It was up to our gunners to keep us alive. No one panicked, though. Over the interphone I could hear the gunners calling out incoming planes as casually as birdwatchers in the woods, "Bandit at 1 o'clock," one would say; "I see him," another would reply. They were calm and cool even as shell casings were piling up around their feet, hotter than fish grease.

Both German fighters were hit hard by our gunners. One of the pilots ejected from his ship and the other one fled, a trail of black smoke following him to the north. Seconds after ditching the Germans, engine no. 4 erupted in flames. We were down to one engine. I felt we still had a chance to make it if the fuel could hold out. We burned three-quarters of it getting to Toulon due to strong headwinds and the heavy payload we were carrying and lost more out of shredded fuel lines. Joe closed off the 1, 3, and 4 valves, stemming the flow of fuel to those engines.

The navigation system was destroyed and we were unsure of our bearings. The radio worked but we were reluctant to use it. We needed to call in for coordinates but the longer we stayed on the airwaves, the greater the chances the Germans could track the signal and find us.

Joe wanted to head for the Island of Corsica for an emergency landing. "Big Fence, over," Joe called out to Amendola. "Need coordinates for safe haven," referring to Corsica. All we heard was static and then silence. We quickly got off the air. We called in again. No response.

Joe and I were doing all we could to keep our bird in the air. We called out to our radio operator for help. "RO, you've got to make contact. Keep trying . . ." No response. "RO, do you copy?"

Finally, I called back to Johnson, our navigator. "Check on Knobbie. He's not responding."

Bill reported back. "He's unconscious."

"Check his tube," Joe instructed. Oxygen tubes iced over due to warm breath passing through cold air; frozen spit and drool clogged them too. You had to pay attention to your tube, check it regularly, and pinch it frequently to break up the ice. Without the oxygen flow, guys passed out. Some guys, none of ours, suffered from hypoxia, returning to base without a scratch but dead nonetheless.

We heard over the intercom, "Tube's frozen!" Bill pulled out an emergency bottle of oxygen and held the mask over Knoble's mouth and nose. "Eyes open! . . . He's up. . . He's okay, skip," came the report.

We never made radio contact with the base, so we dropped below the clouds to see what we could see. Soon we had CAVU-ceiling and visibility unlimited, and before long the French island came into view. It was dumb luck that we found it. As we began our descent, the fourth engine started to sputter. I feathered it back, nursing it along. It quit too. With no power, I had to fly the plane dead stick with only the drag of the flaps to slow us down.

Even though it was cold, sweat fell into my eyes as I struggled to maintain control of the ship. I could keep her airborne but had trouble with her speed. Too slow and we would sink. Too fast and we would overshoot the island and crash into the sea. As the plane descended we came in at a hard angle, smoke spewing from the engines. The dirt airstrip was short and narrow, more of a pick and shovel project. There were no signs of a tractor blade or the skill of an engineer. We were going to hit hard and hoped the brakes would stop the plane before the runway ran out. Joe dropped the landing gear on the approach but only the right tire emerged, and it had been obliterated. When the plane touched down, the metal rods of the landing gear post-holed the earth on impact, jerking the plane into a sudden, violent revolution. We spun around several times until the plane was spit out like a child on a funhouse ride. The plane skipped and skidded on its belly across a field some distance from the airstrip before coming to an abrupt stop. Pebbles and rocks pinged against the fuselage as a blanket of dirt rained down on the plane.

Dazed and disoriented, no one said a word. Had we cheated death? None of us knew for sure until Joe's voice broke the spell. Over the interphone he asked for a report. We were numbered one through ten, starting with the tail end.

We heard, "One. Okay, skipper."

"Two Alive and well, skip." When all ten of us were accounted for, the plane erupted with laughter and jubilation.

Joe said, "Gentlemen, let us give thanks to God that we are alive." Our navigator replied, "And don't forget to thank him for "Dead Stick" Kirkland. You got us home, Kirk! We're alive!" The plane rocked and swayed with joyful noise.

When the dust settled, we noticed a truck approaching in the distance, slowly zigzagging, until it stopped about fifty yards from the plane. It was fitted with a large mine sweeper extending from the front bumper. I opened the hatch to jump down when someone called out over a bullhorn, "Don't move! You are in danger!"

A tall redheaded soldier slid down from the hood of the truck. He was holding a bullhorn in one hand and a long metal rod in the other. He followed another soldier who was waving a metal detector back and forth over the ground as they approached the plane. They stopped occasionally, looking closely at the ground, probing with the rod.

When they got halfway to the plane, the redheaded soldier raised the bullhorn to his face, "That was quite the landing, boys. Don't think I've seen one quite like it," he joked, and then explained we had stopped in the middle of a restricted area, a minefield, left over from the German occupation of Corsica. He told us to stay in the plane until the mines could be cleared.

Sappers worked feverishly until dusk, clearing most but not all of the mines. We slept on the plane that night and stayed there until mid-morning. With the field cleared, we jumped into a truck and rode to camp, ending up at a Quonset hut where we rested and ate.

The corporal who helped us the night before stopped by to see how we were doing. He kept looking at me even as he was talking to other guys. "Do I know you?" he asked. I looked at him closely. His red hair stood out in my mind.

"You look familiar but I can't place you," I replied.

We retraced the places we'd been in the military, "No that's not it." And then I told him I was from Arizona. He was too. "I'm from Phoenix."

"Me too," he said astonishingly.

"I know who you are," he continued. "You're Frank Kirkland from Mrs. May's class."

I slapped my knee and nodded my head, "And you're Rex Earl."

We were friends in the first grade and hadn't seen each other for eighteen years. I never saw him again after that, but I took our chance meeting as a good omen, concluding that I was leading a charmed existence.

Notes

1. Stanley Sandler, *Segregated Skies: All-Black Combat Squadrons of WWII* (Washington, DC: The Smithsonian Institute Press, 1996), 122.

2. Alexander Jefferson and Lewis H. Carlson, *Red Tail Captured, Red Tail Free: Memoirs of a Tuskegee Airman and POW* (New York: Fordham University Press, 2005), xviii.

CHAPTER 19

As far as I could tell, the sign of the cross was one of the steps on the official operational check list for B-17 pilots because Joe checked out the plane and crossed himself religiously. There were seventeen items to check before we even started the engines, beginning with a pre-flight inspection and a review of Form 1A. Then there were seven more checkpoints. After that we started the engines—"both magnetos on, check"—and five more inspection points, including a crew report. Then five more checks for the engine run-up and three before take-off, "Tail wheel locked, check"; "Gyro set, check"; "Generators on, check." Once in the air, Joe always crossed himself before completing the rest of the checklist: wheels up, reduce power, close cowl flaps—check, check, check!

There were more than twenty other things on the checklist that had to be done before landing a Fort. Joe and I only managed to do a few of them when we crash landed on Corsica. Some steps couldn't be done because the equipment was shot up. Other steps were overlooked or forgotten in the pandemonium. Except for one: as we made our final approach Joe was tapping his forehead, chest, and shoulders. He did it again after we landed.

He insisted that surviving the Toulon raid was a matter of providence. "Kirk, we need God's blessing, and I don't plan to fly again without it," he said. By then we were back at Amendola figuring out what to do on a three-day pass. Joe asked me to go with him on a pilgrimage of sorts to seek a blessing from Padre Pio who lived two hours to the north.

"Who is Padre Pio?" I asked.

"He is the only priest in the history of the church with the stigmata. He bears the wounds of Christ on his hands, feet, and side."[1]

Although skeptical, I agreed to go with him on one condition: that we make a stop at San Severo Airfield where, rumor had it, Phil Cochran was flying Spitfires.

"After all we've been through, you're still itching to get into fighters, Kirk?" he asked.

"Joe, let me put it this way. It's as important to me as getting the padre's blessing is to you," I told him.

Padre Pio lived with six other Capuchin Friars in a small mountain monastery, although they called it a *convento*. He arrived there in 1916 at the age of twenty-nine and lived an austere life, conducting mass, hearing confessions, caring for the poor. He attracted thousands of the faithful, drawn by stories of his supernatural gifts.

The monastery was located in San Giovanni Rotondo. The town was established in 1095 A.D., the year the Pope launched the First Crusade to recapture Jerusalem. We entered the town in uniform, driving a jeep with a white star on the side. The town folk welcomed us, reaching out to shake our hands or touch our shoulders as we slowly passed by them on the crowded streets. This was heady stuff. I was from the newest state of a young country entering an ancient town with a history that pre-dated Christ. They shouted, "A-me-ri-ca bellissimo, bellissimo!"

We were their saviors fighting to recapture Rome.

A long dirt road, hedged up by mortarless stone walls and clusters of olive trees, connected the monastery and town. We turned on to it, passing poorly clad peasants on foot and a rusty flatbed truck puttering down the road. As we got closer to the monastery we passed a domed roadside shrine on the side of the road. Women were kneeling before it, their heads covered with black scarves.

It wasn't what I expected, the monastery and church. Grand and glorious they were not. The church was two-stories, squat with a single front door over which a small bell tower was perched. There were no stained glass windows, statuary, or sculpted gardens. The grounds and surrounding lands were barren and rocky.

The monastery was contiguous to the church, and it was just as plain. No adornments of any kind except for an arch-shape over the standard front door, roughly matching the one over the door of the church. Its windows were covered with bars, its plaster grimy.

The dirt courtyard was filled with people, civilians and servicemen, waiting to enter the church. A tin lizzie, its black paint badly faded, and a beautifully lacquered covered carriage were parked to the side. Small children sat in large wheel barrels, in between rakes and hoes. They could not attend mass because of their age, giving their fathers reason to stay outside. Carts and wagons with long wooden spokes and wooden wheels shod with steel bands were parked here and there, their beasts of burden still in harness. A couple of other wagons were parked with their tongues dipping to the ground and their beds tail end up, accounting for a wondering ox and horse.

The door to the church opened as we rolled to a stop, and the crowd rushed in to celebrate mass. A few people, including Joe, were turned away when the pews were filled. We waited outside with the young fathers and children for a while, listening to the organ music and choir.

One of the men engaged us in conversation. He spoke English so we asked about mass, when it starts, how long it takes.

"If it is Padre Pio, it takes two hours, un po' più," he said. I couldn't believe it.

"Two hours for mass?" I exclaimed.

"It is true," he continued. Pointing to a wheel on one of the carts that was as tall as a man, he added, "The longer the spoke the bigger the tire." He made a joke at the expense of the priest, and I laughed. Joe, thinking he was talking about the cart, just shrugged his shoulders.

We spent the night at a hotel down the road from the church. The next morning while walking to mass we were joined by a woman wearing a loose-fitting black dress with long sleeves. A silver cross on a chain hung around her neck and her head was covered with a black scarf. She introduced herself as Mary Pyle.

Mary was old, at least she seemed old to me back then—probably in her fifties. Born into a wealthy New Jersey family, she was a world traveler until meeting Padre Pio twenty years before. He asked her to remain in Italy to serve the church, and she did, funding the construction of a convent and seminary in Padre Pio's hometown. When he was assigned to San Giovanni Rotondo, she built a nice home—servicemen called it the Pink Castle close to the monastery. She attended mass daily and served as a secretary to the Capuchin priests. Her main duty was helping Padre Pio respond to the deluge of letters from people around the world asking for his blessing.

"You're going to mass today, are you boys?" Mary said. "Come to my home afterwards for some lunch, won't you? There will be other servicemen there too. They come all the time to the *convento*, hoping to meet Padre Pio and somehow end up at my table. My home is the pink one just down the way. You can't miss it," nodding her head in its direction.

I was planning to let Joe go into the church by himself, preferring to stay outside with the fathers and children. I liked being with them. Anyway, it seemed a whole lot better than spending two hours in a church meeting.

The prospect of a warm meal prepared by an American woman changed my plans.

"We would like that very much, wouldn't we, Joe? Would you mind showing us around the church?" I asked.

The interior of the church looked more like a church than the outside, reflecting the work of fine craftsmen. The walls and columns were clad with wainscoting, some of it wood-stained, other parts perfectly painted white with gold trim. Wooden panels adorned the front wall of the chapel. Each one ornately framed a painting of a religious figure, John the Baptist, Mary, Peter, and a few saints unknown to me. Arched alcoves bearing candelabras flanked the panels. Constructed below them were rows of long shelves filled with white flowers and tall candles. A large pedestal was centered in the front. It was skirted with gold embroidered cloth and a large figurine of Christ hanging from the cross that rested upon it. In front of the pedestal stood a long white alter decorated with a beautiful lace tablecloth.

Padre Pio entered the chapel and stood in front of the main alter. He had black, thinning hair and dark eyes. His face was mostly covered with a salt and pepper beard. His vestments were intricate and ornate, his hands covered with fingerless gloves. If there were wounds in his feet, hands, and side, they were covered. Raising his arms he began to speak, losing me after his first word, "*Bambini . . .*" For almost an hour he spoke sincerely, reverently, smiling, causing people to smile, even laugh. Although I didn't know what he was saying, I could tell when his words changed and his tone became more formal. Joe told me the padre had switched to Latin.

Joe followed along perfectly, genuflecting, kneeling, and standing like the rest of the faithful flock. I mostly sat but I did stand for some parts, not knowing why but enjoying it nonetheless, especially the part where we turned around and shook hands and exchanged embraces with the friendly people sitting behind us. An hour later, Joe and the others received communion, partaking of a wafer and a sip of wine from a common cup. Padre Pio then crossed their foreheads with his thumb, and they returned to their seats. The padre concluded with some kind of blessing and a prayer. I heard "*Ave Maria*" and then more Latin, or Italian.

Mary led us to a room she called the sacristy to meet Padre Pio. A handful of other servicemen greeted us as we entered. Soon the padre walked into the room and we all stood up. Wearing a simple white hooded robe with a sash tied to the side, his hands and feet still covered, he looked shorter and smaller than he appeared in the chapel. He did not speak English so Mary translated for us.

We stood in a row and he walked down the line handing out medals of the Virgin Mary and the Sacred Heart of Jesus. Joe asked if he could have a blessing instead of a medal, explaining that we had crash landed a few days before and needed his intercession. The padre was kind but firm, saying he was too tired to bless all of us and that it would be unfair to bless only one. Instead, he offered to bless our medals or anything else we had. Mary handed around a plate on which the men dropped dog tags, pilot wings, and the medals Padre Pio had just given them. Joe removed from his pocket two St. Christopher medals on chains and set them on the plate. The padre extended the plate heavenward and pronounced a blessing, speaking in solemn, earnest tones, and then handed the plate back to Mary. He was kind and courtly with us and then excused himself, saying it was time to hear confession. Joe retrieved his medals, handing one of them to me. "This is for you, Kirk. St. Christopher is the patron saint for soldiers. Wear it for safety," he said. I thanked him and slipped it into the side pocket of my jacket.

Joe got what he wanted and then it was my turn. After lunch we headed for San Severo Airfield, arriving late in the afternoon. Major Cochran was not there. He was in Burma, leading the 1st Commando Unit. I got the story from the commanding officer of the 31st Fighter Group, and a friend of Phil.

A new unit had been formed to provide air support for troops fighting the Japanese in Burma. When General Hap Arnold informed Phil he was being considered to head up the group, Cochran expressed his strong opposition to the assignment, emphasizing his wish to fly fighters in England.

"Phil told the General, 'I don't want to go to some side-alley fight over in some jungle in Burma . . . The big show is in England, and I've got this job ready to go over there. I want to do it, and I want to fulfill it, because I think it is my destiny, and I think it's my life,'" is the way the colonel put it.[2]

After the meeting, Cochran pulled every string he had to get out of it. He asked General Vandeberg to intercede, telling him that being sent to Burma would be an "injustice." He told his friends that he wouldn't go, that he didn't care about the consequences. In the end, General Arnold gave the order and Cochran obeyed.

I was frustrated as we headed back to Amendola. Joe got what he wanted from the trip while my high expectations were crushed. If I had confessed my feelings to our base chaplain he would have had every reason to chastise me for the twin sins of pride and envy. I am sure Joe must have felt that way about me. He asked if I had heard Mary's explanation of Padre Pio's homily during mass. I hadn't.

"He quoted from the Holy Bible, Luke 16:13," Joe said.

"Sorry, Joe, you might as well be speaking Italian or Latin for that matter. I have no idea what that means."

"Take a look for yourself. My Bible's in my duffel bag."

I opened the Good Book and read out loud the words underlined in red pencil, "*No servant can serve two masters: for either he will hate the one, and love the other; or else he will hold to the one, and despise the other.*"

"So what's the point, Joe?" I asked.

"I think it's pretty clear: you can't love God and love the things of this world. To do one excludes the other, but you can't have it both ways and be right with God."

"I get it, but why did you bring it up? Why did you have me read it?"

"Listen, Kirk. Ever since we've been together you've been moping about having to fly heavies. You're aching to get back into fighters, and now your ticket out is in Asia. What's that done to your head?"

"So that's what this is about? You're mad at me because I want to fly fighters?"

"I'm not mad. I am concerned, concerned for you and more concerned about our crew. I don't like to think you're double minded when we're in the air."

"When have I been double minded?"

"I see your reaction when we have fighter cover . . ."

"What on earth are you talking about? Since when has that affected my flying?"

"Never, but I need to know which way you stand. With us or with some fighter squadron you are not even a part of."

"I was with the 56th Fighter Squadron before I was with the 429th. Anyways, I am absolutely with you every time we go up. I'm with the crew, helping them, encouraging them all the time," I said.

"I know, and nobody knows better than me what you mean to our crew. Maybe I'm overreacting . . ." Joe dropped the subject. Confrontation wasn't his style. Instead he switched back to Padre Pio and *his* frustration over not getting a blessing from him as he had hoped.

"I was counting on that blessing. I felt impressed to go there. . . . I have a funny feeling we're going to need the good Lord's help in the days ahead," Joe explained.

"Every crew does, Joe. Most of us will die. I see no reason for God to favor us over any of the other boys. Let's keep our heads up, and drop as many eggs as we can for as long as we can. What else can we do? There's no easy way out. You fly the missions until you die or until you hit the magic number and go home," I said.

"So you don't think my prayers and faith are enough to get us home?" Joe asked.

"I think you should do what helps you feel at peace. Our crew needs you to be calm, to lead. But as far as God's intervention, I don't see that it would be fair for him to single us out over other crews. I'll trust that whatever happens is supposed to happen, and I'm content to live or die that way."

We arrived at the base at dusk. Before going to sleep, I reached in my jacket pocket and pulled out the St. Christopher medal Joe had given me. Slipping it over my head, I silently prayed for protection so I could finish seventeen more missions and get into fighters. I wore it for the rest of the war.

Notes

1.   "Saint Padre Pio da Pietrelcina," *Caccioppoli*, accessed March 5, 2014, http://cac cioppoli.com/.

2.   John Allison, "Phil Cochran: The Most Unforgettable Character I've Met!," *Air Commando Association*, accessed March 19, 2014, http://www.specialoperations.net /ColCochran.htm; "U.S. Air Force Oral History Interview-Col. Philip G. Cochran (November, 1975)," *Air Force Special Operations Command*, accessed February 3, 2016, http://www.afsoc.af.mil/AboutUs/AFSOCHeritage.aspx.

CHAPTER 20

President Roosevelt established a commission in August 1943 to work with the military to safeguard European art and monuments from theft and destruction.[1] The theft was at the hands of the Nazis; the destruction was the fault of both sides, most of it accidental.

In Italy, the job was enormous. In addition to the master works of artists like da Vinci, Michelangelo, and Raphael, there were ancient churches filled with iconic treasures that were vulnerable to indiscriminate warfare. These sacred sites were identified in the Army Service Forces Manual,[2] and the Army Air Corps went out of its way to avoid bombing them.

The Abbey at Monte Cassino was on the list of protected properties. It was one the most magnificent monasteries in the world. Built in 529 A.D., the abbey housed valuable manuscripts and works of art, including the Beuronese murals. It was also the thirteenth century home of the philosopher and theologian St. Thomas Aquinas. He was sent there when he was five years old to study with the Benedictine monks and remained there until he was thirteen.[3]

Historically, Monte Cassino Abbey had been a victim of its strategic hilltop location, 1,700 feet above the town of Cassino. Overlooking the Liri Valley, Monte Cassino was a prominent defensive location. By controlling the high ground, an army could control the valley below. As a result, the abbey was destroyed three times in battles prior to World War II, the last time by the Normans in 1046.[4] The church rebuilt the abbey each time, adding to the grandeur of the building with each successive effort.

In early 1944 the town of Cassino became an integral part of the Gustav Line, Germany's hundred-mile defensive line that stretched from coast to coast and Germany's last, best hope to prevent the Allies from advancing further north. There were four bloody assaults on the Gustav Line from January 17 to May 18, 1944. One of the fiercest battles was at Monte Cassino, resulting in 75,000 casualties from both sides.[5]

The German 1st Parachute Division demolished every building and cleared away the trees below its defensive position so any Allied movement coming up the valley could be detected. The Rapido River was swollen which narrowed the landmass on which Allied troops could advance. Adding to the difficulty, the Germans filled the passable land with mines and assembled nests of machine guns on higher, nearby ground.

The abbey was a key defensive component since it overlooked Highway 6, the surest way to Rome for the Allies. German soldiers dug into the hillsides around the abbey and fired down on the advancing troops while spotters were directing German artillery fire from within the abbey.

On January 24th, the 100th Battalion, an all Japanese-American unit, was given the task of taking the town of Cassino.[6] They were fierce and determined fighters. Their commitment was made all the more remarkable because of what had happened to their families back home. After Pearl Harbor, President Roosevelt ordered them into relocation camps. By 1944, there were more than 110,000 Japanese-Americans living in barracks behind barbed wire fences, mostly in Utah, California, and Arizona.[7] In the process they lost their jobs, homes, lands, and businesses.

The 100th Battalion was known as the "Purple Heart Battalion." Its 1,300 soldiers were awarded 1,700 Purple Hearts.[8] Their bravery became legendary at Cassino. At some point during the battle, Companies A and C made it to the river. The 187 men of B Company tried to follow them but got caught in machine gun and artillery fire. Only fourteen of them made it to the river.[9]

With so many men getting killed in Liri Valley, Allied commanders made the controversial decision to bomb Monte Cassino and take out the abbey. On February 14, Allied artillery shot leaflets around the town and abbey, warning the civilians of the imminent bombing. US planes dropped warning notices too.

Early the next day, I was in the briefing room at Amendola when the mission to bomb Monte Casino Abbey was announced. We knew of its historic significance but debating the wisdom of the mission was above our rank and pay grade. We just flew the missions. It wasn't our job to analyze the morality of them. But we were aware of the perilous conditions facing our troops there and were anxious to help them out.

My crew didn't fly that day. Anxious to get more missions, I volunteered to fly copilot with another crew. Thirty-six Forts took off, each carrying twelve 500-pound bombs. We came in low as we approached Monte Cassino, flying at around 6,000 feet. Surprisingly, there was no interference from enemy aircraft. The flak field was brimming, though.

We got off our bombs and banked toward home. Just then a chunk of shrapnel ripped through the port side of our plane and sliced through the navigator's skull. Blood spurted everywhere. The bombardier injected him with morphine, sprinkled sulfa powder into the wound, and wrapped his head with pressure bandages. The bandages were submerged in blood within seconds. The navigator was unconscious, his face ashen. He was dying.

We didn't think he could make it to Amendola so we decided to break from the formation and head to Madna Airfield, just south of Termoli near the Adriatic coast. We reported the situation and headed east.

Our pilot radioed to the crew, "We're on our own, fellas, watch out for Jerry."

Within minutes two P-40s appeared. A voice came over our radio frequency: "We'll escort you to Madna. Don't worry about E/As; we've got you covered!" They got so close we could see them.

A crewmember said, "Check it out, skip. Night Riders!" Our escorts were black pilots from the 99th Fighter Squadron.

They stayed with us until our final approach to the airfield. Tipping their wings, the fighter pilots said good-bye and returned to their base at Capodichino. A medical team was waiting for us when we landed, and they rushed the navigator to the hospital where he died a few hours later.

Three days after the abbey was destroyed, the 100th Battalion began the final assault on Monte Casino. A platoon of forty men rushed up the hill but was repulsed at the halfway point, and only five returned. After days of intense fighting and considerable reinforcements from the 34th Division, the 100th took Monte Cassino.

After the war, President Truman addressed the 500 survivors of the Purple Heart Battalion during a Presidential Unit Citation ceremony. "You fought not only the enemy, but you fought prejudice, and you won,"[10] he said. Whether known to the president or not, the battalion had another nickname. Anglo troops called them "the little iron men." The tag was better than "Night Riders," which had nothing to do with the time of day or color of the sky.

We were grounded by bad weather many times. The downtime was frustrating to me, irritating really, like a fisherman feels untangling a bird's nest, angry about the fish getting away.

There was a way to make up for lost missions, though. You could get double credit for flying extremely perilous ones. The intensity of these was a notch or two above the run of the mill dangerous kind to which we were accustomed.

Crews that flew during Operation Argument between February 20 and 25, 1944, got double credit. The operation targeted German aircraft manufacturing facilities in Leipzig, Brunswick, Gotha, Regensburg, Schweinfurt, Augsburg, Stuttgart, and Steyr. The objective was two-fold: destroy the plants and wipe out the Luftwaffe that would be sent up to defend them. If successful, the Allies would have air superiority for the invasion of Europe that was to follow.

In what became known as Big Week, the 8th Air Force flew 3,000 sorties during Operation Argument, losing 140 bombers and a dozen fighters. The 15th flew 500 sorties, losing 90 bombers and a couple of dozen fighters. On the other side, Germany lost more than 355 fighter planes trying to protect the targeted factories.[11]

On February 24th, heavies from the 5th Bomb Wing flew over the Alps to Steyr, Austria. Our target was an aircraft components factory. It was defended by 150 enemy aircraft, mostly Me-109s, and heavy flak. Fourteen of our Forts were shot down that day, half of them from the 49th Squadron. When we got back to Amendola, Major Kutchera told us we got double credit for the mission. It was his 50th, and last, mission, and I went from 12 to 14.

Weather conditions improved in early March. We flew three missions in three days. After that, more rain. The skies were clear early in the morning of March 11th as we took our seats in the briefing room. The target that day was a railroad marshalling yard located in Padua, a city in northern Italy. In addition to the usual briefing business, the CO pointed to a large aerial photograph. A building near the rail yard was circled in red.

With pointer in hand, the CO tapped the red circle. "Gentlemen, this is the Church of the Eremitani, a very famous church. It is on the list of protected properties, three stars out of three![12] You must be extremely careful to avoid it. We're catching flak for Monte Cassino Abbey. The Krauts are using it for propaganda, claiming we're trying to destroy European culture. I can also tell you the Pope was not too happy about it, that's for sure. So stay clear of the church! Got it?"

The ground crew was waiting for us as we pulled up to the plane. They were all smiles standing in front of our shiny, new B-17 G, excited about the plane's first mission. One of them had a camera and wanted to take a picture. "We'll take it when we get back, Hal," Joe told him. "We gotta get going." And with that the ground crew jumped into action.

It looked much like the old Forts we'd been flying, except for its pristine condition and the addition of a chin turret. This modification was a reaction to the Luftwaffe's new tactic of flying its fighters through the front of our formations. Since there was a gun pointing in every other direction, it made sense to come at us directly. Now we had a counter-measure, a forward-facing gun.

The other difference was the name on the plane. Up to that point, we hadn't bothered naming our ship like a lot of outfits had. Names were painted on the noses of planes, often with some kind of artwork. Some names symbolized the damages the planes had endured, like *Leak'in Lena*, *Flak Happy*, and *Hangar Queen*. A lot of them were named for women, real or imagined: *Sahara Sue*, *Shady Lady*, *Raggedy Ann*, *Sky Witch*. Others were calls to arms, like *V for Victory*, *Winged Fury*, and *War Eagle*.

We looked up at the plane and saw, written in script, *My Eva*. There was no portrait of a pin-up model or a lingerie-wearing vixen, there was just plain, *My Eva*.

One of the waist gunners, Freeburn Jones, asked, "Who is Eva?"

"Isn't that Hitler's girlfriend?" someone said. Everyone laughed, except the crew chief.

"That puts a whole new twist on *Kraut Chaser*," I added, referring to another Fort we had seen around. We laughed some more. The chief was turning red at this point.

"Wait a second, fellas," Joe piped in. He had given the honor of naming the new bird to the chief. "Who is Eva, chief?" Joe asked.

"She's named after my mom," the chief said. "I can't wait to tell her. She'll be so proud."

We had seen a *My Gal Sal* and a *My Baby*, but no references to anyone's mother. Everyone ganged up on the chief, giving him a hard time for the squishy name on our plane.

"Just take care of Ma and Ma'll take care of you. I expect her back in fine form this afternoon," he told us.

We all groaned as we made ready for take-off.

Notes

1.   *Records of the American Commission for the Protection and Salvage of Artistic and Historic Monuments in War Areas (The Roberts Commission), 1943–1946* (Washington, DC: National Archives and Records Administration).

2.   *Civil Affairs Handbook, Italy, Section 17A: Cultural Institutions Central Italy* (Washington, DC: Army Services Forces, 1944).

3.   "Monte Cassino," *The Order of Saint Benedict*, accessed March 25, 2014, http://www.osb.org/gen/monte.html.

4.   Ibid.

5.   "Battle of Monte Cassino," *Wikipedia*, accessed March 24, 2014, https://en.wikipedia.org/wiki/Battle_of_Monte_Cassino.

6.   "Nisei," *Monte Cassino Tours*, accessed February 16, 2016, http://montecassino-tours.com/index.php/page/id/6/nisei.html.

7.   "War Relocation Authority Camps in Arizona, 1942–1946," *Through Our Parents' Eyes: History & Culture of Southern Arizona*, accessed February 3, 2016, http://www.parentseyes.arizona.edu/wracamps/.

8.   "Nisei Soldiers of Hawaii," *100th Infantry Battalion Veterans Education Center*, accessed February 3, 2016, http://www.100thbattalion.org/history/stories/nisei-soldiers-hawaii/.

9.   Ibid.; "100th Infantry Battalion (Untied States)," *Wikipedia*, accessed February 3, 2016, https://en.wikipedia.org/wiki/100th_Infantry_Battalion_(United_States).

10.   "Nisei Soldiers of Hawaii."

11.   Martin W. Bowman, *USAAF Handbook, 1939–1945* (Mechanicsburg, Pennsylvania: Stackpole Books, 1997), 27, 256; "'Big Week'—Daily USAAF Raids on German Factories," *World War II Today*, accessed January 22, 2014, http://ww2today.com/24-february-1944-big-week-daily-usaaf-raids-on-german-factories; Williamson Murray, "Attrition and the Luftwaffe," *Air University Review*, accessed January 22, 2014, http://www.au.af.mil/au/afri/aspj/airchronicles/aureview/1983/mar-apr/murray.htm.

12.   *Civil Affairs Handbook, Italy, Section 17A: Cultural Institutions Central Italy.*

CHAPTER 21

The Padua mission turned into a mess. The planes in the forward half of our formation passed over the marshalling yards without dropping their bombs because another group attacking from a lower, different axis was in the drop zone. They were clear of the target by the time the second half of the formation crossed over the target, so it was bombs away for us. The lead element did a 360 to the IP and back so the planes in the first half of the formation could drop their bombs. We in the second half mechanically followed like cars on a roller coaster.

When we reached the Adriatic Sea, the fighter squadron that escorted us to Padua was gone and the first sixteen Forts were far ahead of us. We tried to catch up but were intercepted by an armada of Junker Ju 88 bombers surrounded by Me-109s, Ma-202s, and Fw-190s. Some of the Messerschmitts and Focke-Wulfs peeled off, and attacked us in three groups of six, dropping their wing tanks to increase speed and agility.

Hitting us from behind, they fired their cannons and rockets from every button hole. The rockets were housed under the wings in bazooka-like launchers. In order to fire them, the 109s and 190s had to fly about 500 feet above us at a range of no more than 3,000 feet. The trajectory of the rockets was not always accurate but if they scored a hit, the damage was devastating. Even if they missed, the detonations were so powerful they could break up a formation, giving the Germans what they wanted, a single Fort to attack.

About half of the Forts took cannon fire. Bill Peters's plane was hit by a rocket, leaving a two-foot hole between engine nos. 1 and 2. The plane began to lose speed and altitude as a huge fire consumed the wing, and then the rest of the plane on the way down. The entire crew was killed.[1]

Gunners from the various Forts returned the fire, knocking down an E/A on each of the first two passes. Another wave of them came at us. Cannon shells pounded *My Eva's* fuselage and one shell whizzed past my ear, ripping the oxygen mask off my face. Seconds later, our wing was strafed and started to unravel. But we held steady for another ten minutes after that, still firing our cannons. Then a rocket slammed into our tail section and a fire erupted in engine no. 3, followed by more fire in engine nos. 1 and 4. Even though engine no. 2 was operating, we were unable to control the plane any longer. She started to plummet. Joe held her steady, pointing her to the coast of Yugoslavia. At 4,000 feet, he ordered us to get ready to bail. The guys in the ball turrets rolled out and had just enough time to put on their chutes.

The waist gunners had a hard time jettisoning the waist door, which was their way out. The tail gunner, Carl Anderson, removed the tail door easily but didn't want to jump, fearing the waist door might break free and hit him as he bailed out. He moved to the middle of the plane and watched as the other guys jumped. At 3,000 feet Joe pointed the nose of the plane downward to ensure an imminent crash.

I didn't hesitate when it was my turn to jump. It wasn't that hard of a decision since the alternative was dying in a fiery ball in a matter of seconds. Carl was sitting calmly at the waist door preparing to jump as Joe launched out the nose hatch behind me. Seconds later Carl's legs were jerked out of the plane by the slipstream. His head smashed into the side of the waist door. His chute never opened.[2]

It was the first time any of us had jumped from a plane. At Randolph Field we practiced on the ground. We learned how to don a parachute, a clumsy process at first. Standing in rows, we were taught how to open our chutes, reaching for the rip cord ring over and over with each blast of a whistle. We learned to gather the chute as if we had just landed, pulling it inward and rolling it up. We also received classroom instruction about the fundamentals like altitude, distance, timing, and speed.

The first parachute jump from an Army plane happened at Kelly Field in 1917. An enlisted man named Rodman Law jumped out of a Jenny at 2,000 feet.[3] He landed on the roof of a hangar and broke his leg. I didn't do any better on my first attempt.

As my canopy blossomed I looked around to get my bearings. My crew was scattered to the wind, and I was being jerked around by turbulent winds. I couldn't see anyone's chute except Joe's, and he was half a mile away. I could see German vehicles in the distance. No doubt the German pilots radioed our location and their soldiers were already looking for us. I was on my own and began planning my escape. I looked at my watch. It was not quite 2:30 p.m. I could see a woman plowing a field. *Perhaps she would help me*, I thought. I had money, American cigarettes, and chocolate with which to barter. It was also possible I could get help from one of the resistance groups but I didn't know if I was in Partisan or Chetnik territory.

The ground was rising fast and I braced myself for the impact, slamming hard into the rocky ground on the side of a steep hill. The wind dragged me toward a low slung wall. I frantically tried to gather my *Switlik*[4] before the Germans spotted me. Scanning the landscape, I saw movement. A big man was darting across the hill from tree to tree. He would run, drop to the ground, and roll behind cover. I crawled to the wall and pulled out my Colt .45. I heard a clicking sound. It came from about fifty feet away. My heart pounded as I considered my options. Then another *click, click*. It was the sound you might hear a cowboy make to his horse, as in, *giddy up Diablo, click, click*. The man looked nothing like a cowboy—no hat, no western-style boots—but he sure clicked like one. He had a thick beard and wore a white tunic and loose fitting pants that ballooned at the knees. Since he was not in uniform I knew he wasn't a German soldier. Still I couldn't tell if he was Ustashi or some other kind of German sympathizer.

Again, *click, click*. I set my jaw and clicked, clicked back. He called out, "Tadeski?"

I remained silent, having no idea what he saying.

Then he said, "Deutsch?"

I yelled back, "No!"

"Engleska?"

"No!"

"Americki?"

"Yes!"

He darted from behind a boulder and headed for the wall. I could hear him shimmying along the other side of the wall, heading my way. I was on my back, holding my .45 in my hands, both arms fully extended, the way Uncle Jim held his pistol in his day. The man suddenly rose above the wall and seemed surprised to be looking into the barrel of my pistol. His eyes narrowed as he put up his hands. He was unarmed. He glanced quickly at my legs and feet. His face contorted. I looked down and noticed for the first time my right foot was twisted backwards: toes to the ground.[5] This wouldn't have been a problem if I was on my stomach but I was sunny side up. The stranger stepped over the wall and kneeled beside me. He patted the ground, signaling me to put the gun down. I complied, dropping it just as the pain found me. I closed my eyes: *think, Frank, think!* Without warning, he grabbed my foot, yanked it downward and twisted it clockwise. I lost consciousness, overcome with pain and the grating sound of shattered bone.

When I came to, the man was kneeling beside me, holding my gun. I thought he was going to use it on me. Instead, he pointed down the hill and put his fingers to his lips, telling me to be quiet. Wheeling around me, he lifted me up from behind so I could get a glimpse of what was happening. A truck was screeching to a stop. Half a dozen German soldiers jumped out and headed up the hill toward the wall, toward me.

Suddenly, gunfire rained down on them. I turned around to see where the shots were coming from. Two young women with machine guns were running down the hill, their guns waist high, spraying bullets. They were in uniform and wore dark green caps with red stars at the crest. They were Partisans. A dozen teenaged boys, no more than fifteen or sixteen years old, emerged from a thicket with grenades in each hand and more dangling from theirs trousers, like bunches of swollen grapes. They were running pell-mell, heaving grenades with deadly accuracy. They ran passed the south side of the wall, taking the fight to the Germans and diverting them away from me. The Germans returned the fire but seemed uncertain and disorganized, running in circles as if tethered to a pole—each movement shortening their lives.

Even though I was immobile, the astounding scene caused me to twitch and sway with the forward surge. My heart was pounding, connected piston-like to my brain, which was telling my body to move, to fight. My sense of sight and sound intensified as fire sprayed from gun muzzles and bullets bellowed out in angry bursts. The German volleys sheared off tree limbs, ricocheted off rocks, and clipped my covering place, but the downward assault was unrelenting.

My ears were still ringing when the shooting and explosions stopped. I propped an elbow over the wall to survey the scene. The Germans lay dead, some in a heap and others splattered and sprinkled across the landscape, appearing as lumps of grey-green wool, their steel helmets mostly covering their faces. It must have been such a surprise to them. It was to be a routine operation: capture a downed pilot and send him to a stalag. What could be easier?

The skirmish over, I fell to the earth as bits of spent gunpowder filled the air. The sweet, metallic smell was indelible, like cut grass or desert rain. For the first time I noticed how cold it was. I could see my breath hit the wall and disappear. A sheet of crusty snow lay in the shadow of the wall. All of a sudden, hot air hit my neck, disappeared, and returned. Rolling away from the wall I came nose to nose with a bewhiskered old workhorse. Without warning the Yugoslavian cowboy picked me up by the waist and slung me over the horse's bare back like a sack of cracked wheat, my arms and legs dangling down from each side. One of the young women led the horse up the hill, a machine gun slung over her back. The cowboy took up the rear, my gun in his waistband, never to be returned. The other girl and the boys disappeared into the woods.

I was an eyewitness to many acts of heroism during the war. My crew and squadron exhibited unthinkable courage for men so young and inexperienced. I met bona fide heroes too: generals, a Congressional Medal of Honor winner, aces with columns of kill marks painted on the sides of their fighters. But gallantry was never more evident to me than that morning on an obscure hillside in Yugoslavia when young strangers ran headlong into fury for me.

The horse walked haltingly, the roll of each step causing a hot prod of pain in my leg. I arched my back and strained my neck to look up to see where we were going. After a quarter mile I gave up. Exhausted, I lay my head on the heaving ribcage of the poor animal and watched as the snow level increased against the trunks of the trees as we climbed higher up into the mountains.

Notes

1. Charles W. Richards, *The Second Was First* (Bend, Oregon: Maverick Publications, 1999), 217–18.

2. Ibid., 218–19.

3. WPA Texas, *Randolph Field: A History and Guide* (New York: The Devin-Adair Company, 1942), 36.

4. When he returned to the United States, Frank applied to the Switlik Company for membership in the Caterpillar Club, an association of people who successfully used a parachute to bail out of a disabled aircraft. His application states he was using a chest type parachute, serial no. 4299974. On the back of the application he wrote his "Emergency Jump Story," in his elegant handwriting. It states in part, "On March 11, 1944 after making run on target and dropping bombs on assigned target we were hit by cannon fire from fighter type aircraft. We maintained altitude as long as possible with three engines badly hit . . . " The original membership certificate was found in the WWII files of Frank J. Kirkland Jr. The Switlik Parachute Co., Inc., kindly provided the original application for club membership to the author on April 8, 2015.

5. Kirkland and five other members of his crew were awarded Purple Hearts: William J. Johnson, George Lund, Joseph F. Senta, Herman J. Le Grand, Floyd M. Le Master. General Orders No. 11, Headquarters, Second Bomb Group, Army Air Forces, Office of Commanding Officer, March 25, 1944, from the WWII files of Frank J. Kirkland Jr. Kirkland's citation reads, in part, "For wounds received in action against an armed enemy while participating in an aerial bombardment mission over Italy, on March 11, 1944. Lieutenant Kirkland, a copilot of a B-17 type aircraft was forced to parachute from his plane after vain attempts to feather an engine. At 2,000 feet the engine burst into flames and the aircraft became uncontrollable. The parachute descent was made during high winds and into rocky ground, and as a result, Lieutenant Kirkland was injured. His courage and devotion to duty reflect great credit on himself and the Army Air Forces."

CHAPTER 22

They gently lowered me into a bed. It was warm, an old lady having occupied it just seconds before. After settling in, I injected my leg with morphine. When the pain subsided, my head was clear enough to take in my surroundings. I was in a small log cabin. A ribbon of mortar closed the gaps between each log. A stone fireplace occupied the main room. Wood crackled in the fire, a large copper pot rested on the flames. I was offered soup and black bread. I tried to eat but had no appetite. The bread was filled with straw, the soup, mostly water.

The next day I awoke to a convention of folks. A middle-aged man came forward. He had worked in the coal mines of Pennsylvania and returned to his homeland to live out his retirement years. In broken English he explained that I was in an area heavily patrolled by the Germans, and that the Partisans would take me to another village soon.

A slender hand with a missing index finger fell on his shoulder and he stepped back from the bed. One of my hillside heroines came forward. She bent over and kissed me on both cheeks, a Star of David dangled down from a chain around her neck. Her name was Regina. Looking to my translator, I asked him to tell her how grateful I was to her for rescuing me.

She looked at me closely, her face weathered and drawn. Slowly she spoke, her dark eyes boring into mine. The man explained, "She did not do it for you. She did it for her people. You are here to kill Germans. She is here to kill Germans."

She had been fighting for nearly three years, ever since her Jewish father was killed by the Ustashi and her mother and sisters were interned by the Germans at Lobor-grad, a concentration camp of sorts, along with 1,600 other Jewish women and children.[1] She said she would continue to fight until she was dead or the Germans were gone. Without emotion she told of German and Ustashi atrocities against the Jews: firing squads that murdered innocent civilians, children torn apart by hungry dogs as entertainment for sadistic guards, and people buried alive in large pits. She was only twenty-one yet there was nothing youthful about her.

I was carried outside and placed on the back of a waiting motorcycle. Regina removed her red star cap and handed it to me. I gave her all the money I had. She handed it to someone else and walked away. The driver kick-started the bike and we set off. I had no idea where we were going. I was a helpless babe, unable to communicate, unable to walk, no way to protect myself.

I never saw Regina again. I hope she lived a long life. If she did, she was most likely without the companionship of her mother and sisters. I learned later that many Lobor-grad internees were shipped to death camps.[2]

The next week was spent evading Krauts. More precisely, I was carried and carted away from them, over mountains, across streams, through the woods. At one point I was slung over the back of another horse and led over a mountain by a twelve-year-old boy. It seemed we were in a chess match, and the Germans were anticipating all our moves. We were headed for the Adriatic Sea, and they knew it, so they heavily patrolled the marked roads leading to the sea. We had one advantage though: the Partisans knew the woods, each pass and switch back, every cave and hiding place.

I arrived at a village one night in a *kola*, a wooden cart, and was carried to a barn next to a stone cottage. Joe was inside, resting on some straw. Holding up my St. Christopher medal away from my neck I asked him, "What happened to our patron saint?"

"You're alive, aren't you?" he retorted.

"Yeah, but it seems we had a better time of it at Corsica—before Padre Pio or the great Saint Christopher ever got involved," I responded.

"It's good to see you, Kirk," Joe said.

"It's really good to see you too, Joe!"

Joe could speak a little Serbian and had news about the fate of our crew. Some locals told him they found Carl's body and gave him a proper burial in a church cemetery. The rest of the crew was under the protection of the Partisans in the mountains somewhere. We were going to join them at some point, but the details of the escape plan were not divulged.

I asked Joe for some morphine. He didn't have any. His leg was broken too. By the time we jumped from the plane we had less altitude to work with, leading to our rough landings. It would be a long, cold night without some pain relief. A woman came in with two small boiled potatoes, some cheese, and black bread. We devoured the food. She handed us tall tin cups full of amber liquid made from plums called slivovic. Joe said it was to ease the pain. It burned like fire all the way down but it did take my mind off the leg. There was plenty of clean straw on which to rest but no fire. I slept well anyway.

Smoke was rising across the valley the next morning. Stukas had bombed and strafed the village I had been in the day before. Large and angular, Stuka aircraft were manned by a single pilot and a rear gunner. Their landing gears were fitted with sirens called Jericho-Trumpets, making them sound like screaming banshees as they hurtled toward their target, adding to the terror.

They were in the air every morning patrolling the mountain, looking for us. When my guides shouted, "aviani!" I knew to look for the menacing machines and came to expect a sudden jump into the woods.

I had an Arizona connection with these rugged mountain men. A prosperous Phoenix businessman immigrated to the Arizona Territory from Yugoslavia in 1879. His name was Martin Gold. Like my father he worked as a teamster hauling supplies and materials around the territory. And like my father he married a Mexican woman. He developed land south of Van Buren Street into a desirable Mexican neighborhood and a successful business district known as "Gold's Alley." He also built the 1000-seat Ramona Theater on 3rd Street and Washington. It featured movies, vaudeville shows, and on Fridays, amateur night for musicians and artists.[3] While the entertainment was terrific, the greatest draw to me was its air conditioning, and I slipped into the icy air whenever I could come up with a dime.

Mr. Gold's land holdings included 320 acres north of the Salt River, land near my grandparents' place, land that became part of Sky Harbor Airport, land that I played on as a boy, and the land where I discovered airplanes.[4]

Martin's homeland was called Croatia, not Yugoslavia, when he left for America. It existed in one form or another from the days the Greeks settled the Dalmatian coast in the fourth century. For hundreds of years, the people of that region, Slavs, Croats, and Serbs, were caught regularly in the crossfire of wars, battles, and conflicts between neighboring states and kingdoms. It was the stomping ground for Crusaders and Mongol invaders. For a time, the fragments of Croatia were under the control of the Ottoman Empire, and repeatedly, the kingdom of Croatia was on the chopping block of rival kings and conquerors like Charlemagne and Napoleon who divided the spoils of their conquests among their allies.[5] In 1914, Serbian militants, wanting to sever Austria-Hungary's ties with its south Slav provinces, conspired to assassinate Archduke Ferdinand, heir to the Austro-Hungarian throne. His death triggered World War I. In the aftermath of the Great War, the State of Slovenes, Croats, and Serbs existed for a time before merging into the Kingdom of Yugoslavia.[6]

As Joe and I were winding our way through the mountains, we were surprised to see an OSS officer emerge from the trees. He was waiting for us. He shared some food and supplies and told us we were getting close to the coast. We were to assemble there with the rest of our crew, although he couldn't tell us exactly where. "The Partisans know where they're going," he told us. "That's all you need to know." We were being kept in the dark in case we got picked up by Germans. We were still in danger.

A few hours later the Dalmatian Coast came into view, the shades of alpine green giving way to gray rock and mottled blue water. Closely spaced islets jutted into the sapphire sea, looking like a footpath to nowhere.

We waited for hours in the hills, watching as German patrols rolled past us. We had to cross over a main road to get down to the rendez-vous point, a lighthouse. It had been an hour since the last patrol, so we began to cross, thinking Jerry had turned in for the night. A light rounded the bend, and we heard the roar of an engine heading our way. Soon, a motorcycle with a sidecar sped past. We waited another hour and tried again.

We got close to the lighthouse in the middle of the night. It appeared empty as we approached. There was no light and no sound except for a gentle splash at the seashore. Joe and I waited in the brush as our guides tried to make contact with someone inside, hopefully friendlies. They returned with Lieutenants Lund and Johnson who carried us to the lighthouse on their backs.

The rest of the crew quietly gathered round as we entered. Joe asked us to join him in prayer. With bowed head Joe began to pray, his words taking on a more deliberate tone at the end: "And lead us not into temptation, but deliver us from evil." He crossed himself, as did a couple of other men. We all said amen.

There was no time for catching up. Fishing boats were on the way to pick us up. One was coming up from the south, another down from the north. One boat was already there, anchored 300 hundred yards off the shore, waiting for Joe and me. The rest of the guys were to split up in the other two boats as they arrived.

The lighthouse rose up from a rocky promontory. A stone stairway led to the sea. We were rowed out to the fishing boat in a dinghy and hoisted aboard with a rope rig. Forty feet long, the ship's overall complexion was marred by imperfections: rust, a broken window, a patched-up hull, deep scratches, and chips exposing layers of paint. A tall, narrow cabin sat atop the front third of the deck under a single mast, the sail unfurled. Metal handrails enclosed most of the deck. There were a few bunks in the quarters below, next to the engine room, and below that, a well for storing fish.

The Germans allowed fishermen their living by plying the waters of the Adriatic. So it was in the normal course of things that boats could be seen line fishing or trawling. Joe and I were asleep below while the fishing crew went about its normal routine on deck. Suddenly one of them had me by the shoulders, shaking me. "Nimski! Nimski!" he screamed into my face. "Germans," Joe said. An S-boat was approaching rapidly. We were carried to the fish locker and told to lie down. We complied, not knowing what to expect. We heard a swooshing sound as fish started sliding down the chute. We were being buried under a pile of fish and placed our arms over our faces to create pockets of air. It became our sanctuary.

The Germans tied their boat to ours and came aboard. We could hear the conversation. The tone seemed even, nothing strident. We could hear the heavy footsteps above us. They grew louder as someone descended the steps. There was a pause, I'm guessing at the bunks, and then more steps down to the storage area. A three-foot wall of flopping fish separated us from whoever was lurking above. Next, I heard the sound of metal hitting a hard surface. I heard it again, and again. Straining to recognize the odd sound, it finally came to me. It was the sound of a bayonet blade passing through fish and striking the tank. Then there was another jabbing sound and another thud against the tank. Randomly, but methodically, the blade jabbed up and down. Clink. Clink. Clink. There was nothing to be done except lie there, and hope for the best. I decided if I were hit I would not make a sound, hoping Joe would not be found. Clinching my teeth I prepared myself for the deadly steel blade. Suddenly, the grating sound was replaced by the sounds of boots climbing stairs and the guttural whirr of the S-boat pulling away, our sanctuary rocking in its wake. We did not move or make a sound until the fisherman pulled us up out of the tank.

We arrived at Vis, a small island about eight miles wide and fourteen miles long. It was Tito's headquarters for a time and was occupied by British and American forces when we got there. A short landing strip in the middle of the island cut through acres of what had once been a vineyard that produced the region's best champagne. There were still remnants of the vines growing in terraced plots carved into the hillsides. A submarine pen emerged from one end of the island.

When I entered the medic's tent, I had two objectives: eat and bathe. My foot still flopped loosely below my calf, so the medics had something else in mind. After administering morphine, they twisted and pulled my foot into place, and then put my leg in a splint.

After that, I was allowed to clean up and eat, and then found my way to a cot. Two OSS officers sat down next to me. They were joined by an Army colonel and someone who said he was a liaison to the Royal Air Force. They asked for details about my ordeal and pressed me for information about German locations and tactics. The debriefing over, the men stood up to leave. The British chap asked if he could have a few more minutes. He said he belonged to a special society of airmen who had been shot down and evaded capture. He handed me a small gold patch in the shape of a boot and said, "It is my high honor and great pleasure to present you with this Winged Boot, emblematic of the courage, great strength, and good fortune of those who find their way to freedom. It is indeed my hope that this token will cause you to remember and never forget the many 'Helpers' who risked their lives in your behalf."

Notes

1. Harriet Freidenreich, "Yugoslavia," *Jewish Women's Archive*, accessed May 17, 2014, http://jwa.org/encyclopedia/article/yugoslavia.

2. Ibid.

3. David R. Dean and Jean A. Reynolds, "Migration, Marginalization, and Community Development, 1900–1939," accessed March 18, 2014, https://www.phoenix.gov /pddsite/.../pdd_hp_pdf_00045.pdf.

4. Ibid.

5. Joel M. Halpern and David A. Kideckel, Neighbors at War: Anthropological Perspectives on Yugoslav Ethnicity, Culture, and History (University Park, Pennsylvania: Pennsylvania State University Press, 2000), 86–88.

6. "Croatia," *The History Files*, accessed March 13, 2013, http://www.historyfiles .co.uk/KingListsEurope/EasternCroatia.htm; "Kingdom of Yugoslavia," *Wikipedia*, accessed March 13, 2013, https://en.wikipedia.org/wiki/Kingdom_of_Yugoslavia.

CHAPTER 23

J oe and I were placed on stretchers and carried off a British ship that had taken us from Vis to the Bay of Bari. Both of us were headed to the hospital. Our ground crew chief was waiting for us at the pier. After a friendly greeting he walked alongside us without saying a word. The hospital came into view and the medic told Chief he couldn't accompany us any further.

"Sergeant Anderson?" he asked. "Dead," Joe replied.

"*My Eva?*"

"A thousand pieces," I told him. "I hope you didn't already tell your mom you named our ship after her."

"Too late," he replied.

"Well," Joe added, "you can tell her *My Eva* was a magnificent fighting machine the short time we had her in the air." We all laughed.

We had been in Bari a few days when the order to return home came. The order of March 23, 1944, read

> Pursuant to auth. contained in letter, NATOUSA, File AG 383.6/384 A-O, dated 8 Feb 1944, Subject: "Return to the United States of US Personnel who have Evaded Capture by the Enemy," the following named Off and EM now casually at this station having evaded capture in enemy territory WP via mil or commercial aircraft, surface vessel, belligerent or otherwise, and/or rail from present station to US.[1]

This did not go over well with me. I protested to my commanding officer, expressing my fervent desire to remain in Italy, recuperate from my injuries, and finish my mission quota. I was so close to getting back into fighters, it was all I could think about.[2]

"Your commitment is, admirable, lieutenant but your orders are to return home. You will finish you service stateside," the CO said.

"But I need to finish my twenty-five missions here. I've been promised the opportunity to fly fighters after that . . ."

"If you ever get back in fighters, it will have to be stateside. You are finished over here and we are finished with this discussion. You are dismissed, lieutenant."

I offered a weak salute, turned, and left the building.

The reason for this strict policy of sending rescued flyers home finally sunk into my head on my journey home. If we had remained in the field and were shot down a second time and captured, the Germans would have leaned into us to extract vital information about the underground rescue operation. We knew enough about escape routes and Partisan methods and means, manpower, and weaponry to compromise their work and endanger their lives. And so we were sent home to avoid such outcomes, and the Germans knew it.

I flew from Bari to Casablanca in a C-47. While making arrangements there to travel to New York, I was warned about German spies, that they frequented local bars and cafés, hoping to strike up conversations with airmen or overhear their conversations which, after a few drinks, could be useful to them. I was told to be guarded in the things I said, even to men and women in uniform, since it was believed German spies were donning US military uniforms and in perfect English, trying to befriend airmen. There was also a recent story about an airman in transit who was beaten badly by a spy trying to extract information about the underground in the Balkans, and so we were encouraged to stay in groups.[3]

Although I didn't like it, I came to understand the wisdom of the policy that was sending me home. Lives were in the balance: American and Yugoslavian. Over the course of the war, more than 2,300 airmen were rescued in Yugoslavia by Partisans and Chetniks and successfully evacuated by the Air Crew Rescue Unit of the 15th Air Force.[4] The most spectacular rescue effort happened after I got home, during the summer of 1944. In a daring plan called Operation Halyard, 512 US airmen rescued by Chetniks were airlifted out by the Air Crew Rescue Unit.[5]

Four years after Operation Halyard, President Truman awarded the Chetnik leader Mihailovic the Legion of Merit for his role in the evacuation of the US airmen and his contributions to the war effort. The award was given two years after Mihailovic was executed for treason by Tito's communist government. Numerous US airmen rescued in Operation Halyard petitioned the Yugoslav government to testify at Mihailovic's trial for treason. Their petitions were denied.[6]

From Casablanca, I flew to New York, where I received more medical attention for my broken leg.

Adjutant General Dunlap sent a telegram to Peg on April 6, 1944. It read

> *Am pleased to inform you report received states your husband First Lieutenant Frank J. Kirkland Jr who was previously reported missing in action has returned to military control Undoubtedly he will communicate with you at an early date his welfare and whereabouts.*[7]

The telegram was a little behind schedule. I arrived in Texas just two days later.

While waiting for a bus to arrive at the Alamo Station in San Antonio, I saw a young, black woman with two small girls holding on to her skirt and an infant in her arms. As the bus approached, I watched as this frail woman pushed a large upholstered bag and a leather valise with her feet while trying to maintain her balance, looking as though she might stumble over her children.

"Can I give you a hand?" I asked. The girls scurried behind their mother, peering out from behind her. The woman looked at me with plaintive eyes, puffy and red. I don't know how far she had come but she seemed nowhere near home. I was in my dress uniform. My leg was in a walking cast. She surveyed the people queuing up to the bus stop. I don't know if she was nervous talking to me or doubted my ability to help. Maybe she was hoping someone else would come to her aid. No one did.

"Thank you, sir," she said, stepping away from the bags.

The bus was half full when we boarded. There were a number of servicemen, black and white, on board. The black ones were sitting in the back. I followed the mother and her kids as they headed to the back of the bus. They took their seats and I squared away their luggage. Behind them sat a man in dress uniform, captain bars on his collar, pilots' wings on his chest. I acknowledged him with a salute and walked up the aisle to find a seat.

He called out to me, "Good work, lieutenant!"

I turned back and spoke to him a few minutes, sharing that I had just returned from Italy after being shot down over the Balkans. He told me he flew fighters with the 99th in North Africa and Italy and, yes, he knew Phil Cochran. He let me know he'd been shot down too. "I managed to land without busting up my leg, though," he said, smiling. The bus driver spoke up, telling everyone to take their seats. I found mine next to a civilian in the white section of the bus.

He was reading a copy of *Stars and Stripes*, and barely looked up as I pushed past him and sat down by the window. He would shake his head occasionally, smile, and sigh. Fifteen minutes into the journey he said his first words to me: "It's a heckava thing; you won't believe this story," handing me the newspaper, its masthead decorated with American flags on crossing staffs.

I began to scan over it. It contained the usual sort of things: summary of battles, a cartoon poking fun at Hitler, a variety of human interest stories. The gentleman took the paper back, folded back the first two pages and said, "Read this one; you won't believe it," pointing to the headline, "Rescued Flyer Returns to Texas." I began to read it. It was my story, and then I remembered the reporter when I was recovering in the hospital in Bari.

My leg was in traction at the time. A private walked into the room I shared with a dozen other wounded soldiers, including Joe. We were joined by two of the commandos we met on Vis. Both of them had been wounded on a reconnaissance mission looking for potential invasions sites in the Balkans. The private wore a patch on his sleeve that said, "Stars and Stripes US Army." He told me he was from Texas and was looking for a story about a local boy. He heard about the rescue of the *My Eva* crew from some staffers in the OSS office. I told him I was from Phoenix and only trained in Texas. He said, "With your permission, sir, I'd like to tell your story and if it's all the same to you, I'll leave out your place of birth."

The story was devoid of details. There was no mention of Tito's Partisans or any aspect of the underground network that led us to our safety. Still it was a compelling read, if I do say so myself. It focused on the dogfight, the jump, the crash, the broken leg, and the hillside heroics that saved me.

I handed the newspaper back to the man sitting next to me and told him it was my story, that I was the pilot rescued by the girls and boys. He shook my hand and called out to the bus driver, "We have a real-life American hero on board," and then recounted the *Stars and Stripes* story.

The bus driver shouted to the passengers, "Ladies and Gentlemen: We have a hero among us. I'm going to let this gentleman explain." My seatmate stood up and faced the back of the bus. He said, pointing to me, "This here's Lieutenant Frank Kirkland. He was shot down after a bombing mission over Italy and got rescued by a couple of girls and a buncha boys in Europe somewhere." I was a little embarrassed by all the attention. He then said. "Stand up, lieutenant, so everyone can see you." I stood. The passengers applauded and cheered.

Amid the hoopla I remembered who else was on the bus, sitting in the back. I made eye contact with the young mother. She nodded her approval. I searched for the captain among the smiling faces. He was staring out the window the whole time. I couldn't understand what he was feeling then but I think I do now. He had saved lots of guys like me from the Luftwaffe but I was the one getting the attention. Having returned home to America after so much success overseas, he was now like the son who seeks his father's approval. He worked hard, played by the rules, made sacrifices. He was smart, talented, accomplished. After doing all that he could do to distinguish himself, no one seemed to notice him, least of all his father, or in this case, Uncle Sam.

Notes

1. This order is from the WWII files of Frank J. Kirkland Jr.

2. There were other bomber pilots in the 2nd Air Force who had originally trained to be fighter pilots and wanted to return to fighters. Those who had not been shot down were allowed to return to fighters when they met the minimum number of missions as bomber pilots. Charles W. Richards, *The Second was First*, 203-4 (Bend, Oregon: Maverick Publications, 1999), 203–4.

3. Ibid, 222.

4. Thomas T. Matteson, *An Analysis of the Circumstances Surrounding the Rescue and Evacuation of Allied Aircrewmen from Yugoslavia, 1941–1941* (Maxwell Air Force Base, Alabama: Air War College, 1977), 2, 20.

5. Gregory A. Freeman, *The Forgotten 500: The Untold Story of the Men Who Risked All for the Greatest Rescue Mission of World War II* (New York: NAL Caliber, 2007), 238–39.

6. Matteson, *An Analysis of the Circumstances*, 2.

7. This telegram is from the WWII files of Frank J. Kirkland Jr.

EPILOGUE

It pleased me to think my posterity would share my war stories after I was gone, as I had so often done in retelling Grandfather's tales of glory. That would be my son's job. He was the repository now.

"What do you think?" I asked him. He looked at me kind of funny, puzzled at the question. I probed further, "Did you learn anything new today?"

He responded, "Well, Dad, I suppose I've learned more about your life. I have a new appreciation for what you went through. I feel closer to you."

His tepid reaction was disappointing. I didn't expect an ovation but an "atta boy" wouldn't have killed him. But then again, he wasn't exactly raised on a diet of praise either.

I got up from my chair and walked back to the front window, not really agitated, just unsettled. The bright sun and blue morning sky had faded into twilight, and then blackness. My thoughts turned to Amendola and the men who didn't make it home. If the length of their lives could have matched their promise, the world would be better place. What would this band from beyond say to children never born or, worse, to the ones they left behind?

In the window's reflection I saw the table behind me and my son sitting to the side of it. Outside, the rising moon revealed mountain peaks, connecting heaven and earth. Staring back into the night I saw myself sitting with Carl Anderson at a table in the mess tent. We were having breakfast, waiting for a briefing session to begin. We talked about life and the paths that brought us together. I hashed over my heartbreak at Walla Walla and confessed my plan to get back into fighters after twenty-five missions.

He smiled and stared down at his coffee. "This war is not about you, Kirk," he said. "You better get used to the idea." It was our last conversation before flying to Padua. I never spoke to him again. His death spiral to earth is one of those images I wish I could forget.

I turned away from the window, dragging my chair across the carpet to get closer to my son. One of the legs got hung up on the shag, and he got up to dislodge it. I placed the chair directly in front of his and we both sat down. Scooting closer until we were knee to knee, I said, "I'm about played out, kid. I don't know when it will end but I feel like my time is short."

"Dad, don't say that," he chided.

"You don't know what it's like to live this long. I wake up each day wondering why. Why must I live so long? What is my purpose? Maybe it's because I needed to tell you these stories, and now we have finally had our moment together."

"We're not ready to let you go! Not yet."

"You've got to listen to me. My stories are of no value to me at this stage of my life unless they add meaning to your life. I want our family to be strengthened by the things I've experienced, to know there is more to life than just living. That hope outlasts despair every time if you just hang on to it."

He replied, "I know, Dad. You've taught us that all of our lives."

I thought, *How many times have I heard him say, 'I know, Dad'?* I replied with words he had heard from me just as often, "You don't know nothing about nothing!"—I got his attention, and he looked like he had something to say, but he just stared straight into my eyes.

I continued, "I want you to take hold of what I'm telling you today, right now, this very moment! Okay? I've got one more story, and if you don't get it after that, I'll let it go. We'll call it quits."

"Okay, Dad, I'm not sure what's got you so riled up in the last few minutes, but go ahead. Tell another story. After that, I've got to get going."

I then recounted the little-known story from my last mission on March 11, 1944. During the pre-flight briefing session, we were informed about a church near the target zone that was on the list of protected properties. Built in 1276, the Church of the Eremitani[1] was the home of a large fresco painted by Andrea Mantegna, a native of Padua and a master artist from the Renaissance era.² Unfortunately some errant bombs hit the church, destroying the chapel and the fresco.³

After the war, the people of Padua carefully sifted through the rubble to find the fragments of their native son's famous work.⁴ They found 88,000 fragments, none bigger than a coin. Unable to piece the huge puzzle of broken plaster together, the people stored them in dozens of crates, not knowing what would become of the shredded fresco. Six decades later, after digital cameras were invented, they got their answer.

Forensic specialists photographed each shattered piece of plaster. With these digital images, a mathematician was able to write an algorithm that created a precise blueprint for the location of each piece of painted plaster. Using a black-and-white photograph taken in the 1920s as a guide, artisans recreated the painting in black, gray, and white hues on the walls of the rebuilt church and then reattached the original colored pieces in their proper places, restoring significant portions of the masterpiece to its former brilliance.

It was the advancements in science and technology that made the recovery of the fresco possible, but it was the unconquerable spirit of the people that inspires me. They safeguarded the worthless fragments of the priceless painting year after year with no reason to believe it could be restored. They held on to them anyway until the impossible became possible.

Lives are shattered every day. The work of a lifetime is often lost. Life's masterpieces painted with careful strokes can be destroyed overnight through the careless acts of another. We may never be exactly the same in the aftermath, but we can choose to be happy despite our sorrow. Eventually, we may be in an even better place than before, added upon in the most unexpected and even unwelcomed ways.

Nearly 160 years before American bombs dropped on Padua, the German writer Johann Goethe called Mantegna's work "astounding" and suggested it inspired later painters to "rise above the earth and create heavenly forms which are still real."⁵ Today the restored painting is pleasing not only to the eye, but to the heart. It inspires in ways never intended by the artist. It is a reminder of what is possible: we too can mend the broken pieces of our lives. We may not know how it will be done but in time and with hopeful hearts, our lives can be rebuilt and their beauty restored.

When I finished with the story my son jumped up to embrace me. I tried to stand and he reached out to steady me.

"I get it, Dad. We're going to be okay. You don't have to worry about us."

"I know, son. I know," I said, patting him on the back. "I used to say 'don't look back' but I don't believe it anymore. We need to look back. What's the point of our lives if we don't learn from our experiences, good and bad?"

His arms wrapped around me snuggly like a belt in need of an extra notch. He said softly, "I'll be thinking about these stories the rest of my life. And I'll try to learn from them. I've gained a new perspective on life's trials. They seem to have shaped you more than I realized."

I thought about it for a minute and said, "You have to put trials in their proper place. They are never the end of the world. I've learned that economies eventually recover and wars do end, so you can't let hardships color your outlook on life. It's taken me awhile but I know now that people are just people, no matter the color of their skin. Every group has a few bad apples and a lot of good ones too. I've learned that dreams do come true, if you're willing to work hard and make sacrifices along the way. And that regrets should not last forever. You've got to get past life's disappointments to have joy in the here and now and hope for the future."

"The 'getting past it' part is not as easy as it sounds," he said. "Sometimes I get stuck on my failures, and I can't get those thoughts out of my head."

"There's nothing wrong with remembering your mistakes," I told him. "But when your heart's harrowed up like that, you've got to plant something that will replace the pain: honesty for a lie, virtue for vice, patience for anger, forgiveness for hate. If you can find a way to turn your weaknesses into strengths, then in due time wisdom will replace the pain."

"I'm not sure what you are saying. What do you mean, harrowed up?" he asked. I had raised a city boy, and it was showing.

I replied, "Nothing grows in hard ground. The old boys farming cotton in Laveen used to break the ground up with a harrow, kind of like a plow except wider, with disks that cut into the earth. The farmer would hitch a harrow to a team of horses and follow behind while holding on to the reins, walking over the freshly tilled ground, getting it ready for planting. Our hearts can become hardened and proud, and when they do, they, like the ground, need harrowing so we can grow. Life is the implement. It has a way of breaking our hearts in one way or another. So my point is you're going to make mistakes, you're going to fail. When your heart feels run over by something, learn from it, grow. Keep moving forward."

"I'm trying, Dad, but sometimes it feels like I can't get past the past."

"Our failings make us human, not failures. We cannot fail so long as we have the will to get up each time we're knocked down." I started to laugh as I thought about it. "I've been knocked down so many times I've lost count."

We embraced again. He thanked me and reminded me of the late hour. As he opened the door to leave, he teased me about my thin frame. "I think I might finally be able to take you."

"Don't be so sure!" I fired back, putting up my dukes in Brown Bomber fashion.

He continued: "You need to put some meat on those old bones of yours. Can you come over for Sunday dinner?"

I said that I would.

"And bring a few things from your footlocker, like your uniform. I would like my kids to see your stuff."

I eased back into my chair as the door closed shut. The house was silent, except for the ticking of the clock. It had been a long day. I was tired, the kind of tired that comes from an honest day's work: you're drained but full. I looked up at the charcoal portrait of my mother. It hung over the spinet piano my wife once played. My medals and ribbons were on display on the same wall, a Purple Heart, the Presidential Unit Citation, the Air Service Medal with two oak leaf clusters. They were mounted behind glass atop red velvet in a shadow box of my making. The walnut framed box had become just another decoration in the house, blending in with my wife Donna's menagerie of porcelain owls and the vintage airplane models I made out of wood.

I felt alone but not because the house was empty. It was as though I was the last man on earth, longing for my own kind, thinking what it would be like to encounter someone else who knows. Maybe such a fellow would understand what I was feeling. I had given my son the best I had in me, pouring out my life to him. Hoary wounds were on the mend, my war stories the balm of reconciliation. As is the case with most transfusions, what made him stronger had left me weak. Despite my sermonizing about overcoming adversity, I had to admit there was one setback that had gotten the best of me. Time had made me wiser but it had not put a dent in my attitude about the raw deal I got at Walla Walla. *Heaven*, I thought, *is going to be hell if I don't recover from the day I got yanked out of fighters.*

Notes

1.   *Civil Affairs Handbook, Italy, Section 17A: Cultural Institutions Central Italy* (Washington, DC: Army Services Forces, 1944).

2.   "Andrea Mantegna," *Italian Renaissance Art*, accessed October 9, 2013, http://www.italian-renaissance-art.com/Mantegna.html.

3.   "Bombed Fresco: Using Math To Piece Together a Lost Treasure," S*piegal Online International*, accessed October 9, 2013, http://www.spiegel.de/international/zeitgeist/bombed-fresco-using-math-to-piece-together-a-lost-treasure-a-792781.html.

4.   Ibid.

5.   "Johann Wolfgang von Goethe (1749–1832): Italian Journey, 1786–7, published 1816–7," *DJ Lee*, accessed December 10, 2013, http://debbiejlee.com/ageofwonder/goethe.pdf.

ABOUT THE AUTHOR

He is not *that* Ron White. He is no comedian, that is. Ron grew up in Covina, California, in a neighborhood carved out of a huge orange grove. Most of the three-bedroom homes there were purchased by WWII vets under the GI Bill for less than 19,000 dollars. Boys in the neighborhood smuggled their dad's war mementoes to play "Army Man" in the grove across from Ron's house. The bounty included helmets, bayonets, hand grenades, ammunition boxes, parachutes, hand-cranked radios—most everything a kid would need to while away the hours on long summer days.

Ron left Covina for college and then law school. His work as a lawyer and mediator has provided a living for his family while allowing him to do some good, as he sees it, for others. He was proud to champion the cause of victims of unscrupulous businesses that resulted in seven figure recoveries for his clients. He is just as happy when he successfully mediates business disputes, allowing adversaries to move beyond the conflict.

Headlong into Fury is Ron's first book. Writing it was like going back to the old neighborhood for him: Figuring out how military equipment works, trying to imagine what it was like to be in battle, and wondering if he could be so brave. The only thing missing from those halcyon days was the cool stream water running over his bare feet on a blazing hot day and the sweet taste of a fresh-picked orange, its sticky juice trickling down his chin and arm.